BWH
93

IN THE COLD
LIGHT OF DAY

IN THE COLD LIGHT OF DAY

ann williams

LeFleur's Bluff Publications, Inc.
Jackson, Mississippi

Library of Congress Catalog Card Number: 97-80660

ISBN: 0-9661268-0-7

LeFleur's Bluff Publications, Inc.
Post Office Box 55442
Jackson, Mississippi 39296

Printed in the United States of America

This book is respectfully dedicated to the memory of Gene Tate, and to my friends, the children of the neighborhood.

ACKNOWLEDGEMENTS

I want to thank my family, including Sam, for their consistent love, moral support and encouragement. For urging me on and generously advising me, I thank Doug Magee, Walt Moeller, Esq., and Harley McNair, all gentlemen and scholars, whose friendship I value.

My friends, who have always "been there," I thank you: Yanah, Barbara, Joan, Halal, Jean, Myra, Carolyn R., Carolyn B., Kitty, and Gretchie, of course. And thanks to the entrepreneurs of "Dare to Succeed," who encouraged me and this project along - Chris Carley, Karen Werbelow, Nancy Morris.

For the many people, who wish to remain anonymous, I interviewed for this book, I greatly appreciate your help and hope you are pleased with the result.

I also want to thank my editor Jo Barksdale. Chuck Galey, thanks for a uniquely striking dust jacket design. In addition, much thanks to "investigator," Todd Pollard, and a special thanks to the gifted, consultant, Jeanne Borgen. And for their courteous, always friendly help - which can be critical - at Office Depot, the past two years, I thank Pat and Addean - the copy ladies.

Ann has written a book about a murder that happened a long time ago. She was 10 when the murder happened and lived down the street from the murdered woman, the mother of her friends in the neighborhood. The startling murder and subsequent murder trials and murder plot against my life rocked Mississippi and the South and changed the lives of many, many people forever, and, still, even now, makes people shake when it is mentioned.

January 31, 1960, Mrs. Gene Tate was strangled with a coat hanger, to the horror of everybody. "Prominent Socialite Garroted to Death" the headlines read.

I stood in total shock as I heard it on the radio standing in my dormitory room. Surely there must be some mistake, I thought, things like this don't happen to people like me! In my 19 years of growing up in a small Mississippi town, there had never been a murder. I thought murders only happened in New York. Was it possible that I knew what I knew?

In the end, my utter innocence is all that saved my life.

PREFACE

After my graduation from college, I moved to California, and after some years, I began the practice of law there. During my stay of over twenty years, I discovered that Rob Tate was also living in the San Francisco area, and we renewed our childhood friendship with periodic visits and telephone conversations. We delighted in reliving our neighborhood adventures: playing cowboys, football, army, kick-the-can. Rob and I agreed that we were lucky to have had such a great neighborhood to live in - all the other kids, all the stories, peppered with the "bathroom" humor we dared to shock each other with back then.

But almost every time we met or talked, I was compelled to bring up the subject of his mother's death. We would discuss it briefly, with bitter recall.

In 1994, I moved back to Mississippi. On the occasions that I drove up to the old neighborhood in Columbus, still a beautiful town, it was impossible to avoid those bad memories of that time in 1960. The houses that once belonged to the Tate's and Mattox's remained to me colorless reminders of sorrow, cowardice, and injustice.

But there were many unanswered questions. After all, I was a child when it happened. So, I decided to visit the state archives to read the public records: court transcripts and old newspaper articles about the case.

One thing led to another, and I contacted old friends, acquaintances, and others who were involved at the time. I suppose my most surprising discovery has been that, like myself, most of those I interviewed expressed an unresolved need, almost an eagerness, to talk about the murder and air their long buried thoughts and feelings.

Some mysteries remain. However, I have described events as I believe they happened, based largely on the public record and information gathered from interviews. I should add that, with few exceptions, those people who were gracious enough to talk with me wish to remain anonymous.

In addition, I have fictionalized the true names of several people. These include the first names of the Tate brothers and their father, the names of Gene Tate's mother and father, and the neighbors referred to as Doug and Jane Hamilton. Also fictionalized, are the names of three friends of Sarah Grayson, in Chapter Three, referred to as Barbara, Sally, and Jack.

I have also created some fictional characters in order to reflect the true atmosphere, and to articulate my latter day interpretation of certain facts. Those fictional characters are Hank Walker, Emmett McRae, Frank Hardy, and the reporters, Reed and Shea.

The reader should also be informed that many times I have reflected on the fact that Gene Tate was only thirty years old when she was murdered. And yet, compared to women of today, she, like many homemakers in 1960, was more comparable to a woman of forty - I think that perhaps her maturity and sense of responsibility reflected the stability of that time - when the "American Dream" was a middle-class reality.

There is a newspaper article, quoted in Chapter One, which describes her funeral, and states that after the cortege left the church to go to the cemetery, a single rose remained on the church steps, among bits of petals and fronds . . . And I thought it an appropriate metaphor - that for the many people who loved Gene Tate, she truly was a rose among the fronds - thus, the single rose on the spine of the book jacket.

ONE

I hated going to church as far back as I can remember. But for my mother, it was the central focus of her life, and my brother and I were forced to go with her every time the doors opened.

"Lillian Ann? . . . Rise and shine! It's the Lord's day," my mother half sang outside my bedroom door early in the morning.

"You in there? . . ."

"Yes, ma'am." Where else would I be.

By the time I was ten, like my older brother Buxton, I had learned to console myself by climbing out of the church basement window after Sunday school.

Meanwhile, the preacher, who was less forgiving than Jesus, spewed threatening admonitions about sin and hell to the obediently attentive congregation. How on earth grown people voluntarily absorbed this weekly punishment was a mystery to me. My father, who knew better, stayed home and relaxed.

Maybe it was because, beside the wrath of God, there wasn't much else to worry about back then. Life was predictable in 1960, for most residents of Columbus, a small Mississippi town. Controversy was limited to family squabbles, farm prices, or business disputes.

There was an occasional car wreck and a burglary here and there, but for the most part, reports of any serious crime, like murder, were confined to the big cities far away. And the smaller crimes of the sinful were prayed away every Sunday in churches all over town and at the only temple on the Sabbath.

When the Sunday service was over and the church doors opened, Buxton and I casually walked into the departing crowd and pretended to have been there all along. If my mother suspected anything, we never knew it.

My mother, in an attempt to make our church trips more desirable, let Buxton and me take turns steering the car to and from the service. On this last Sunday in January, it was Buxton's turn to steer home, which was just as well to me. Recently, he had begun to torment me when I steered. He would crouch down in the backseat and yell out the car window at pedestrians along the way. In a loud, deliberately high-pitched voice, "Hey! Want a ride?"

So Buxton steered, and I stared out the window and looked forward to the rest of the day, as we passed the familiar places along our route home. We turned by the mammoth county courthouse with the confederate soldier monument which towered overhead. I think for many it served as a constant reminder that we had lost the war - which was still a sore subject.

Along the way, we passed some houses that were built before the Civil War and were well-kept. The owners' worked hard on them year 'round. In the spring, when the dogwood trees, azaleas and magnolia trees were in bloom, the city hosted the Columbus Pilgrimage, and people came from all over to tour the antebellum houses. The historic homes, on the south side of town, that were built high above the Tombigbee River were particularly picturesque. At that time of year, Columbus was full of soft color and tradition and was quite beautiful.

It was a cold, but sunny January day after nearly a week of ice and rain. And on a Sunday like this, my friends in the neighborhood usually gathered in someone's yard to play football or army, or maybe we would meet to build a hut in the woods. All of us looked the same in our blue jeans and jackets, sometimes five or six of us together, running and yelling, with a couple of yapping dogs in tow. No place or yard was off limits.

Rounding the corner by the Sanders' house, we were suddenly surprised to see some of our neighbors up the street standing out in their yards, facing an ambulance parked near the Hamilton's. My mother was the first to notice.

"Hey y'all, look at that ambulance! Dr. Hamilton must have had a heart attack or something. Poor Doug and Jane. I hope not."

Mama stopped the car when we got closer and called out of the window to Mary Dell Gardner, who was nearby.

"Mary Dell, what's going on?"

Mrs. Gardner, a petite, sandy-haired woman, turned in the direction of my mother's voice and walked toward the car, with her arms crossed, as though she was holding herself together. Her brow was furled and she bore a pained expression.

In a sharp, cracked voice, Mrs. Gardner exclaimed, "We've had a murder!"

Mama stared at first and then looked dumb-founded, as her mouth fell open. Buxton and I shot up straight in our seats transfixed on Mrs. Gardner. My mother spoke slowly, almost in a whisper, and asked, "Who? . . ."

Solemnly, sadly, Mrs. Gardner said, ". . . Gene Tate."

After a moment of taking it in, Mama, locked in Mrs. Gardner's gaze, inquired as to how it happened . . . and did they catch anybody. Such awkward sounding questions. The whole exchange seemed suspended in another dimension.

"She was found by the children after church on the garage floor . . . strangled with a coat hanger . . . They don't know who did it, Virginia."

Again, another pause. Buxton and I looked at each other. Oh, no . . . not Mrs.Tate! Murdered! And our friends found her . . . their mother . . . I looked down the street at the Tate's house. Now I noticed that some of the people standing outside were strangers. Men in suits. Maybe the police.

When we got home, we ran into the house to tell Daddy. He had been asleep on the couch. "What? . . . you don't mean it! Gene Tate? Martin's wife? . . . Judas Priest . . . "

Daddy let out a low whistle and took off his glasses to think about it. He and Mama exchanged comments as she told him what Mrs. Gardner had said. I went to my room to change clothes before dinner.

We ate our noon meal with less conversation than usual, although my mother talked nervously about safety in the neighborhood and kept wondering aloud who could have done such a horrible thing. Daddy would nod or shake his head.

"That's really a shame . . . hard to believe . . . I didn't know Gene that well, but I always thought she was a cute-looking, nice girl . . . I'd see her out in the yard sometime, and we'd wave at each other," he said.

My mind was active with alternating thoughts of Mrs. Tate, and then Rob. I pictured her as she usually looked, wearing pedal pushers with her blonde hair put up in a French twist. She smiled a big pretty smile and was always friendly, the kind of neighborhood mother who asked questions about what you were doing and was genuinely interested in your answers.

I remembered one of the times I was in the Tate's house: I went over looking for Rob, and Mrs. Tate took me down in the basement family room where she had been playing with Genie. She held up a drawing Genie had just finished.

"Isn't that good, Lillian Ann? I'm so proud of her!"

Genie was shy - she beamed with her mother's praise. She was a cute little girl, four or five then, and had blonde hair like Mrs. Tate's. I smiled and said "Yes, ma'am," even though it looked like just an ordinary, little girl kind of drawing. But I thought it was sweet of Mrs. Tate to say that, and I always liked her for it.

The last time I'd seen Rob, I had gone to his house to return his 8 mm movie projector and monster movies that he had gotten for Christmas a few weeks before. He had gotten the idea to ask for it because of Don Furr who lived a couple of houses away from him. The previous spring, Don had acquired a 16mm sound movie projector along with some good movies like "Abbott and Costello Meet Frankenstein," "The Creature from the Black Lagoon," and "The Bowery Boys."

Don turned his basement into a little movie theater, with a screen and more than a half dozen odd chairs arranged in rows. He covered the basement windows with dark colored material.

Don was about thirteen then and very imaginative. He bought M&M's, Hershey bars, and Sugar Babies down at Mrs. Brown's store on Military Road and sold them to us for a few pennies over his retail cost. He charged a nickel to watch the movies. None of them were feature length, but nobody cared. The shorter, edited versions completely entertained us. Almost every kid in the neighborhood came to watch.

Once after one of the showings, Don's older brother, Bill told us he was building an airplane in their garage. He was mad at T.C. Ward for some reason and wanted to fly over his house and bomb him with pinecones. Bill was a few years older than Don, and we believed him.

"Hey Bill. When it's ready, I'll go with ya." offered Jerry Gardner. Rob and some of the others laughed. We liked T.C., but we liked the idea better.

We peered into the Furr's small garage and saw some kind of engine and a couple of sawhorses, with some tools and boards laying on the floor. Maybe it wouldn't take too long to finish. But, as the days and weeks passed, we sort of forgot about it. When I did remember, I just figured it was taking Bill a lot longer than he thought.

Rob's looks favored his mother's especially when he smiled widely like she did. But he also had a temper that frequently got him into trouble at home - like the time he hurled a baseball bat down the stairs and smashed a picture hanging above the landing. In spite of it, he remained his mother's favorite. Maybe it was because he was her first born, or maybe it was his confidence and independence or his easy sense of humor that made him special to her. Whatever it was, Rob knew he had an edge with his mother.

Some of the arguments he got into were with his brother Danny, who was two years younger and also resembled Mrs. Tate. Once when we were playing baseball over at the Hutchinson's yard, they got into it.

Danny was up to bat, and Rob had just made it to second base. We were behind a couple of runs. Danny, who was usually a good player, missed the first two pitches, and Rob started getting irritated.

"Come on, Danny. Watch the ball!"

"Why don't you just shut up, Rob!"

The rest of us looked around at each other. Here we go again.

"Why don't you make me, you little baby!"

Rob's and Danny's voices seemed to get deeper, louder, and more menacing. The threats and insults escalated. David Witt tried to intervene: "Come on, y'all. You're gonna get us in trouble!"

About that time, we heard the Hutchinson's screen door open, and Mrs. Hutchinson came walking over to the top of the stairs on the porch. She looked tall, and she had her hands on her hips, and her lips were tight together . . . she stared in our direction.

"All right now. I told you children you couldn't play here if you were gonna argue."

"It wasn't my fault, Mrs Hutchinson. It was Danny's!" yelled Rob as he turned to point at Danny, who was fuming, still standing on home base with the bat in one hand, hanging at his side.

Mrs. Hutchinson interrupted him. "Ya'll just go on home now. You can't play if you're going to argue." She waved at us like she was shooing a fly. "Go on now." She turned and walked casually back in the house, but we knew she meant business. We heard the screen door bang shut, and then there was momentary silence.

We picked up our gloves and things and began walking out of the yard, heads hung in disappointment. Destination unknown.

"You're gonna get it when we get home!" Rob angrily yelled at Danny.

This was not the first time, or the last, that we would get kicked out of someone's yard. When that would happen, some of us would head home, and others would walk off together, which is what George Witt and I did - to go play with his little army men. George was only eight, but he was my best neighborhood friend - when we played "Tarzan and Jane," I didn't always have to be Jane.

Danny and Rob continued to bicker as they walked down the street with their brother Stan, who usually managed to stay neutral.

Stan, the next to oldest, and Genie, the baby, looked more like their daddy, who seemed quieter than his wife and more serious. Mr. Tate worked hard at the family business, an office supply company in town, but sometimes I'd see him in the front yard pitching the ball for the boys. And sometimes, he would pile the whole family in the car and take them to the drive-in movies.

But on this Sunday afternoon . . . those memories seemed a long time ago. Within minutes after rounding the corner, coming home from church, everything had changed forever.

After my family and I finished eating, I left the house. Mama and Daddy were reading the paper and talking about the murder, and Buxton was going over to Willy Wash Lott's house, a few streets over. I walked up 12th street. There were cars parked outside the Tate's house and up and down the street. People were going into the Tate's.

I saw Rob standing outside. He was throwing a football up in the air and catching it by himself. He still had on his Sunday pants, shoes, and a white long-sleeved shirt. I decided to walk over to see him.

"Hey Rob . . . "

"Hey."

"You want to go in the backyard and look for clues or something?" I asked tentatively.

"Yeah, okay," he answered and began walking toward the back of his house. I followed.

Silently, slowly - we walked along the fence-line in the backyard of the white, two-story, clapboard house - heads down, scanning the grass.

"Wonder if we'll find any footprints, or cigarette butts, or things like that?" I asked Rob. He looked up at me and then down again, noticing the area along the bottom of the fence that met the weedy, unmowed grass next to it.

"I don't know. Maybe we'll find a piece of cloth or something on the fence - that got torn off." Rob seemed to be frowning, but his eyes looked too distant and somehow unfocused to call it frowning. I searched his face . . . and then looked away from my friend.

We moved along not saying much - hoping to find a clue, something that might catch our eye. It was a big, long backyard that sloped downward from the back of the house. But we were mainly looking in the right-side area, not too far from a little gate in the fence that opened into another backyard. This was closest to the garage backdoor that apparently had been left wide open by the killer.

It was getting colder outside and after a little while, Mr. Tate appeared at the backdoor.

"Come on in and get a jacket, Rob'. It's too cold out there for ya, Son."

We hadn't found anything, and I'm not sure we really expected to. Rob decided he would go on inside . . . so I walked back around the house to the street.

I was surprised by a long parade of cars slowly passing by the house. People from Columbus and other outlying communities had heard about Mrs. Tate's murder on the radio. They had to see the place that had suddenly become extraordinary and shocking. For the next week, and many Sunday afternoons after that, there was a steady stream of the curious, silently driving by the Tate's. It seemed like an endless funeral procession.

There were still a few cars parked on the street, and I recognized Mrs. Baker's, Rob's maternal grandmother. Mr. Baker had died years before. After the Tate's had moved to the neighborhood, Mrs. Baker was there visiting her daughter and grandchildren every day. She had a little shaggy dog named Suzette that she took with her in the car.

Often when Mrs. Baker drove up the street, Suzette would be draped over her arm, head out the window. Mrs. Baker always smiled cheerfully and waved as she drove past with one or more grandchildren yelling at me from inside the car.

I walked toward home and thought about what my mother had mentioned earlier that day: Gene had been Mrs. Baker's only child.

That night, for the first time, porch lights were left on all night . . . and doors were locked shut. The next afternoon, the Columbus newspaper, the *Commercial Dispatch*, ran the story by reporter Rachel Shute, with a large photograph of Mrs. Martin D. Tate under the front page headline:

YOUNG COLUMBUS MATRON MURDERED AT HOME

"Into the churchly quiet of Sunday morning a killer came - struck and vanished - leaving horror behind. Stunned Columbians gathered in solemn groups yesterday morning on 12th Street North at the scene following the news of the murder of Mrs.Martin D. Tate, lovely young Columbus matron . . . The groups shifted uneasily while inside the utility-garage dresses of a small girl swung from coat hangers, and from these the killer had wrenched one out of shape and cruelly twisted it around the victim's neck to bring death - and leave four children motherless . . . a headline story on front pages of newspapers over the nation. Calls from Chicago, Memphis, Birmingham, New York and other cities began pouring in seeking information, pictures, background . . ."

An accompanying article gave more detail;

"The body of the strikingly handsome mother of four children was found in the combination garage and utility room at 11 o'clock yesterday morning by her son, Danny, 8, when he returned home from Sunday school with his father, Martin D. Tate, and his brothers Rob, 10, and Stan, 9.   His screams of 'something's happened to Mother' brought his father, and an employee John Montgomery, from the car in the front of the house to the scene, where they discovered the victim in the garage, which is joined to the house.

Mrs. Tate was lying on the concrete floor dressed in pedal pushers and blouse, her clothes not disarrayed. Officers said she had not been criminally assaulted. Mr. Tate told newsmen, 'I first thought she had fainted. Then I saw the coat hanger around her neck.'   A neighboring physician was called immediately. 'I can think of no earthly reason why anyone would kill her,' her husband said . . . Officers reported there was no known outcry from the victim, nor had anyone been reported observed leaving the scene. They said the house had not been ransacked.

Mrs. Tate, a native of Columbus, was graduated from S.D. Lee High School, where she was homecoming queen and attended Missouri's Stephens College and Mississippi State College for Women, where she was elected Most Stylish.

She was a member of the Junior Auxiliary, the Four Seasons Garden Club, and church groups. She has appeared in Junior Auxiliary pageant balls and served as hostess in pilgrimage homes.

Services for Mrs. Tate were held this afternoon at the First Presbyterian Church. Neighbor and friend, Mrs. Jane Hamilton, voice choked with tears, sang the only hymn, 'Safe in the Arms of Jesus.'

The church was filled to capacity, and after the service flowers upon flowers were taken from the church bucket-brigade fashion by a line extending from the street into the deep recesses of the church.

A single white rose lay amid small bits of fronds and petals below the steps to the chapel as the final car in the unusually long funeral cortege turned the corner to head for the cemetery."

It was the first newspaper article I had ever read. The picture of Mrs. Tate was taken of her when she was a hostess in the pilgrimage. She was smiling, wearing a formal dress. I sat there for a while feeling very sad.

For months to come, the murder story would occupy the front page of the newspaper many times. Late that afternoon, as we watched television, Walter Cronkite broadcast the news of the murder of Gene Tate to audiences across the country. Our neighborhood tragedy had become a national concern.

Supper was interrupted that night by a phone call from my married sister, Ginger, who lived in Jackson, the state's capital. She was 14 years older than I. Mama came back to the table after talking with Ginger.

"Ginger called to say she heard the news about Gene's murder, and she said she thinks Jonny Mattox killed her," she reported doubtfully.

Jonny was a college boy who lived with his parents next door to the Tate's. They had lived there as long as my family had, close to fifteen years.

"Jonny Mattox? . . . Why on earth does she think he did it?" Daddy asked as he reached to get some butter for his cornbread.

I looked up from my plate and waited to hear more. Buxton continued to eat - and watched my mother.

"She said that when she and Bill lived here, and Elizabeth was just a toddler, she was outside one afternoon, and Bonnie Jean Lavender was outside with a policeman. They were standing in Bonnie Jean's yard, next door, where the policeman had just shot this stray dog that the Lavender's had been worried about. He thought it was rabid or something . . ."

Buxton's eyebrows shot up and he became quite excited.

"I remember that, Mama! I saw that dog, too. That's that dog Jonny killed! I ran home crying. He wanted to kill it. After the policeman shot the dog, it wasn't dead, and Jonny came walking over. And the poor dog walked right over to him, and Jonny started beating it in the head with a pipe! That's when I ran home."

"Goodnight, Buxton . . . Well, your sister said he took out a knife and slit it's throat . . . ." My mother shuddered at the thought. "That must have happened after you left. But she said Jonny came walking up and said 'I'll kill it for ya!' She said it made her sick, and she thought 'You cruel little so and so . . . ' and took Elizabeth inside in a hurry."

Buxton said Jonny was mean and he hated him. He said there was another time that he was across the street at the Nabors', in their basement watching Louis Jr. fool with something, and Jonny was over there. He said Jonny, who was about fifteen then, took an electric cord and tied some knots in it. Then he put the cord around Buxton's neck, and Louis Jr., who was a couple of years older than Jonny, told him to leave Buxton alone.

"He should have beat him up," I offered.

"Why don't you shut up, stupid. You don't know anything."

My brother decided to take it out on me, so I kicked him under the table and got sent to my room.

The next afternoon, riding home from school, Dorothy Anne White, who lived across the street, told me that she and her brother, Jimmy were sleeping on the floor in their parent's room. I was surprised.

"Really? Why are you scared? The murderer only tries to get grown-up's. He doesn't care about us." I was only afraid of made-up monsters.

When we got home, for the first and only time, I persuaded Dorothy Anne to play cowboys with George and me. She would only play store, or dolls, or games with me, usually. We went and got George, but before we started playing, I told them what Ginger and Buxton had said the night before. They looked very upset while I told them about the dog. George thought about it a minute.

"Hey, remember that cat we found in the vacant lot? You know, the one that had been burned? . . . "

"Yeah . . . " It was a gruesome memory. "You think Jonny did it? . . . Look at what he did to that dog! . . . "

We explained to Dorothy Anne how we had been playing over at the vacant lot, which adjoined several backyards near the Tate's. The grass and weeds there were knee high, and I had found a dead cat lying there. It had a stake-like stick that had been pierced through the nape of its neck, and it had been burned alive. It was stiff and charred all over. I had picked it up with the stick and showed it to George. Somebody had just thrown it in the vacant lot, probably, because none of the grass was burned.

George then told us that he had seen two other cats in the vacant lot at different times. One of them was hanging from a broomstick - with a coat hanger around its neck, and the other one had been buried up to its neck and looked like it had been run over by a lawn mower. We were mortified. George, Dorothy Anne, and I left and went to the vacant lot to see if the burned cat was still there, but we weren't surprised that it was gone.

Meanwhile, the police had been interviewing the Tate's neighbors on 12th Street. Even though my house was only three houses away from Rob's, on 12th Avenue, my parents were never questioned. Neither were any of the other residents of our street, except George and me.

He and I had been standing at the top of the hill, on 12th Street, watching the cars drive by the Tate's, when a stranger approached us. He asked us about the murder and wanted to know any details we might know. George and I didn't talk to him long because we didn't know very much, but I was suspicious. On "Perry Mason," the police said the villain always returns to the scene of the crime. When I got home I told Mama what had happened.

The next day, a man from the F.B.I. came to our house and asked me to describe the man. I told him he had sandy colored hair and was wearing a purple jacket. George told him the jacket was green. We didn't hear any more about it.

George and I got busy setting a trap for the killer. He helped me dig a hole by my backdoor. It was about two feet deep and a foot wide. We laid twigs and leaves across the opening to disguise it. If the killer tried to break in the house, he would step into the hole and get hurt.

This had been tried twice before. Once when Buxton was mad at Daddy, he dug a hole and disguised it by the driver's side of his truck. Daddy left for work early in the morning, so when it was time for him to come home late that afternoon, Buxton hid in the woods behind the house for a while in case he was going to punish him. But, finally, when Buxton went inside, nothing was said about it. I figured it hadn't worked.

So then I tried it on the garbage man - by digging a hole next to the garbage can in the backyard. That one worked, but luckily he wasn't hurt. I had a heck of a time explaining to Daddy my reason for doing it: to see if it would work.

It turned out that we were too late. That afternoon, there was another headline story - and the news spread like wildfire around the block and all throughout Columbus:

COLUMBUS YOUTH ARRESTED IN TATE MURDER

"Jon Neville Mattox has been arrested for the murder of Mrs. Gene Tate. 'All evidence upon which the arrest was made will not be discussed at this time,' said Chief of Police Mahlon Vickery in a statement issued late last night. Arrest was made at 11:30 p.m. Thursday, February 4th, Vickery disclosed, following the return of evidence from Washington which had been analyzed in F.B.I. laboratories.

Jon Mattox, 20, lives with his parents, Mr. and Mrs. James Mattox, next door to the Tate home. He is a day student at Mississippi State University, where he is a physics major, earning average grades. Mattox belongs to no fraternities or organizations. He is being held in the city jail."

Jonny's high school graduation picture was printed next to the article. He had brown hair, cut in a crew-cut style, and looked very pleasant and harmless. Some even thought he was handsome.

Rumors began to circulate about Jonny. There were other stories about his cruelty to animals, and some said he had done even more horrible things, but I wasn't sure what they were.

The newspaper continued to give daily reports about the case, and Mr. Mattox made the headlines in defense of his son who he said was "in an area removed from the scene" and added that he and his family were "morally convinced of the innocence of their son, Jonny Mattox."

No one was surprised that his family would defend him, but the neighborhood wasn't so sympathetic, and after Jonny's arrest, life almost returned to normal.

Dorothy Anne and Jimmy were sleeping in their own beds again, and Buxton wasn't afraid to get up in the dark on Sunday morning to deliver newspapers.

Mrs. Baker had moved into the Tate's, to help Mr. Tate take care of the four children, and offer a comforting presence to somehow help fill the agonizing void left by their mother's sudden and terrible death. Living next door to the family of the suspected killer was an added test of endurance.

Thirteen days after his arrest, the *Commercial Dispatch* once again startled the fragile neighborhood:

OFFICIALS RELEASE JON MATTOX IN TATE MURDER CASE
"County Attorney Lowery Lucas and Chief of Police Mahlon Vickery released a statement to explain: '. . . Mattox was arrested after laboratory reports and other evidence
was submitted to the F.B.I. laboratory, and their second finding, in a most unusual
particular, tended to weakened the evidence of guilt . . .' "

When Daddy got home from work that afternoon, my mother met him at the door holding the newspaper.

"What in heaven's name is going on? Have you heard anything?" She questioned Daddy looking for reassurance. He said he had heard it on the radio and didn't know any more.

"Oh my word! And just think of that poor family up there having to live next door to that."

Later, when Buxton and I came in for supper, we were told to stay put. No more playing outside after dark.

Few days would pass without the mention of either the murder or the progress of the police investigation. Soon enough, all of the major news-papers, from Dallas to Atlanta, would once again carry daily front page reports of the life-changing horror that occurred only a short walk from my home. In time, I would learn that the inherent darkness of infamy, which nurtures deceit and controversy, can stain the most innocent and conceal the truth in its shadow until finally exposed to the light. But it would be much later before that task would be undertaken - that I would be placed in a position to learn the truth, to complete the picture - and tell the story, as it has been revealed to me, of the murder of Gene Tate.

TWO

Jonny Mattox lowered his rifle and walked toward the deer. One shot expertly fired had brought her down. He looked her over. Boy, she's perfect. A real beauty.

Mattox stood over her and fired two more times. It was one of his rules: Kill it three times, just to make sure it's dead. He chewed on a piece of dried straw he had snatched off the ground.

"Well, ole girl, guess you won't be nursin' any babies next spring."

Mattox was a tall, muscular, twenty year old. A Mississippi State college student who lived with his parents, but had his own private entrance to his bedroom and his own automobile that he had skillfully rebuilt from junk parts, both of which gave him a feeling of relative independence. And when he wasn't attending classes on campus, he was often in the woods hunting alone. A physics major . . . with a minor in stalking and killing.

Jonny had no close friends. Never had, and that's the way he liked it. Every once in a while, he would go on a hunting drive with some local men, but other than that and friendly small talk, they had few interests in common.

There had been talk about Mattox among his hunting acquaintances, how he sometimes appeared covered in blood after a drive. Odd for an experienced hunter, they had uneasily agreed.

Jonny kneeled over the doe and, with his right hand, reached for his hunting knife which he had meticulously sharpened. He placed his left hand on her side, not to steady himself, but to feel the warmth of her body. It was part of the thrill for him, an intimate confirmation of his power: this lifeless creature was an instant ago, a breathing, living being.

He ripped open her body. Warm blood spilled out onto the ground - and covered the fallen leaves in an ever widening pool. Methodically, he began to remove the inner organs.

Whew! The old man is gonna be mad - killing a deer out of season and with the freezer already full . . . he speculated. But, then again, the old man was usually mad at him about something. Jon smiled and shook his head as he drove back to town.

He changed out of his hunting clothes, and as he turned on the television, Jon heard a car drive up next door. He went out the backdoor of his bedroom and walked around toward the carport on the side of the house - just in time.

The Mattox's next door neighbor, Gene Tate, was carrying a bag of groceries into her house. He watched her from the shadows where he knew he couldn't be seen. He had tested it to make sure. Had to be more careful now.

Jon crossed his arms, noticed the rock hardness of his biceps, and enjoyed the view. Gene always looked good, even in her casual clothes. Her blonde hair was swept up off of her neck and pinned into place. The back of her coat collar, stylishly pulled up against her neck. Always a slight smile on her pretty, full lips. Gene reminded him of that doe he had seen earlier. Dignified. Beautiful. Almost untouchable.

She quickly disappeared from sight, and Mattox, lost in dark thought, absent-mindedly studied the ground as he kicked at a dirt clod. Suddenly, he was surprised by the sound of footsteps rapidly moving in his direction. He looked up. Gene Tate was headed right toward him.

Her sunglasses hid her eyes, but her rigid gait and posture spoke volumes. She was steaming. She stopped a few feet away.

A moment passed, as she apparently calmed herself. He was amused.

Gene spoke slowly in a controlled even tone. "I know what you're doing and I want it to stop. Now."

To throw her off balance, Mattox refused to look her in the eye and instead deliberately focused on the movement of her lips. Mm-m-m.

He looked back down at his feet and back again at her and coyly grinned. "What am I doing?"

Her anger resurfaced. "Jon, I've tried to be nice about this, but you obviously can't take a hint." She shook her finger at him. "I know you're watching me, and I know you're following me. I'm sick of it! . . . I can't even come over to visit with your mother any more for fear of what you might make of it . . . You need to find a girl your own age."

Silence followed. Mattox wasn't grinning now. He blushed a scarlet red that crept up his neck into his face. He said nothing.

Gene pretended not to notice his discomfort. She had wanted to avoid this kind of confrontation. She turned to leave and said, "I'm sorry, Jon. I had hoped we could be friends, but I mean it."

He watched her walk away . . . Pure rage pulsed through his veins. His eyes quickly darted around. Did anybody see what happened? . . . Didn't see anybody. His rage slowly dissolved into anger.

To hell with what she wants. Nobody could tell him what to do. He'd already gotten her message loud and clear.

That's okay. He didn't care. So what if she was mad - He had a message for her, too!

"Hey, Mary Dell!" Her voice interrupted his thoughts. "Are the boys over at your house?," referring to her three young sons. Gene was yelling to another neighbor, Mary Dell Gardner, who was outside sweeping her drive-way. Jonny couldn't hear the response.

"Okay. Well, I'm fixin' to cook supper, so just send 'em home when you're ready . . . Warren and Jerry are welcome to join us," she said, inviting Mary Dell's children. "I've got plenty. Martin won't be home till late, and Genie's staying over at Mother's."

He could hear her and Mary Dell laughing about something. Then Gene opened the front door, which she hadn't bothered to lock, and went into the house.

Jonny walked over and sat on the stoop by the side door to his house. Mary Dell spotted him and yelled in his direction.

"Hey Jonny! What have you been up to today?"

"Hey. Not a whole lot. Working on my car." Sometimes he didn't know what she was thinking, the way she looked at him - a serious look, it was like she knew. Nah. She doesn't know squat. He was good at reassuring himself.

Mary Dell kidded him about how much he worked on his car. Said maybe he ought to hire a tow truck to follow him around. He laughed, told her she was probably right. Blah, blah, blah. She went inside.

Like Gene, Mary Dell was just one of his mother's friends. He joked around with all of them. Once he had overheard one of them say, "Jonny's so cute, Elizabeth. Why isn't he dating anybody?" He had almost laughed out loud when he heard that. He thought, 'cause I've got better things to do than spend my time and money on some empty-headed female . . . Get serious.

The truth was that most girls weren't interested in Jon Mattox. In high school, he was considered strange . . . Theoretically, he could have fit in. He grew up with them in the small town, came from a respectable family, was good-looking. But there was something in his eyes - A look that put girls off. And he didn't participate in the usual teenage pursuits: sports, football games, parties, dating. Jonny just didn't show any interest in his classmates, male or female.

He reflected there on the stoop while he chewed the inside of his lip. She's going to be sorry. Real sorry. He began to feel agitated and angry thinking about it. Began tapping his foot, wringing his hands. Nobody's gonna make me look stupid. He looked around. Nobody outside now. Cool down, boy. You're gonna enjoy this one. He thought about his plan and was proud of himself. Preparation, that was the key. He had run it over again and again in his head. Even practiced some.

And that smart-ass husband of hers, Martin Tate. Mr. Big Shot. I'll give him something to smirk about . . . Jonny couldn't wait. Thinking about it made him feel better. Back in control.

The house had felt chilly when Gene returned home. She started a fire in the living room fireplace and admired the fresh-cut Christmas tree that filled the house with the fragrance of outdoors. She wanted to take her mind off the conversation with Jon. At least, she had taken care of it.

On occasion, Gene had certainly been aware that a man or two found her attractive, but they had the maturity and good manners not to assert their interest in her, a married woman.

Jonny Mattox, on the other hand, didn't even fit into that category. He had gone from being an admiring teenager to just plain obnoxious and disturbing. He was too aggressive anyway. Too rough with the children. Mary Dell had told her boys to stay away from him, and Gene surmised that she should do the same.

While she unpacked the groceries in the kitchen, she tried to enjoy the smell and sound of the fire as the burning wood crackled, hissed, and spit. It was one of those rare occasions when Gene was alone in the house. But even though she knew better, feelings of guilt caused her to question herself.

Have I said something or done something to encourage him? When she had coffee with Elizabeth, she sometimes talked to Jonny and joked around with him. Or out in the yard, he would come over and talk to her while she watched the children . . . A couple of years before, when she and Martin and the children had just moved to the neighborhood, she was outside washing the car with the boys, and Jonny had popped her on the backend with a towel. Gene had wanted to be a good sport, but it embarrassed her. Wasn't appropriate. She let him know, in a kind way, that she didn't like it. Oh, for Pete's sake. Encouraged him? That's ridiculous. He's just got a screw loose or something.

As she wiped off the counter, she decided it would soon blow over anyway. But the thought of Jonny Mattox bothered her.

Suddenly, the front door swung open followed by her mother's voice.

"Gene?"

"I'm in the kitchen, Mother." As she turned to go into the living room, little Genie ran up and threw her arms around her waist.

"Well, hey Sweetheart! What are ya'll doin' home now?"

With her little arms firmly around her mother's waist, Genie placed her feet on top of Gene's, and the two of them struggled forward across the room.

"Genie, I swear, my feet are gonna be as flat as pancakes! I'm gonna look like Daisy Duck! Is that what you want?" She looked down into her daughter's face and kissed her forehead.

"No, ma'am." The little girl giggled and revealed a vacant space in her smile that had been recently rewarded by the tooth fairy. She had just turned six.

"She said she wanted to talk to her daddy about Santa Claus, because he works for him." Mrs. Baker gave Gene that look that suggested someone had been pulling Genie's leg.

"Oh-h-h. Well, Martin told Genie that sometimes he's late coming home because he has to stop by after work and help Santa Claus get ready for Christmas. But I don't know about tonight, Genie, we'll see . . . Why don't you stay and have supper with us, Mother?"

"No, I've got to get going. But, I thought I better bring her home. She seemed so distressed that she might miss some news about Santa. Is Martin gonna be late tonight?"

"Yeah. With the company growing, he has a lot to do. He works so hard, I guess it's a good thing he takes all those vitamins." On the Tate's breakfast table sat a ceramic Lazy Susan, and each cupped compartment was filled with various vitamins. Her husband liked to keep physically fit.

"Well, it's just a shame he has to travel so much."

Gene nodded. "It won't last forever . . . But right now, I've got to get over to Jane's. She's saving some big pinecones for us to decorate." Jane Hamilton and her family lived across the street. She and Gene had become good friends.

It was getting close to supper time, and Gene was very respectful of other people's family schedules. She had her own. With four children, it was a necessity. The children were fed at the same times every day. Good meals. And no goofing off until their homework was done.

But it was really Gene's down-to-earth manner and sense of humor that kept the household together. She was the glue.

Once her oldest son, Rob, who had just turned ten, told her that their's were the only family photographs he had ever seen where everyone was laughing in them. He apparently had made a study of it when he went to his friends' homes. His observations often surprised her.

The middle boy, Stan, who was nine, rough-housed with his brothers, but thankfully he was generally quieter and spent time developing his talent for drawing. Danny, eight, the youngest son, was the family comedian and of late was perfecting his Elvis Presley impersonation, accompanied by "Hound Dog" at high volume on the record player.

Her husband Martin took a more serious view of life. He had grown up differently. His mother was a cold woman, and some thought her snobbish. But she was smart at business and had taught her children practical values. She had put Martin to work when he was eleven, and he had never stopped.

When he started dating Gene Baker in high school, it was probably the best thing that had happened to him. The balance in his life that he needed: warmth, caring, and thoughtfulness. And she had a good head on her shoulders and a quick wit.

They had fun together, and when Gene was elected Homecoming Queen for the second time, the only time the school had so honored a student, he was especially proud.

Gene and Martin were a popular and handsome couple. They had fallen in love and, after going together a while, decided to get married. In a few months, the couple would celebrate their twelfth wedding anniversary.

Sunday Morning
January 31, 1960

As they drove away, Gene waved good-bye to her daughter and mother. Mrs. Baker was taking Genie to church, then out to eat. She looked at the kitchen clock. Ten-thirty. Hm-m, she thought, I've got about a half-hour before Martin and the boys get home from Sunday school.

Gene shook with a long yawn as she went into the bedroom to put on make-up and fix her hair before she finished cooking dinner. Early most every morning, she hit the ground running to perform all the tasks necessary to get everyone out the door on time: from cooking a large breakfast to locating the proverbial lost shoe or jacket. It was a friendly form of organized chaos which had steadily improved as the children grew older.

She heard a faint rapping sound. She went back into the living room. Maybe her mother had forgotten something. She was about to open the front door when she realized the knock was at the back door. It was a door from the kitchen going into the garage. She frowned. Who could that be?

When she opened the door . . . no one was there, but she noticed the other door opening out to the back patio was wide open. Cold winter air was blowing into the garage.

"Br-r-r." She crossed her arms against the cold. "Elizabeth?" Gene walked toward the patio door. Maybe it was Elizabeth Mattox, her next door neighbor . . . That would be strange on a Sunday morning.

"It's me, Gene." A low male voice. She almost jumped out of her skin! Jon Mattox was standing behind her on the other side of the dark garage. With the only light coming from the patio door, it was no wonder she hadn't seen him.

"Jon! You scared me half to death." Gene was more than annoyed. She had tried to be nice about it, but he wouldn't quit bothering her, hanging around.

Her anger mounted and her jaw tightened. She glared at him, her fists on her hips. Mattox smiled - that quirky smile.

She headed back toward the kitchen door. "Look Jonny, I've had enough of this. I'm tired of telling you. You're not welcome here any more. Enough is enough. Just go on home."

He stepped forward and planted himself in front of her. She was startled. "What do you think you're doing?" she demanded. Jon wasn't going to budge. He stood firmly like a brick wall. And his eyes. Piercing, angry eyes. Cruel eyes. He didn't look like himself.

"Jon," she tried to stay calm, "please . . . just get out of the way." She was unnerved.

"I brought you this." He held up a coat hanger he had spread open. There was a black scarf hanging from it, or something. She couldn't quite make it out. What was he doing? She was becoming more frightened.

Suddenly, she understood . . . And charged with a rush of adrenalin, she lunged forward. Her heart pounded as she tried to push by him to get to the kitchen door.

It was too late. Instantly, he was on her from behind, and the hanger was slipped over her head.

Gene started to scream out, but in one rapid movement, he pulled her against his body and twisted the hanger against the back of her neck. He was in total control. Grunting, and with the strength of both hands, he twisted it - one, two, three times. And let go.

In less than five seconds, he had shut off her breath, her vocal chords, even her blood supply. Frantically, futilely, she scratched at her neck.

Jonny stood back, and his eyes brightened as he watched her. He had imagined it many times.

Then, just like he planned it, Gene Tate slumped down, out cold. The last thing she had seen was the light from her kitchen: Home.

It was over.

Across the street, a world away, Jane Hamilton washed the morning's breakfast dishes and remarked to her mother-in-law about the pretty weather outside.

Across town, little Genie Tate sat on a church pew beside her grandmother and stared up at the back of a lady's Sunday hat, fascinated with the small colorful feathers that adorned its band.

Back home in the dark garage, on the cold, gritty concrete, Gene Tate lay helpless . . . unconscious . . . and dying. Separated from her life by a thin, unyielding garrote.

And Jonny Mattox quietly completed his evil business of death and desecration.

He pulled her across the garage floor and left her lying on her back between the station wagon and the washer/dryer.

Quick! Quick! Gotta move quick. Gotta be careful.

But, he couldn't resist admiring his handiwork. Mattox leaned down, ungloved a hand and placed it on her cheek. Warm.

But, not for long. She would be dead in a few minutes. He was sure of that. The wire couldn't have been tighter. It would take a while for anybody to get that off.

Mattox looked around. He could feel the blood pounding in his own neck, and he was breathing heavily. Everything looked okay. Probably hadn't been there more than five minutes. He walked quickly but quietly, out the patio door, through the gate in the hedge and into his backyard. He looked around again and listened. Everything was quiet. Good.

Jonny noticed his hands were shaking when he opened the backdoor to his bedroom. He had to calm down. Think! He took a deep breath. Now you call Otho's and get out of here! . . . Oh. Gotta get my radio so I can hear it on the news . . . He began to relax.

It wasn't until he was driving away from his house, that he could think about what he had done. It was perfect. Just like he planned. He felt proud of himself. Exhilarated.

It's okay. Everything's gonna be okay.

"You boys stop that bouncin' around back there," Martin Tate admonished his sons.

Along with John Montgomery, a salesman from his company, they were riding in a brand new Volkswagen van that Martin had purchased that week for the business. He had promised his sons that he would take them for a ride so, after Sunday school, he stopped by the office to get the van and drive them home. Montgomery, who had been there catching up on some work, agreed to drive it back to the office for him later. Besides, it would give them a chance to discuss business.

Rob, Stan, and Danny, who were ten, nine, and eight years old respectively, sat on the backseat in their Sunday clothes, with fresh crew haircuts, and tried to contain their excitement.

"Hey Daddy, wasn't this made in Germany?" Asked Rob, as his eyes wandered around the interior of the van. Unmarred new vinyl. New car smell. It wasn't like his mother's station wagon. It had an exotic look, and he had never seen one before.

"That's right. They ship 'em over here."

Danny asked Stan, "Where's Germany?"

Rob smiled wryly and confided, "It's next to Alabama, Dumbo."

"It is not! Daddy, where's Germany?"

Stan and Rob laughed and opened the back windows all the way. "Hey, Mrs. Hamilton!" Stan waved at their neighbor, Jane Hamilton, who passed by them in her car. Martin parked the van on the street in front of the house.

"You got that tape measure, John? I want to measure the dimensions in back."

Three pairs of hands grabbed at the door handle as the boys fought to slide open the side door of the van. "I'm gonna be first in the house to get Mother!" challenged Stan, his teeth clenched as he struggled with the handle.

"Oh, no, you're not!" yelled one of his brothers. They couldn't wait to show Gene the new van. When the door gave way, all three almost tumbled out on to the curb. They ran toward the house, neck and neck. When they reached the front door a shoving match ensued, but all three made it inside.

The boys anticipated their mother's reaction to the new van as they ran through the house calling for her - Gene almost always made a big show of enthusiasm for anything that brought joy to her children. They could imagine her look of surprise, her big smile, her laughter.

"Mother?. . . Mother?"

They ran shouting from room to room . . . until they found her.

And nothing in the world could have prepared them for that.

THREE

Heading west out of Columbus, across the Tombigbee River and twenty miles of rolling green farmland, lies Starkville - home of Mississippi State University. Originally, "State" had been an agricultural college for men and complimented the historic women's liberal arts college, Mississippi State College for Women, in Columbus. But by the late fifties, "State" had become a university with a diverse offering of curricula, an ever-growing campus which attracted a number of female students.

Eighteen year old Sarah Grayson transferred to "State" from a junior college in the fall of 1959. Her father and mother were school teachers in the small rural town of Bay Springs, where Sarah grew up. And for a period of that time her father, Curt Grayson, was elected and reelected as County Superintendent of Education.

The Grayson's natural desire that their children pursue academic excellence was satisfied not only by their son Bill, a nuclear physicist, but also by young Sarah. The year before her transfer, she received an award for her work in chemistry and continued to please her family with her disciplined approach to college demands.

Sarah easily made the transition to "State" and gained a spot on the staff of the school newspaper, the *Reflector*. She had tried to persuade her father to let her attend the University of California in Berkeley, having spent the summer there visiting her brother. Curt insisted, however, that she return home for school, and Sarah had chosen "State". It was a three hour drive from her hometown, and a fair compromise with her father.

And Sarah was enjoying her new social life at "State". Before her summer trip to California, she had broken-up with her steady boyfriend of four years and had now begun to date again on a casual basis. She was conservative in dress in an old-fashioned way. Her thick curly, dark brown hair set off her clear blue eyes, said to be remarkable for the maturity they seemed to reflect in such a young person. And she possessed an engaging, clever personality, which insured her an active life on the campus.

On the Sunday afternoon of January 31st, Sarah and her friends, Sally and Barbara were relaxing in Magruder Hall, the dorm where they lived.

They had just finished first semester final exams about a week before. Sarah was sewing curtains and listening to the radio while the other girls discussed where they were going to eat that night. They were tired of the dining hall, having survived another lunch there after church.

"Hey, I know, let's go over to Rubin's and get some catfish tonight."

"Hm-m-m . . . Are you sure they're open, Barbara? . . . Do you know, Sarah?"

"No, I don't. Sorry. Whose car are we going to use anyhow?"

"Hey wait, ya'll . . . Sh-h-h. I love that song!" A look of romantic rapture fell over Sally, while they listened to "Blue Moon" on the radio and softly sang along.

As the singer crooned the words, " . . . you saw me standing alone, without a dream in my heart, without a love . . ." The voice of the DJ abruptly announced:

"Ladies and Gentlemen, we interrupt this broadcast to bring you the following News Flash Bulletin: At approximately 11 a.m. today, the lifeless body of Mrs. Gene Tate was found on the garage floor of her home at 1216 12th Street North in Columbus. Mrs. Tate was murdered by an unknown assailant who apparently strangled her with a coat hanger. The 30 year old mother of four was found after church by her young children and her husband, Martin D. Tate, a prominent Columbus businessman. The Columbus Police Department, in a statement by Chief Mahlon Vickery, said there are no known suspects at this time, and the department is conducting a full-scale investigation to track down the killer . . . There is no more information at this time, ladies and gentlemen, but you can be sure that we will update you on this most frightening and tragic situation as soon as more news becomes available . . . Let me repeat, we interrupt this broadcast to bring you the following News Flash Bulletin . . ." The DJ continued with the repeat story.

After a pause, during which the girls looked around the room at each other, Sally was the first to speak:

"My gosh y'all . . . I can't believe it!"

"Oo-o-oh, me either. And he said her children found her. That's awful . . . wonder who she was . . . wonder if anybody around here knows her. You know? Somebody from Columbus?" Barbara waited on a response.

Sarah sat on her bed and slowly shook her head, stunned. Finally she said, "I would imagine a lot of people would know her, coming from a prominent family and all . . . That is such a . . . oh, terrible."

"Well, that kind of scares me . . . Doesn't it scare ya'll? I mean who knows what kind of crazy thing would kill somebody like that? Maybe he'll run off now and come here to Starkville." Barbara wanted to be reassured.

Just then, the old steam radiator began clanging and hissing. The girls all jumped, and Sally and Barbara burst out laughing.

"Oh Barbara, you know Jack will protect you from those ole booger bears! . . ." Sally teased.

"Hell, poor Jack, bless his heart, couldn't fight his way out of a paper bag. But he is real sweet." Barbara thought about the big stuffed bulldog, "State's" mascot, that he had given her for Christmas. "And, I'm sure he'd die trying . . . Of course, I might too. "

Sarah fidgeted a bit and laid aside her sewing.

"I'm going to get some water."

In the hallway, lost in a fog of shock and alarm, she stood over the water fountain, not drinking - as the water trickled out. This can't be true . . . It must be some enormous mistake. He couldn't have done it.

Jon Mattox, her classmate and friend, had told her of his "perfect plan" to murder the woman he claimed had rejected him. The news report matched what he had said about his intended victim: married, mother of four, prominent . . . It was his neighborhood, the address given . . . Sarah hadn't believed him. Who would have!

She paced the empty corridor . . . His smiling handsome face flashed in her mind - her stomach knotted. A Murderer!

The impact of the revelation numbed her thought processes. She stood silently before a window at the end of the hall. Suddenly, the obvious dawned on her: He must be thinking about her - what she knows. Sarah caught her breath.

Thank God her instincts had kicked in, and she hadn't blurted it out to her friends. Maybe, as long as Jon didn't think she'd tell - she might be safe . . . until they caught him. If she knew he did it, someone else must know. It's just a matter of time

She could not tell anybody. Not at "State." Her thoughts turned to home . . . What about Mother and Daddy? . . . No. They'll be too worried. What could they do? Daddy isn't well.

In her confused panic, Sarah could not think clearly about her dangerous predicament. One thing was certain - her innocent, sheltered life was shattered the instant she heard the news broadcast.

The ice cold wind lashed at her legs as Sarah walked to class a few days later. It was Wednesday morning, three days after the murder. She wished she had thought to wear her knee socks and was grateful that all of her morning classes were in the same building. It seemed like she had been cold ever since Sunday - and she had barely slept.

Robert Stone spotted her coming down the sidewalk.

"Hey Sarah!" She brightened when she saw him. Robert was tall, blonde - had nice features.

"Hey Robert! Boy, isn't this something! We look like two Eskimos bundled up. Are you going to Lee Hall?"

"No, but that's okay. I don't have a class till ten. How ya doin'?" He draped his arm around her as they walked.

"Pretty good. Well, actually I have felt better. Not enough sleep I guess. But I'll be fine." She smiled up at him. "How have you been doing, Robert? Did you have fun last weekend?"

"I had a good weekend, and boy, I'm sure glad those damn exams are over! . . . How about that murder in Columbus? I hear they don't have any idea who did it . . . I'll be glad when they catch him though. I hope they fry him."

"I guess a lot of people feel that way, besides being afraid. I hope they catch him, too. It's just so unbelievable." Sarah had carefully prepared herself for conversation about the murder.

They continued talking, occasionally yelling "Hey!" at friends along their route, passing under the stark leafless trees and the shadows of the brick campus buildings.

When French class was over, Sarah picked up her books to move to another desk and get prepared for her German class - which met in the same room. As she turned to move, she looked up and saw Jon Mattox standing in the doorway. He looked startled to see her.

Her knees felt weak. "Hello, Jon." Attempting to hide her own anxiety, she was tentative but friendly. "Are you taking German this period?"

He rocked back and forth on his feet, his eyes darted around the room. Sarah noticed he was blushing scarlet.

"Well, yeah . . . are you? I haven't been to school this week before today . . ." She nodded and looked past the door and back at him. Since Sunday, she had dreaded seeing him. Every time she turned a corner, or entered a classroom, she had held her breath. And now, here he was.

"Ah," he said, "I didn't know we had a class together this week. I mean this semester."

She looked down. "Neither did I, Jon . . . Well, I better get ready for class." She walked around him and smiled.

"Yeah, I guess I better find a desk . . . See ya later."

Sarah wanted to collapse into her chair. Her heart was pounding. This is crazy! But, you've got to calm down. If you act nervous - he's going to notice. She needed to leave, but knew she couldn't, so she pretended to focus on the lecture.

When the class was over, Sarah gathered her things and was relieved to see Jon standing near the professor's desk waiting to talk to him. She left the building and walked to the "Grill" where there would be other people. She sought superficial comfort in a banana split. Nothing seemed real.

But as long as he couldn't catch her alone. In the company of friends or at the dormitory, she should be safe.

The next morning Sarah felt better, more composed. Her roommate, Sharon had come back to the dorm the night before and told her about a girl on the first floor who had come in drunk Saturday night, and her roommate had short-sheeted her bed. The girl apparently made repeated attempts to get into bed, cursing and confused. Sarah had laughed with Sharon and welcomed the distraction.

Thursday came and went with the usual routine and pretense. But, Friday morning she was awakened early, around 7 o'clock, when a friend appeared at the door.

"Sarah, Jon's been arrested for the murder of Mrs. Tate!" It was announced on the early morning radio news.

"Oh, no, I can't believe it!" She sat back on the bed. Her surprise was genuine. She didn't have to pretend about that. But it was immense relief that she felt, an almost giddy feeling, although she feigned sympathetic concern for their friend Jon.

A great weight had been lifted. Pretending to know nothing about the murder would be easier now that Jon was locked up. It meant the police must know what she knew.

She resumed her studies and began dating Robert. But, two weeks later . . . Jon was released from custody due to insufficient evidence. He moved on campus.

She discovered that, although Jon had dropped the German class, he was now enrolled in her psychology class. Sarah tried to avoid him as much as possible, tried not to appear obvious, but fear gnawed at her day and night. Almost daily he was able to find her - just to let her know he was there and watching. To others he was a curious figure - a suspected murderer. Still, with his good looks and attractive physique, he could fit in with his classmates. But to her, he was a towering, menacing presence.

She constantly remembered him telling her that she had to promise not to tell anyone if he murdered this lady. Sarah had righteously informed him that he should stop talking nonsense.

"But if you did do it, Jon, you also know that I will never let an innocent person be hurt. If you were to do a terrible thing like that, I would expect you to turn yourself in." He knew she didn't believe him. He persisted.

Finally, annoyed and exasperated, Sarah had agreed.

"Okay, Jon, I promise!" He was angered by her attitude and stormed away.

By then, in mid-January, three months after they had met, Sarah decided to end their friendship. Clearly, he was emotionally disturbed: dramatic mood swings. angry outbursts. His obsessive need to talk about his murder plan. This behavior had become troublesome and overshadowed his initially sweet, agreeable disposition. But not in her wildest dreams had Sarah thought Jon could murder anyone.

The next week at school when Sarah was leaving a classroom, she noticed, out of the corner of her eye, Jon standing in the hallway as other students walked past her up and down the hall.

She turned away from him, as though she had not seen him, and began walking. "Sarah!" It was his voice. "Sarah!" He was following her down the crowded corridor.

Panicked, she turned the corner and quickly ran up a stairway and out of sight.

She leaned against the wall and clutched her books to her chest, out of breath. How could this be happening to her? There was no experience Sarah could draw from to make sense of it all. She had grown up in a very small town where everybody knew her and her family. She had no experience with criminals . . . and certainly not killers!

Sarah was suffocating emotionally, being overpowered by fear, on one hand, and a desperate desire for protection and the familiar, on the other.

Day to day, she tried to keep her mind busy with school work and off of Mattox, but escape from reality was impossible. Lately, various scenarios of her own murder occupied her thoughts. What ploy would he use? What weapon? When she was alone in her room, noises and sounds previously unnoticed were now cause for panic.

The time finally arrived as she knew it would. It had been exactly two months since Gene Tate had been murdered. Two months of sleepless nights. Two months of keeping it bottled-up inside herself.

Sarah was standing in line at the "Grill" with her good friend, Judy Jenkins, when Judy asked her if she had heard the latest rumors about Jon.

"People are saying he was involved in other murders - the boy from Columbus who died in the Old Main fire last year, and this junk dealer in Columbus who was murdered a few years ago."

"What! Other murders - I can't hear this. I know too much about this already."

Judy was puzzled. "What?"

Sarah quickly got hold of herself and hoped Judy hadn't understood. "Oh, I'm sorry. I wasn't paying attention." Then . . . she awkwardly changed the subject.

After lunch, she returned to her empty room and closed the door. Sarah sat with head in hands and stared at her reflection in the dresser mirror. Now nineteen - going on a hundred. Her eyes were dull and puffy. Look at what she had become. She sat slumped, depressed. With her face buried in her hands. She couldn't take it any more. It had been a long time.

That night, she had once again summoned strength - from where she didn't know. Judy dropped by and asked her to go to the school library to study. Sarah decided to get out. A walk in the cool night air would do her good.

In the library, Sarah picked up the Sunday paper. As fate would have it, there was an article advertising a $1000 reward for information leading to the conviction of Gene Tate's killer . . . Why? The police must be stalled in their investigation. He could actually get away with it! What if Jon thought she would be tempted by the money?

It was the final straw.

"I need to talk to you about something." She moved next to her friend and looked around to see if anyone was nearby.

In a whisper, she said, "You can not tell anybody what I'm going to tell you . . . I could be killed, Judy."

"What, Sarah? . . . My God! . . . "

"It's about the murder of Mrs. Tate . . . I know Jon did it. He told me he was going to, but I didn't believe him!"

Judy was astonished. "When did he tell you this?"

"Well, I've been thinking about it so much . . . He first told me about her on that picnic last fall. But, Judy, he seemed like such a nice boy. I just didn't believe him." Judy nodded sympathetically. "You know, I thought he was only talking . . . blowing off steam. And now she's dead."

"You have to go to the police, Sarah." Judy was firm. "I'll go with you. We should go to Columbus tonight."

They talked a while longer. Sarah agreed with Judy and called a long-time friend, James Donald, from her hometown to ask if she could borrow his car. When she explained to him her reasons for needing it, he tried to dissuade her.

"Sarah, I don't think this is something you want to get involved in. Why haven't you told your parents? You need to call them first."

She told him she just couldn't. They were getting old, and it might affect their health. Besides, what could they do? No, she wasn't going to burden them with this, especially if she didn't have to. Her friend still disapproved, but agreed to loan her the car.

Then she decided to call Harley McNair, the editor of the school newspaper where she and Judy were both on staff. Harley was someone they could trust. He was responsible, intelligent, and a good listener.

As a journalist, Harley had taught them the rules about confidentiality and protecting news sources. And importantly, they regarded him with respect and affection.

Harley agreed to meet them at the newspaper office.

Judy drove the car over to the old house on campus that had been converted into a make-shift office for the student paper. Sarah waited while Judy went inside. Harley was busy, as usual, at the typewriter when Judy walked in the door. He looked up at her through black, horn-rimmed glasses, smiling and curious.

"Where's Sarah?"

"She's waiting in the car. Come on and go for a ride with us."

"What . . . are ya'll trying to get me out on some dark lonely road?" he kidded.

"No such luck," she smirked a grin, "Just come on. We want to tell you something."

Intrigued and amused, Harley put away his work and left with Judy. They climbed into the old car with Judy driving and Harley seated between her and Sarah. He quickly realized the seriousness of the situation when he saw Sarah's worried expression.

They told Harley the whole story. It seemed as if they drove for hours. Sarah was clearly afraid for her life and didn't want to get involved. After some discussion, it was decided by all that it would be best if Harley went to the police in his role as a reporter to keep Sarah's identity a secret for the time being.

"I've got to tell you, I had a class with Jon. We were friends, in that sense, and I thought at the time that he was kind of odd."

"You did, Harley?" This surprised Sarah. Why hadn't she noticed this "oddity" sooner herself.

"Yeah. I'll tell ya why. When I met him, I thought, 'What a handsome guy,' and I noticed how well-built, athletic-looking he was. So, I asked him if he played football or something. You know, like most guys. When he told me he didn't play any sports, not even in high school, I just thought it was odd - he was so muscular and everything. The other reason was that even though I liked Jon okay, thought he was funny, there was something missing inside him. It's like he was a stone inside."

Later, back in his dorm, Harley kept thinking about Sarah's revelation. There was no doubt in his mind that she was telling the truth, but he did have doubts about what Jon had told her: that he had had an affair with Mrs. Tate. It struck him as wrong, just a gut feeling. The details Jon described were not believable. Not the Jon Mattox he knew . . . pretty fishy. But whether he did or not wasn't important. The fact was, he must have murdered her!

Two days later, on Saturday, April 2nd, Harley met with Columbus Police Chief Vickery, a fortyish, heavy-set man with a cherubic face that belied his serious manner. Harley identified himself as a reporter interested in the Tate murder case and asked the chief:

"If a person knew that Jon Mattox had a problem with this lady. If Jon told them that - would that be of value to you?" Chief Vickery told him that such information could be critical to their investigation.

When Harley returned to "State," he told Sarah to prepare a written, unsigned statement detailing everything she knew about Mattox and the murder of Gene Tate. In order to identify the statement as hers, Chief Vickery had said she was to tear the corners off of each page and keep them for a future match-up, if necessary.

It took her almost two weeks to write the lengthy statement. She was able to determine the dates of her interactions with Jon by school schedules for exams, special dates, and the like. On April 12th, Sarah dropped it in the mail before she left school to go home for spring break. She was still feeling reluctant and afraid.

On April 21st, a few days after she returned from break, events began to move fast. Columbus police lieutenant, Louis Harper, arranged to pick-up Sarah and Harley on the campus and drive them to nearby West Point to meet with District Attorney Harvey Buck. He arrived in Starkville in an unmarked car. In spite of the sober nature of their business . . . there was an undeniable air of excitement.

Once both students were in the car, Harper drove away at great speed. They arrived at a motel in West Point. Along with Mr. Buck, Chief Vickery was also there. Sarah talked with them for several hours.

Three days later, she was driven to Birmingham where she underwent a grueling lie detector examination. After six hours of interrogation, the officers concluded she was telling the truth.

That night, when she had returned to the dormitory, Sarah passed her window and noticed a chilling figure. At first, she thought she was imagining it, but no, it was Jon Mattox. He must have sensed something.

Mattox was pacing back and forth in front of Magruder Hall. She had seen him react this way once when he was angry: His gait was bizarre and disjointed. It was a loping kind of walk . . . and as he stepped along with his shoulders hunched over, he would look furtively up at the dorm. It was, for Sarah, a horrifying sight. What was he doing there!

The next day, April 25, 1960, Jon Mattox was indicted by the Lowndes County Grand Jury for the First Degree Murder of Gene Tate. In the company of his attorney, Jesse Stennis, he was arraigned late that afternoon and pleaded, "Not Guilty." Because of his help with the case, Harley was tipped-off by the D.A.'s office about the indictment and was able to scoop the other papers by having the only front page photo of Mattox's arraignment.

The trial was set to begin two days later. . . and once again Mattox was placed in jail.

Sarah maintained a normal school schedule and told no one of her recent alliance with the prosecution.

The grand old Lowndes County Courthouse stood near the center of downtown Columbus. It was a large two story, brick and mortar, building with tall white columns which supported the overhanging roof. And high above the top story was a classic brick clock tower that was visible blocks away. The grounds were shaded by magnolia trees and landscaped with flowering shrubs. At the outer left corner of the property stood the imposing confederate soldier monument.

Housed inside the courthouse were the county offices, the sheriff's office, and the jail, but the second floor was largely occupied by the circuit court. The dark-stained, wooden, double doors opened into a traditional, but simply designed courtroom with rows of spectator benches. They resembled church pews and formed a semi-circle that faced the judge's bench. The attorneys' tables were about six feet from the bench, one on either side of the center aisle, and separated from the spectators' section by a gated bannister. To the judge's left was the witness stand, and further left was the jury box. Above the floor of the courtroom was a balcony area, usually reserved for "colored" spectators.

On any week day, on the lawn outside the courthouse, lawyers and businessmen gathered in small groups to discuss politics and gossip about local goings-on. It was the hub of semi-public debate and deal-making. One wise-cracker called them the "Tri Pi" fraternity - meaning Prognosticators, Pontificators, and Prevaricators, allegedly captivated by their own voices.

Hank Walker, a lawyer whose office was directly across from the courthouse, could be found on an outdoor bench at the county building every morning, eating doughnuts and drinking from a milk carton, as he greeted passers-by. He sat outside on the bench with no jacket and no tie - just his white shirt sleeves rolled up to the elbow, ready for action or gabbing . . . whichever came first.

This particular Thursday morning, up the sidewalk came the president of the Farmers Bank, Emmett McRae, an elderly, distinguished, gentleman.

"Good morning to you, Brother Walker!"

"Hey Emmett. You got any money in that bank for me?"

"Not unless you got some to give me!"

They both cackled, and Emmett sat down next to Hank - suddenly becoming serious.

"Hank, I hear they have the Mattox boy locked up again. You know anything about that?"

"Yeah. He's up there now." Walker pointed up to the barred windows of the courthouse jail. "The grand jury indicted him late yesterday."

"Well, I'll be John Brown . . . What have they got on him, Hank? They had to let him go last time."

"All I know is I saw Harvey Buck looking like the cat that swallowed the canary. And Martin Tate's hired Bill Burgin as a special prosecutor to assist Buck." Burgin was a former state senator and a well-respected trial lawyer.

Walker continued, "Mattox has got himself two pretty damn good lawyers, too - Jesse Stennis and Luther Sims." Both men had strong political connections.

"Huh . . . Well, I'll tell ya, Hank, if that Mattox killed her, then I hope they get him good. You know, I see people every day at the bank, and I swear, I don't believe I've ever seen a little gal like Gene Tate who was so well thought of . . . It's been a damn sad thing - those four little children with no mother."

Frank Hardy walked across the street from his insurance office next to the barber shop.

"How you gentlemen doin' this fine morning?" Emmett and Hank rose from the bench, and each gave him a friendly handshake and sat back down.

"Pretty good, Frank. How's business?"

"Oh, I suspect it could be better, but I'm doin' okay. Just hope I don't get any flood claims this year." Hank and Emmett nodded.

"So what's ole Harvey Buck up to? I hear the grand jury indicted Jonny Mattox yesterday."

"Well, I was just telling Emmett that I don't really know, but Harvey's struttin' around like the cock of the walk."

"No kiddin' . . . Well, it's sure gonna be interesting. You know Jonny has some folks convinced he's innocent. They say it's just circumstantial evidence. Nothin' real."

"Circumstantial or not, they've got something up their sleeve. Besides, what's wrong with circumstantial evidence? You know Frank, criminals don't exactly leave their calling card when they do something. That's the nature of crime - they do it so as not to get caught."

He continued, "And if Mattox didn't do it - you tell me who did. And don't tell me that bullshit, pardon my French, about Martin Tate . . . cause we know he didn't do it."

"For heaven sakes, no." Emmett frowned in disapproval. "Why he was in Sunday school sittin' by Lynn Smith. You couldn't have a better alibi than that." Smith was an F.B.I. agent.

"I'm telling you, Gentlemen, Harvey and Burgin better have something on this boy, because there are some folks who are rootin' for him. And I still haven't heard anything that tells me he really did it."

During the funeral services for Gene Tate, workers had been in the Tate house to change locks and repair windows. And after Jonny Mattox was arrested the first time, Martin Tate had a six foot privacy fence constructed on the narrow strip of land that divided his property from the Mattox's. The fence divided the two drive-ways from the garage to the street.

The Tate children had returned to school a few days after the funeral, and after school, as they had before their mother's death, the boys were back in the neighborhood playing with the other kids. Genie played with her little friends - with her grandmother in attendance.

Even though there was an appearance of normalcy at the Tate house, the neighborhood children noticed a difference in the boys, an emptiness. There was a silent understanding between them . . . more potent than grown-up words of condolence.

FOUR

A crowd began gathering early at the Lowndes County Courthouse. It was Wednesday morning, April 27, 1960 - a beautiful clear spring day that had followed a rainy night of thunderstorms . . . and electric anticipation.

The murder trial of Jon Mattox was, at that time, the most notorious homicide case in the state's history. It was set to begin that morning at 9 o'clock sharp. Almost three months had past since that January when Gene Tate's young sons had returned home from Sunday school and found her body in their garage.

As it would be throughout the trial, the courtroom was filled to capacity with spectators standing in the aisles and along the walls. Among them were members of the press and photographers from all over the South, writers representing detective magazines, and a crew from the local radio station. Six radio leads would be approved to air the trial, some of them to carry the programming to out of state listeners.

Judge John D. Greene, Jr., the presiding judge of the circuit court, was the picture of authority seated at the bench, positioned above all others - his black robe in contrast to his thick white hair.

Jon Mattox, casually attired in a sports shirt, khaki trousers, and loafers, conversed with his lawyers at the defense table. Seated with him were Jesse Stennis and Luther Sims. Attorney Sims was also a member of the state legislature. Jon's parents and other relatives sat nearby.

His mother, Elizabeth Mattox, forty-five, forlorn in posture, lit her first of many cigarettes and peered nervously through her eyeglasses at the packed courtroom. She sat next to her husband James, a quiet, intelligent man who was chief engineer at a local chemical company. The state would be asking for the death penalty for their son.

The lead defense attorney for Mattox, Jesse Stennis, closely linked to his cousin, the state's beloved U.S. Senator John Stennis, was reputed to be one of the most flamboyant trial attorneys in Mississippi.

Pushing past middle-age, Stennis presented an intense figure of expanding girth and jowl. And his facial expressions were often punctuated by the movement of his bushy, graying eyebrows that shot up in profusion like a bramble of black and white exclamation points above his heavy black eyeglasses.

Stennis leaned over toward his client and placed a hand on his shoulder.

"Listen, son. I don't want you, or your mama, or your daddy to worry. Burgin doesn't have a damn thing, and we're gonna prove it. This is just a railroad job, if ever I've seen one. Hell, I don't even know why we're here." He patted Jon's shoulder. "Okay?"

Mattox smiled slightly and nodded. "Yes, sir. I appreciate it. I guess

Mr. Tate's got to pin what he did on somebody, but I sure as hell wish it wasn't me."

" I know. I know." Stennis patted him again and then turned and winked at Jon's parents.

Inwardly, Jon Mattox was a little worried about the case - and angry that he was locked up in jail. The cell was small and his cot was too short - uncomfortable with his long legs. He was spared the jail food. Every day his mother or a relative brought him home-cooked meals and listened to his complaints about the justice system.

What could they have on him, if anything? . . . He was very careful about fingerprints. On top of that, he wore gloves . . . Stennis was right. The police weren't smart enough to have found any evidence anyhow. He'd be home in a week or two, waving good morning every day to Martin Tate.

At night, as he lay on his jail cot, he couldn't help but rack his brain about possible evidence. Every detail of the murder was alive in his memory. There just weren't any mistakes unless somebody saw something. That thought scared the hell out of him. Heart skipped a beat. But it couldn't be. They would know by now if there was an eyewitness.

He reminded himself that it really wasn't so bad being locked up for a short time. And his vivid recall of the murder was almost as satisfying to think about as the actual killing itself.

At the table for the prosecution sat Special Prosecutor Bill Burgin, County Attorney Lowery Lucas, and District Attorney Harvey Buck. Burgin had been hired by Martin Tate as the lead prosecutor. State law provided for that legal option: that a citizen of means, or with access to money, could pay for a special prosecutor. With the heavy hitters hired by Mattox, Martin Tate made sure the state was equally represented.

In contrast to Stennis, Bill Burgin was thirty-five, tall, fit, and preferred tailored suits and french cuffs to Stennis's off the rack gray suit. Both men, however, were dynamic, take-charge trial advocates, at home in the courtroom.

Burgin was relatively young to have already served in the state senate, which was an indication of his driving ambition to someday become a major player among the state's political elite. The unprecedented publicity of the Mattox trial would be a giant step toward this ultimate goal.

The hub-bub in the large old room was suddenly silenced by the crack of Judge Greene's gavel, as he called the court to order. An out of town reporter standing against the wall leaned over to a colleague and whispered, "Let the games begin." The other journalist grinned, "Behave yourself, Reed."

Defense attorneys kicked off the proceedings with a motion for a change of venue to a distant county. They alleged there was a prejudgement in the public mind against their client - the broad shouldered, six foot Mattox, referred to by them as, "this young lad" or, "little feller."

The entire first day was spent with the defense and the prosecution examining and cross-examining over a dozen witnesses called to testify on the subject of community bias. The sheriff estimated that over a thousand spectators had been in and out of the courtroom that day. Later, newspapers, replete with photographs of the key participants, commented that a smiling and friendly Jon Mattox, several times throughout the day, granted permission for the reporters to take his picture and offered them chewing gum.

After more testimony the following morning, Judge Greene denied the defense motion to move the trial and began the tedious process of jury selection. For the next week, 295 prospective jurors were questioned by both sides, and on May 5th, a jury was finally impanelled.

The state began its case and called its first witness to the stand, Mrs. Thomas Baker, the victim's mother. Marie Baker was a pretty, older woman of sixty, who dressed well and wore her graying blonde hair much like Gene had, pinned up in the back.

Earlier that morning she had been taken to the witness room to wait until she was called to testify.

Every morning that she awakened in Gene's house, she was confronted with her absence - her merciless death. Twelve years earlier, her husband Thomas had died leaving her a relatively young widow. Gene had been nineteen then, and his passing had been hard on both of them. The two women, mother and daughter, had grown even closer. Then after her marriage to Martin, Gene had her first child, followed in quick succession by three more. With so many young grandchildren to pamper, and so much to do for Gene, Marie's life had again become meaningful and joyful.

She sat quietly in the witness room and waited to be called. Her hands in her lap, fingers clasped tightly together. Mrs. Baker had lost the other half of all she had.

A respectful hush fell over the courtroom as Mrs. Baker was sworn in. Her usual warmth and friendliness were replaced with a guarded vulnerability.

Prosecutor Burgin courteously exchanged pleasantries with Mrs. Baker and then began his questioning. He had her tell the jury about her final moments with Gene that Sunday morning. She explained, as she had earlier to the police, that she arrived at the Tate home about 10:15 a.m. and sat down to talk with Gene a few minutes. They had talked about the "little new shoes" that Mrs. Baker had bought her granddaughter, Genie.

"Then I told Gene, 'Well, I just must go because I always like to get my regular pew at the church,' and so I said, 'What time is it?', and Genie went into the kitchen and she came back, and she said, 'Gran', she says, 'the little hand is on the ten and the long hand is on the five.'"

Then Mrs. Baker said she noticed Genie didn't have a little purse to take with her to church, so Gene went into the bedroom and found one she could use.

"Then Gene said, 'Mother, don't go so early.' But, I had to get my pew, and also I had to stop on the way to cash a check. So Genie and I left, I would say, about 10:30."

Burgin then inquired about her relationship with Gene, whom she acknowledged was her only child.

"Well, I loved her . . . I adored her."

"And when did you know of her death, Mrs. Baker?"

"In church . . . Mr. Massey, with the police department, called me out of church . . . " Her words became inaudible as Mrs. Baker began to cry. Sheriff Cricket Spruill offered her a kleenex.

After a few moments, Mr. Burgin gently continued his questioning and established that Mrs. Baker visited her daughter every day, usually two or three times a day. To help Gene, she drove her grandchildren to various places, babysat when Gene had to go to meetings or bridge club, and also picked up the housekeeper for her every morning.

Turning to the defendant, Burgin asked if she ever saw Jon Mattox when she was visiting or keeping the children.

"Well, it seems as if he just wanted to hang around in the yard all the time around the children - just all the time. One afternoon, I came out on the walk, and Genie was playing. He picked her up and slung her around by her little arms. And I said to him, I said, 'Jon, I don't ever want to see you do that to Genie. The child doesn't know whether to laugh or cry.' So he flushed - his face flushed, and he gave me a sullen look, and he stomped on over to his property."

Burgin asked, "While you were visiting there, did you have occasion to see the defendant when your daughter was in the yard or on the porch?"

"Well, as I have stated, it looked like he just wanted to hang around, just all the time - just like he was on guard duty. So many times, he was standing in his driveway or on the stoop, the side entrance of the Mattox house."

"Thank you, Mrs. Baker."

Burgin passed the witness to the defense. Mr. Stennis rose slowly from the table, shuffled his papers, and cleared his throat. He wanted to change the atmosphere in the courtroom from one of sympathy for the witness, to a serious look at the facts favorable to his client. He knew his presence could command a certain respect. As he intended, courtroom eyes shifted from Mrs. Baker to Jesse Stennis.

Stennis then stood erect, smiled directly at Mrs. Baker, and nodded deferentially.

"Good mornin', ma'am." Ever the Southern gentleman, butter would have melted in his mouth. Mrs. Baker was paying close attention.

He began his cross-examination by asking Mrs. Baker to again tell the jury about her time with her daughter on January 31st. After many questions, he was unable to poke any holes in her testimony. She further testified that she had not seen Jon Mattox, or his car, either that morning or later in the day. She explained that Sunday afternoon she was so "flustered and grief stricken" that she only remembered sitting in the back bedroom of the Tate home, being comforted by close friends.

"Now I will ask you, please ma'am, if your daughter, that morning, had a black scarf on?"

"She did not." In response to further questions, she stated that Gene owned many scarves, including black ones, but that she wore them over her hair - not around her neck.

"Now you were in the home every day. I will ask you, please ma'am, if you ever saw Jon Mattox in the Tate house . . . ever?"

"One time when they first moved over there, about three years ago when he was still in high school, I guess."

Mr. Stennis changed subjects and asked her about the nature of Mr. and Mrs. Tate's relationship.

"It was very good."

"Isn't it true, Mrs. Baker, that Mr. and Mrs. Tate had separated in that house, and he was sleeping upstairs, and she was sleeping downstairs?"

She was startled by the question. Her eyes narrowed as she looked suspiciously at Stennis. She had no idea what he was getting at, but she knew she didn't like it.

"Well, I was there every day, . . . but not to my knowledge. I know nothing about it." Mrs. Baker said she never heard them "fuss" or observed any marital differences between them.

"Of course, I know they probably did because all couples do . . . But I didn't know of any trouble between them."

Returning to the incident when Jon had swung Genie by her arms - "When you told this young man not to do it, Mrs. Baker, to put her down, he put her down, didn't he?" His voice was sympathetic and soothing. She wasn't impressed.

"And got furious!"

"I didn't ask you that."

"And got furious because I had told him not to do it again. His face flushed - his whole face flushed."

"Did you see him, on any other occasion after that, take any of the other children and swing them around?"

"Well, I think he played with our children more than any others, because the other neighbors had had trouble before with him about their children."

This was going in the wrong direction, and he was losing control of the witness. Stennis paced the floor.

"I am now going to ask the court to instruct the jury to disregard that statement. You are bitter against this boy, aren't you?"

"Well, I had seen him pick up his little dog by the ears."

"I didn't ask you that, Mrs. Baker."

Ignoring the defense attorney, the witness continued - "I had seen him do that not one time, but a lot of times."

Exasperated, Mr. Stennis asked the court to admonish the witness, but Judge Greene said that her answers were probably proper.

Before Stennis could say more than, "I mean . . . ," Mrs. Baker added, "A cute little dog, cute little dog."

"I am not asking you this, Mrs. Baker."

"And the little dog adored him. It followed him all the time."

"Your Honor, I am objecting to that."

"He would pick her up by her little ears." Mrs. Baker may have been down, but she could hold her own.

Finally, he moved on and asked, "Mrs. Baker, you don't know of your own knowledge, do you, who is guilty of this crime? You don't know do you?"

"Yes - I think he is the killer."

"I didn't ask you that. Do you know of your own personal knowledge who did it?"

"Well, I couldn't say . . . but he is the killer."

"And you cannot swear that this boy did it either, can you, because you don't know, do you? Isn't that true?"

"Well, things really pointed that way."

"You can't swear he did it, can you, Mrs. Baker. Yes, or no?"

The witness did not respond . . . and was then excused.

After a brief recess called by the judge, so the jurors could use the facilities and get a Coca Cola, if they wanted to, the court reconvened. The prosecution called its second witness to the stand, Mr. Martin Tate.

He was a nice-looking man, well-built, dressed in a dark business suit. His light brown hair was cut short, and his face was angular with a thin, prominent nose and narrow eyes and mouth, which appeared even more so as he took the stand. Mr. Tate did not look toward the defense table.

Mr. Burgin asked him general questions about his family. He responded with the names and ages of his four children, and that he and Gene would have been married twelve years on the past February 4th. Mr. Tate said he had loved his wife very much.

Prosecutor Burgin asked, "Would you describe the location of your house and the Mattox home?"

"The Mattox house is next door, and it sits on a corner lot, to the north of us. Both houses face west, and there are approximately five or six feet between them - the carport of their home and the garage of our house. Very close, hedge between the backyards, driveways are almost one."

"I see. What type of carport is on the Mattox house?"

"Well, I recall an open type carport - has no back or side or front - supported by steel pipe or columns."

"How was your house laid out?"

"Our bedroom was on the front south corner of the house, downstairs. There is a bathroom and fairly large hallway between our room and Genie's room, which is on the backside of the house. We have a living room, kitchen, and breakfast room, and then there is a stairway between them going down to a den, or basement, where the T.V. is."

"Upstairs from the living room are two bedrooms and a bath. The two oldest boys sleep in one bedroom. We had quit using the other one because we were afraid of fire."

"It is hard to hear from one bedroom to the other, or upstairs and downstairs, and we had an alarm system and intercom, but we were still afraid of getting trapped in the back room, so we had the youngest boy sleeping downstairs with the girl."

"Tell the court and the jury what, if anything, took place Saturday evening, January 30th. Who was home?"

"Well, I got home from work at approximately six o'clock. My wife and children were home- ate supper, of course. There was a lot of paperwork to be done because I travel a lot. I had done a lot of it at the office at night time, but my wife had requested, in the last few months, that I bring it home. So I had made a habit in November, December, and January of doing all the work at home at night, rather than at the office. So we had supper, watched T.V. for a little while, and Gene had a book and read there in bed. And I had a desk there in the bedroom, and I worked on some bids I had to get up."

"Where were the children?"

"At that time, the kids had gone to bed."

"What time did you and your wife retire that evening?"

"I couldn't be specific. I would say probably 9:30 or ten o'clock, after they had watched a few T.V. programs."

"All right. What did you do then?"

"Sat down at the desk, next to the bed. She got dressed for bed, had a book and read. We discussed small things, maybe something about the book - I don't recall. I don't even recall the book she was reading, and she went to sleep while she was reading."

"How late did you work?"

"I worked until about, oh, ten or quarter to eleven maybe, took a bath and went to bed."

"All right. What did you do the next morning, Mr. Tate?"

"Got up about 7 o'clock, had breakfast. Gene got out the kids' clothes for Sunday school. While we were having breakfast, Mrs. Baker, Gene's mother, called at the breakfast table. She had promised to take Genie to church, and she and Gene talked about that. I asked Genie didn't she want to go to Sunday school - but Gene didn't want her to. After breakfast, we got up and got the kids dressed, and I got dressed. Genie wasn't dressed. We left the house to go to Sunday school, with the three boys - left Gene and Genie at home. We left and went to the Presbyterian Church, left the house around 9:30."

"Did you go to Sunday school?"

"Yes. Took the kids to their class, went on to Sunday school. It was over around 10:30. I stayed just a minute to talk to Mrs. Pope, the Sunday school teacher, two or three minutes, left and picked up the kids. They were ready - waiting out front on the lawn, which was unusual."

The witness said that after Sunday school he went by his office and decided to take the children home in the new Volkswagen van that the business had just purchased. The boys had been asking to ride in it.

Because the van didn't have a gas gauge, and the gas key had been misplaced, Mr. Tate asked an employee, John Montgomery, to ride with them. In case they ran out of gas, he could help push the van. But, they were able to drive to the Tate's without any problem and arrived home about 10:55 a.m.

"What happened then?"

If anyone noticed, a slight smile had crept across Mattox's face. He had been looking forward to this.

"I told John to come on in, and he said no, he would stay and look at the Wagen just a minute. I started towards the house, and I heard one of the children, Danny, calling and saying, 'Daddy, Daddy, come quick! Something is wrong with Mother!' I had already started towards the house. We were parked on the street right in front."

"He was very upset, and he said they were in the house - they had gotten in the house and called her, and she hadn't answered - and when I got to the front door, he was right at the front door. He said, 'She is laying on the floor in the garage. Something is wrong!' I immediately thought maybe she had fainted, or something had happened there, and she had fallen and hurt herself - so I ran out in the garage . . ."

There was no sound in the courtroom except the voice of Martin Tate. Almost everyone appeared sympathetic to the witness except the Mattox supporters, who were discernable by their crossed arms and their looks of cold disdain . . . To many of them, Martin Tate was the killer.

Prosecutor Burgin asked, "What happened then, Mr. Tate?"

"The light in the garage was not on . . . Fairly dark . . . There was a light coming in the garage from the back door. She was fairly close to the back door . . . laying on the floor . . . I could immediately see that something was really bad wrong with her - and I noticed a black scarf and coat hanger were around her neck. She was laid out - as if she had just been completely laid out. She was very unusual looking . . . I noticed blood was coming out of her mouth . . . "

Martin Tate had been testifying as though he was talking directly to Bill Burgin. But now, he seemed to be looking right through him - his speech slower, his eyes drooping. He was reliving it.

The prosecutor looked at the jury and cleared his throat. It was clear that they were moved by his testimony. At the defense table, the attorneys were busy jotting notes, and Mattox, as he had all day, just watched with mild interest.

Mr. Tate continued, "I hollered immediately for John."

"That is John Montgomery?"

"Yeah . . . and I immediately tried, while hollering for John, to get the coat hanger off of her neck . . . but I was upset. It was fairly dark in there, and it was hard to tell which way it was twisted - and I was scared to twist it - turn it - and turn it the wrong way because, naturally, I had hopes she was still alive . . . Then John came in."

"What was around her neck, Martin?"

"A black coat hanger and a black scarf . . . Tight, very tight, three or four times."

"Did you remove the scarf?"

"Not at that time. It was fairly tight, and I couldn't . . . The knot - it was a large knot like a Windsor knot, a slip type knot, and I couldn't, I couldn't get it off . . . and I couldn't get the coat hanger off. I couldn't determine which way it was twisted."

He was wringing his hands and almost staring into space, reliving it again. He looked tormented.

"Had John gotten there by that time?"

Mr. Tate recomposed himself as he spoke. "John had gotten there, and I immediately told John to call an ambulance - and he did right away. Then he came out in the garage and he helped me. We determined which way it was twisted . . . and also, and all in the same time - it all happened very fast, very fast - I told him to go see if Dr. Doug was at home. I don't know whether John or one of the kids went, but in just a short time, Dr. Doug was there - Hamilton, lived across the street. And he told John to call the police, that of course the ambulance would be needed . . . but that she was dead."

"Did you and John succeed in removing the scarf and coat hanger?"

"Yes. We had to cut the kerchief off. John went in the house and got a knife, butcher knife - cut it off. I cut it off. John helped me, and he twisted, and we both removed the coat hanger . . ."

"And then I had the immediate reaction - Genie had been left with Gene. And just a sudden feeling went through me, 'What about Genie!' . . . and I ran through the house, in every room . . ."

" First time I had been through the house - calling for Genie. And I hollered out to somebody to see if Genie was in church with Mrs. Baker -

because I was afraid that something had happened to her - maybe Mrs. Baker hadn't picked her up . . . "

"So someone left, I don't remember who. Anyway, they went up to the church to see if Genie was there with Mrs. Baker - because I had a fear that maybe she had been killed, too. And it was like a nightmare - I really couldn't fathom it. I couldn't believe it. It went to . . ." Suddenly self-conscious about his emotional narrative, Tate looked at Burgin, "Go ahead?"

Mr. Burgin nodded, "What time did Dr. Hamilton come, you say?"

"He was there, it just, it seemed like just two or three minutes. Just a very short time. And it took him . . . not that long to say she was dead . . . Of course, I had hopes she wasn't, even though I knew it in my heart - you could look at her . . . She was white . . . blood out of her mouth and eyes. He told me not to touch anything else, more than I had - wait for the police."

"Did the police arrive?"

"Pretty shortly after. However, there were a lot of people there, you know, before the police arrived. There were cars, quite a few cars there - neighbors, people that weren't neighbors. Maybe they had heard the ambulance, I don't know. But there were alot of people, doors slamming, people walking all over the yard - front yard that is. They kept them out of the garage and out from behind the house."

"I noticed that the door going out of the garage was wide open. It was closed when I left at 9:30 - or was closed when I went out and got wood to put on the fire before I left for Sunday school."

"Now, where was that door located?"

"That door goes out the back of our house onto a patio or concrete terrace. It is access to the back of the house. There was a screen door and a door. The door was not locked, as we usually kept it locked, because it was swollen, and it needed planing down, and we couldn't get it off. If I closed it all the way, then it would be hard for Gene and the cook to open it, so we just pushed it part of the way when we closed it, to keep cool air out. It was still cold weather then. Normally, it was kept locked, but it was open as far as it would go - back against the woodpile - and the screen door was all the way back against the house . . . "

"I noticed a pile of clothes that had come out of the dryer. It was sitting right next to the edge of the dryer and the washer there and the car . . . and Gene was between the washer and dryer and the car - very narrow passage."

"How was her body lying?"

"Both of her legs were together, feet were together . . . her right arm was placed beside her and her left arm was laying across her. Her head was turned to left . . . The coat hanger was off the side - made the coat hanger stick up slightly since her head was turned to the left."

Mr. Burgin asked for a moment to review his notes, and the witness asked for a glass of water. Some of the spectators began to whisper and discuss the testimony. Mattox leaned over to whisper to Stennis, and then smiled at his parents. As the prosecutor resumed his questions, Judge Greene warned those in attendance to get quiet.

Outside the courtroom, there were few radios in homes, cars, and businesses that were not tuned to the trial.

Martin Tate continued his story and told the court and jury that his wife had been in very good spirits when he left her that morning. And, in fact, that ever since late October or November, she had been, "her old self, not as tense as she had been."

"Was it unusual for her not to go to church?"

"She probably went about half the time. She always stayed if there was a child sick, and she stayed, you know, to clean up for dinner - and she always liked to have dinner ready at noon sharp. If she went with us, then we didn't eat till around one o'clock. But since November, she had insisted on one of the children staying home with her. I never asked her why, but it was unusual."

"Did you attend Sunday school regularly?"

"Yes. I probably missed every once in a while, but normally, the children and I attended regularly. But, like I said, Gene wanted one of them to stay home with her, like she did that day. She wouldn't let Genie go to Sunday school."

"Mr. Tate, do you know Jon Mattox, the defendant?"

"Yes."

"How long have you known him?"

"About three years, since we moved into the neighborhood."

"Did he come to your house?"

"Yes. Well, what do you mean by that? Did he come over into our area?"

"Yes."

"Yes. Quite often. Too often."

"Did you have occasion to see him there when you returned home from work?"

"Yes, most of the time since we have lived there. He was constantly in our front yard, or sometimes playing with the kids, sometimes just over there - sitting on the front porch, more than normal this past summer and fall. It seemed I couldn't drive up to my house without seeing him there, or it certainly seemed that way."

"What would he do when you would drive up?"

"Well, nothing in the first part of the year through the summer, but towards the end of the summer he would leave, walk on over to his yard."

"Would your wife be out on the porch, or in the yard on those occasions?"

"Normally - sometimes yes, sometimes no, but the majority of the time. I travel, and in the summer months, just like others, it was lighter longer in the summer, and the kids played out longer. I would usually get back, oh, anywhere from six-thirty to seven, off the road. I would drive back in rather than spend the night out and . . . "

"Was that every night?"

"Every night. I spent the night out occasionally - once or twice a month. Monday night, when I worked Booneville. I would leave Monday, spend Monday night in Booneville, and work my way back down and get in late Tuesday night. Occasionally on Thursday, I went up into Alabama, but I wouldn't spend the night, I would just be late. On Friday . . . But, basically, it would be Mondays and Fridays and some Tuesday nights. It was scattered - depending on the situation."

"I see. When you would return home, and the defendant was in your front yard this past summer, on those occasions when your wife was in the yard, or on the porch, what, if anything, did you notice with regard to his conduct toward her?"

"Well, since we have moved up there, since the time that he popped her with a towel on her rear, I had always watched him very closely."

The defense objected, and the court overruled it.

"When was that, Mr. Tate?"

Stennis interrupted, "Unless it is shown that he was present when such things happened, we object, Your Honor."

"Overruled."

"You say he popped her on the . . . with a towel? When was that, sir?"

"The first summer we moved into the neighborhood. She was washing the car with the kids."

"Unless he was present, we object."

Burgin asked, "Who was present, Martin?"

"Mrs. Mattox and Jon, Gene, and the children. Gene told me about the defendant, what he did."

"You weren't there. I am sorry, Your Honor, I didn't understand that," said Burgin.

"Then we move to strike that testimony, Your Honor, and the jury should be instructed to disregard his entire statement."

The judge was apparently confused and thought the witness was present. The other defense attorney, Mr. Sims, jumped up and oddly withdrew the objection:

"He was not there, Your Honor. He made some reference to popping her with the towel. That's all right."

Mr. Burgin continued. "What if anything did you observe with regard to the defendant's conduct?"

"I observed that he watched my wife constantly. If the front door of our house shut, and she walked out to the car, he followed her constantly with his eyes. He seemed to always be on hand, either in our yard or his. I never saw a person to be more on hand."

"You say in your yard or . . ."

"Well, or in his yard, which is almost one. And he would watch her from the car to the house or from her car back. Or, if she was out in the yard, . . . and even if I would walk from the car to the house with her, if he happened, if he were in the yard, and I would walk with her, he would eye her unnecessarily or just fix his eyes on her."

Stennis was on his feet again. "We object to, 'unnecessarily,' Your Honor," he drawled.

"Overruled."

"For the reason that it calls for an opinion from the witness."

"Overruled."

Stennis shook his head in frustration. Tate resumed, "He eyed her constantly."

Mr. Burgin took over, "During the summer of 1959, and the fall, was your wife home on Friday night?"

"The summer of 1959, and the fall, no. Most Friday nights, no."

"What, if anything, did you observe in that connection?"

"Would she go somewhere?" asked Tate.

"Yes."

"Yes. On Friday nights, she helped the Junior Auxiliary chaperone teen dances."

"What, if anything, did you observe relative to her departure and return, and the departure and return of the defendant's automobile?"

"It wouldn't be five or ten minutes, consistently."

"Mr. Tate, was your marriage with Gene a happy one?"

"Yes, it was a very happy marriage - I was completely happy with Gene . . . We didn't depend on partying and things like that."

"Did you go out much?"

"No, not a great deal. I didn't drink, and Gene didn't either, and a lot of partying consists of that, and we would - just two or three times a year. Of course, church barbeques - carry the kids. Occasionally, there was a bridge club that she belonged to, or Home and Garden Club that would have all of them together, and we would go to something like that. Christmas time, one or two places."

"Did you have any difficulties?"

"No, not until the spring and summer and early fall of '59?"

"Did they continue through the late fall and winter until her death?"

"No. I would say in the first part of November there was a complete change in Gene, and she was very happy and stayed that way until her death."

"Then, how was your relationship strained before then?"

"By the undue attention that Mattox paid my wife and by one particular incident . . ."

Stennis, up from the table, "Just a minute, Mr. Tate, please, sir. The defense has serious doubts as to the admissibility of this evidence and respectfully moves that this evidence be developed out of the hearing of the jury. "

"Overruled. I don't think it is necessary. Continue, Mr. Burgin."

"We, or I, had placed some barbells in the back room that joins the garage, and also joins the patio that the garage opens onto in the back of our house - placed them there for the boys, Rob and Danny. They were interested in learning to use them. So I put them out there and coached them on how to use them."

"That was in the spring, and they used them through the summer . . . I came home one day, and Danny wanted me to go out and see how much he could pick up. We went out, and we went in the room, and I noticed about a hundred and fifty or sixty pounds on the weight and thought it was Mattox using my weights."

"Did you subsequently have a conversation with the defendant about that?"

"Yes, I wanted to make sure that he was using the weights. So this past summer, in the late summer, he was outside with his parents, and I asked him how much he was able to press. He told me a hundred and fifty or sixty pounds. I told him that was pretty good - when you can press your body weight around that much."

"He just said, 'Well, what good does it do you?' or something like that."

"Mr. Tate, did you and your wife and children go to the drive-in movies occasionally?"

"Yes, we would carry them out. Usually it would be on a . . . well in the summer, it would be almost any night, and in the fall of the year or school time, it would be Sunday night."

Then he told about one Sunday night in early fall when Mattox apparently followed him and his family to the drive-in. Mattox was alone in his car and parked behind them.

"I looked back several times. As I said, I watched him because he watched Gene so much. So, in a short time, he moved his car on the same row as ours, but quite a bit of distance down - and he was still parked there when we left, when the show was over."

"Mr. Tate, on this past Halloween of 1959, did your children and wife go out?"

"Yes, they went trick or treating - go around and visit all the houses around in the neighborhood . . . get suckers."

"Now, Mr. Tate, what were you wearing at the time you found your wife's body?"

"A dark charcoal . . . dark blue, navy blue suit."

"What type of material was it?"

"It was basically some sort of Dacron and wool."

"When you found your wife, did you move her body in anyway - other to remove the scarf and coat hanger?"

"No."

"I believe that's all."

It had been a long morning. Martin Tate rose somewhat stiffly from the witness chair, buttoned his suit jacket, and stepped down.

The judge called a recess. "It is about dinner time. It is about twelve o'clock, and these jurors have to go to their room and order their meals, and it takes more time. We are recessed until one- thirty this afternoon."

Martin Tate departed the courtroom - overburdened by persistent grief, anger - and the sharp pain of a man who felt betrayed. His world had completely fallen apart . . . The distraction of his work provided his only relief.

FIVE

"The plot thickened, eh?," quipped Reed to his lunch partner, another out of state reporter. They had joined a crowd of trial-watchers at the Gilmer Hotel Coffee Shop. The local restaurants downtown were doing a booming lunch business. Shop merchants, however, noticed a drop in business - with many locals staying home close to their radios and the broadcast of the proceedings.

"You mean Martin Tate's testimony?" asked Shea. Reed nodded. "What d'ya mean - the stuff he said that suggested some romance between his wife and Mattox?"

"Yeah. Is that what you got? I wasn't sure. I mean, maybe Mattox was just following her around all the time . . . Either way, I'd have had to pin that boy back by his ears if it was my wife."

"Yeah," Shea agreed, "I'd have done more than that. And you know what? Why would she have anything to do with that warped son-of-a-gun?

She was a class act. She could've done better than him by a long shot."
Shea signaled the waitress while Reed took one last bite of his homemade
pecan pie.

"Could you heat up this coffee for us a little bit, please ma'am?"

Reed said, "Well, she wasn't even that type from what I've heard. Very
nice lady. Happily married . . . Nah. That's hard to swallow."

"So, what do you make of it all, so far?"

"Don't know. Not much evidence yet. But all that business about every
Friday night - Tate's watchin' Mattox follow his wife back and forth to those
dances. Strange . . .," Reed shrugged.

The afternoon session began as scheduled. The courtroom was very
crowded, and the heat had overcome the ceiling fan's ability to cool the
room. The tall windows on either side of the room were raised high,
which did not produce the expected breeze, but did offer several observers seating on the window ledges. The balcony area, which was the only
seating available to "colored" spectators, was closed for safety reasons,
and because of the heavy attendance, there was growing concern about
the stability of the courtroom floor in the 113 year old building.

Around the room, standing along the walls and seated almost shoulder
to shoulder, were representatives of every social class in the state - the
well-dressed ladies with expensive jewelry, housewives in shirtwaist dresses
- who were outnumbered by the men, old men in bib overalls, suits, young
men in casual dress, and some who appeared to be college students.

And there was a growing number of college girls in attendance . . . who
were preoccupied with the defendant Jon Mattox. There was the whisper-

ing, staring, and giggling that would have seemed more appropriate if they were enjoying a personal appearance by Elvis Presley, instead of the defendant of a murder trial. It was a curious sight that did not go unnoticed by the others.

Judge Greene ordered quiet in the court, and the proceedings began. Defense Attorney Stennis asked the judge to reserve his right to cross-examine Martin Tate at a later time, before the state rested its case.

John Montgomery, Tate employee, was called as the next witness for the prosecution. Mr. Montgomery's testimony corroborated Martin Tate's as to the events of the morning of January 31st, when the body of Gene Tate was found. He noted that Mr. Tate was so upset upon discovery of his wife's body that everything he said was voiced in a "yell." The only specific statement made by Mr. Tate that Montgomery recalled was "My God! Who could have done this!"

Mr. Montgomery also stated that the Tate boys must have gained entry to the house through the front door, as the large front garage door was down, and they seemed to have gotten into the house quickly.

Later on cross-examination, Mr. Stennis asked the witness whether he had talked with the police on the day of the murder. Montgomery said that an officer asked him to make a written statement.

"Nothing more than to write down what happened when I got there, so the facts would remain in my mind."

"Did you write that down, sir?"

"Yes, sir."

"And did you deliver that to someone, sir?"

"No, sir," said Mr. Montgomery.

"What became of that?" asked the lawyer.

"It was destroyed," responded Montgomery.

"Why did you destroy it, Mr. Montgomery?" asked an intrigued Jesse Stennis.

"Didn't feel it was anybody's business," he said matter-of-factly.

"Didn't think it was anybody's business?" replied Stennis, his mouth beginning to water in anticipation of an unexpected choice morsel to fatten his case.

"No, sir."

"You knew that a lady's life had been lost, didn't you?"

"Yes, sir."

"And on that article that you destroyed, Mr. Montgomery, I will ask you to state what it contained."

"Nothing more than what I have already stated - the facts."

"I see . . . You did state there what time you first saw Mr. Tate that morning?"

"Yes, sir."

"Did it state what time you and Mr. Tate left Besco?" Stennis asked over his shoulder while he paced in front of the witness.

"Yes, sir."

"Did it state what time you arrived at the Tate home?"

"It did."

"It stated time with reference to everything that took place - with you and Mr. Tate . . . and Dr. Hamilton . . . and everybody else - didn't it?"

"To the best of my knowledge, it did," replied Mr. Montgomery, unruffled.

"And that was a time when time was fresh on your mind, wasn't it, Mr. Montgomery?"

"Yes, sir."

"And it also stated many other evidentiary matters of great importance, did it not?"

"I would imagine it did."

"Don't you know it did?"

"It did, yes, sir."

"And you never did deliver that to any member of the investigating force in this case?"

"No, sir."

"And you kept it to yourself, didn't you?"

"Yes, sir."

"For how long did you keep it, sir?"

"It was destroyed right after I gave them the information, after the first interrogation."

"I see . . . You destroyed it on Sunday?"

"No, sir. I was interrogated on Monday. It was destroyed after that."

"In whose presence did you destroy it, sir?"

"I don't believe there was anybody present."

"There wasn't anybody present? . . . Did you burn it up, sir?"

"Yes, sir."

"And was there a like request made of Mr. Martin Tate, sir?"

"Not to my knowledge," stated Montgomery.

"Where were you when you destroyed it?"

"In my home . . . In the backyard."

"And that was on Monday?"

"Monday evening . . . I imagine it was around 7:30."

Mr. Montgomery stated that he was interrogated by the police after the funeral on Monday. Several representatives from law enforcement were present at that time, including Mr. Lucas, the county attorney, Mr. Gwin Cole with the Highway Patrol, and another officer whose name he couldn't recall.

"I would like to ask you this, sir: When you were being interrogated by one of these gentlemen, on the Monday following this great tragedy that has hit Lowndes County, if someone took down what you stated, sir?"

"Yes, sir - the same person that was interrogating. I don't recall his name."

"And you don't know what became of what they took down when you first told them about your movements that day, do you, sir?"

"No, sir."

"Mr. Montgomery, sir, I will ask you if you will tell this court and jury, please, sir, whether, to your knowledge, any footprints were found in or around the garage, or in or around the vicinity of the Tate home?"

"No, sir."

"Did you hear of any strangers being in that neighborhood that morning, sir?"

"No, sir."

"I will ask you if you heard a report that there were several young Negro boys in that neighborhood that day?"

"No, sir."

"You didn't hear that?"

"No, sir."

"I will ask you if you heard a report that Assistant Fire Chief Shields came up there and ran down and overhauled some young Negroes on that very morning?"

"I heard nothing about that."

"You heard nothing about that? . . . Now, Mr. Montgomery, you, of course, have discussed this matter at length with several people, have you not, sir?"

"I have."

"You were interrogated twice by the police?"

"Yes, sir."

"Who was present on the second interrogation, sir?"

"I don't know the party. I would recognize the face, but I don't know the name of the party . . . just two people who came to Starkville where I live."

"Did you talk at length with anyone except these two people that came to Starkville, that you do not know and this person who interrogated you on Monday, that you do not know?"

"No. I had talked . . . I had discussed it with nobody but my wife."

"But your wife? . . . I will ask you - whose scarf did Mr. Tate say that was around his wife's neck?"

"He never stated to me whose scarf it was."

"Mr. Sims?" Stennis turned to his co-counsel, "Do you think of anything else?" The older man shook his head "no." "That is all, Judge," stated Stennis, and John Montgomery was excused.

Next, Dr. Doug Hamilton, who lived across the street from the Tate family, was sworn in as the state's fourth witness. He explained that he was a private family doctor, specializing in "diseases of women," and had been in practice in Columbus since 1926.

He was an older man, professional in appearance, with graying dark hair and a kind thoughtful face. Dr. Hamilton, known around town as "Dr. Doug," testified that he had just returned home from making hospital rounds when the Tate boys and Mr. Montgomery came running over to his house. He was directed to the Tate garage by the children, and had found Mrs. Tate lying flat on her back, between the station wagon and the washer/dryer. He described the scene as "horrific", and it was clear from the solemnity of his voice that his relationship to the Tate's had been one of friendship, rather than professional.

"She was cold . . . beginning rigor mortis. She was dead."

The doctor made this determination at about five minutes of eleven, he recollected, after having checked her vital signs, reflexes, and noted her discoloration. He opined that she had been dead ten to fifteen minutes and had died of strangulation.

"Did you observe any objects there, which could have caused that strangulation?" asked Special Prosecutor Burgin.

"There were two objects there - a scarf, a black scarf and a black wire coat hanger. Martin had just taken it off her neck. The scarf was still loose around her neck when I saw her."

Dr. Hamilton noted that the scarf appeared to have been twisted, as it was not smooth, and the hanger had three complete twists in it, prior to removal.

The defendant was impressed that the doctor had counted . . . Kill it three times to make sure it's dead.

"In your opinion Doctor, how long could Mrs. Tate have remained conscious after the coat hanger was applied?"

"I think she would have lost consciousness immediately. This type of tight constriction would not only cut off her breath, but probably her blood and nerve supply."

"And after loss of consciousness, how long would it take for death to ensue?"

Stennis jumped to his feet objecting that the doctor was not qualified to give an opinion of that nature, but the judge overruled him.

"After loss of consciousness, it would take approximately six minutes. An individual can't be revived after six minutes."

"Doctor, could Mrs. Tate have cried out after the coat hanger was twisted on her neck?"

"No, not from the position of the hanger in relation to her voice box."

"Now Dr. Hamilton, when you examined the body of Mrs. Gene Tate, did you notice any signs of a struggle?"

"The only signs of struggle were the small scratch marks on the sides and back of the neck, in the area of the hanger groove. These were probably a result of Mrs. Tate having clawed at her neck to remove the hanger. I observed that her finger tips were bloody."

"I see. Dr. Hamilton, did you know Mrs. Gene Tate during her lifetime?"

"Yes. I had known Gene since she was a very young child."

"Would you describe her physical appearance to the court and the jury?"

"I think she was about five feet, six inches tall, about 130 pounds, a slender, attractive blonde woman, a good physique, well developed for having had four children. She was a healthy, strong looking individual."

"When you saw the body that morning, were the clothes in disarray?"

"No, sir."

"I see. I believe that's all."

Mr. Stennis rose from his counsel table, and after reviewing his notes, he began his cross-examination. The doctor again went over his medical training and other background information. In questioning him about his observations and opinion regarding the deceased, Dr. Hamilton added little new information, except that Mrs. Tate did not appear to be wearing any make-up.

"Of course she was rather pale . . . When I saw her she had a good deal of blood on her lips and around her face."

The doctor was then excused by the defense, subject to recall.

When he stepped down from the stand, there was the usual mumbling throughout the courtroom, and Mattox, who had apparently become aware of his new fan club of college girls, took the opportunity to flash a couple of smiles at them - much to their delight.

The state called Mr. James Thomas, the county coroner to the stand. After arriving at the Tate house around 11 o'clock, he said he helped Dr. Hamilton keep people out of the garage area prior to the arrival of the police a few minutes later.

The coroner was shown a white blouse and a pair of blue and red checked slacks, which he stated were the clothing he had removed from the body after it was transported by him to the funeral home. He said that he had turned the clothing over to Lieutenant Louis Harper of the Columbus Police Department for analysis.

Cross-examination was deferred by the defense, and Mr. Burgin called his next witness, F.B.I. Special Agent Lynn Smith.

Smith explained that he had been contacted by the Columbus police when it was discovered that their camera was malfunctioning. Lt. Harper asked him to come to the Tate's to take pictures of the murder scene including the garage area, the victim's body, and outside areas.

Each of fourteen black and white, 8x10 photographs were identified and authenticated by the witness as having been those he had taken the morning of the murder.

Everyone in the courtroom watched as the all white, male jury was passed the photographs - one at a time. Many of the jurors slowly shook their heads . . . and some groaned, as they examined the seven photographs of the murder victim.

Her eyes were closed, and her face and neck were discolored by death. In one of the six pictures, the line of a dark crease left by the hanger ran from the right side of her neck and disappeared under her chin. A few inches behind her right ear was a bobby pin . . . holding her blonde hair in place where she had put it up that morning.

Her left arm was draped across her abdomen - with her left hand, adorned by her wedding band, resting on her stomach.

In the seventh photograph of Gene Tate, Coroner James Thomas had lifted her head from the concrete floor to expose the left side of her face which appeared much darker than in the previous photographs. That was due to blood settlement at the lowest gravitational point: after the circulation had stopped with the loss of heart beat.

Significant amounts of blood from her mouth, nose, and a thin line of blood from her left eye, streamed together down the side of her face, forming a dark pool of blood under and next to her head. And there was a deep, narrow, contrastingly white groove encircling her neck where it had been tightly constricted by the wire hanger.

There it was before the jury: cold-blooded murder.

Many of the jurors were perplexed about the presence of blood when there was no apparent struggle, and the cause of death was strangulation. Later, it would be explained by the pathologist that hemorrhaging of the small blood vessels in the eyes, mouth, and nose was a result of the uncommonly tight constriction of the garrote.

All of them were struck with another concern:

Did her children find her this way . . . God, I hope not. Maybe it was too dark . . .

Although the defense strongly objected to the admission of the photographs, the judge overruled their motion, and admitted them into evidence.

Having dispensed with that portion of his testimony relating to his professional expertise, Special Agent Smith was asked by Burgin to state whether or not he attended Sunday school on the morning of January 31st.

"I did, sir. Mrs. Pope's class at the First Presbyterian Church."

"Did you see Mr. Martin Tate on that morning, prior to the time you went to his residence?" Mattox looked up from his note pad, stopped doodling, and shifted his eyes toward the witness.

"I did, sir. He sat in the back row of the Sunday school class."

"What time did the class begin?"

"Approximately ten o'clock."

"What time did it dismiss approximately?"

"Ten-thirty."

"Was Mr. Tate there throughout the class period?"

"He was, sir." The prosecutor stepped back away from the witness and turned toward the defense table - the hint of a gleam in his eye.

"You may take the witness."

Stennis briefly questioned the agent about his photography that day, but did not attempt to challenge Smith's testimony which had confirmed Martin Tate's presence in Sunday school during the time period in which his wife was murdered. Why bother, he figured.

All in all, the defense team was feeling pretty confident. Fiber evidence, which they were aware of, and sympathy for the victim were not enough -

not nearly enough - to convict their handsome young client, whose popularity in the courtroom was beginning to infect the press . . . and some others.

After the witness stepped down, Judge Greene scanned the courtroom and cleared his voice.

"Gentlemen, I see we are all worked down. The lawyers are tired. Court will take a recess until in the morning at nine o'clock."

The spectators slowly emptied out of the courtroom, and some lingered out on the courthouse lawn to talk. About a dozen of those who remained were the college girls who had earlier drawn attention during the trial by their visible adoration of the defendant.

They huddled close to the courthouse steps and waited for Mattox to leave for his trip back to the city jail, two blocks away. He had recently been moved to the more comfortable facility.

Jon and his uniformed escort walked out onto the landing, and as they descended the steps, the young women rushed forward to greet him.

"Hey Jonny! We know you're innocent!"

"Hey Jonny, we love you!"

Everyone turned to see the spectacle, and news photographers snapped pictures. One cursed under his breath, as he frantically tried to reload his camera.

Harley McNair, who was there to cover the trial as a stringer for the *Jackson Daily News*, took notes, and watched in amazement. Jonny grinned from ear to ear.

"Hey! Thank you . . . Thank you. I sure appreciate it, ya'll."

Harley's mouth fell open when one girl broke from the group, dropped to her knees and kissed Jonny's shoe. Mattox laughed, and the deputy escort moved forward.

"Break it up! You young ladies move aside now. Break it up!"

McNair watched Jon and the deputy, followed at a tolerable distance by the giggling fan club, as they walked down the sidewalk and disappeared around the corner.

He thought - what an amazing display of ignorance. If those girls only knew . . . Ole Jon must be lapping it up . . . But then again, it's hard to know what he's thinking.

Sarah Grayson had no desire to listen to the trial or read about it in the newspapers. She knew too much already. And she was bothered by self-doubt.

How could I have let myself get that close to a murderer! What should I have noticed that I didn't? She turned back the covers on her bed in the dorm.

With Mattox in jail, she knew . . . intellectually that she was safe. But somehow that had not been translated to her subconscious. She was either so exhausted from lack of sleep that she practically collapsed onto the bed, or she slept fitfully, adrift in a nightmare, and woke up in the night.

She stared at her ceiling, with the light from the street illuminating it partially.

The Old Main dorm fire . . . Henry Williamson. The unwelcome thoughts popped into her head. Henry Williamson was a student from Columbus who had died in a fire that totally destroyed the huge dormitory the year before - almost exactly a year before Mrs. Tate was murdered.

Of eleven hundred students who lived there, Henry was the only one who died - even though several witnesses reported having seen him leave the dorm after the fire started. The fire apparently had started in an empty room next door to Williamson's, but that night he had slept on a different floor.

His death remained a mystery, but there were more than a few who doubted that it was an accident. Since the time Mattox was first arrested, there was a rumor circulating that Jon Mattox had a grudge against Williamson, and that he had something to do with his death. Unlike what she heard or knew about Jon, Henry Williamson had been well-liked, a genuinely nice guy. Big fellow, too. His family had been devastated.

Jon made a point of talking about that - that he was there that night - the night Henry died, Sarah remembered. He said he had gone over to Old Main to study for final exams, and had gotten into a fight with Henry before the fire started. "Whew! Almost didn't get out myself!" She could still hear Jon's voice. He seemed so casual about it. How would I have known that it meant anything? There was a lot she didn't know then. Sarah pulled the covers up around her.

Mattox's voice intruded again. "You know the junk dealer I bought these parts from was killed a couple of years ago. It's too bad. They don't know who did it. He was murdered, ya know." They were seated in his car that he had partially built from old junk parts. At the time, Sarah thought his remarks were curious, as though again, he wanted to make a point of telling her about it.

Around Christmas 1956, when Jon Mattox was a senior in high school, the body of the elderly Max Silverman was found on the ground outside his junk business. He had been beaten to death. The Lowndes County Coroner had stated that any one of four blows to Mr. Silverman's head would have been lethal. In addition, Mr. Silverman's left arm was broken, which was considered a defensive injury that he sustained as he tried, in vain, to protect himself from the attack. The case remained unsolved.

Henry Williamson, and the junk dealer . . . She rolled over.

Sarah fought to change the dialogue in her head, and reflected on her parents. She had finally told them, earlier that night, that she was asked to testify in the big murder trial they had been reading about. They took it pretty well - after some initial questions and worries were discussed. She also had phoned her brother John, in Tennessee, but he didn't seem to believe her - his baby sister. Condescending . . . at least, she had warned him.

Wonder if they'll call me tomorrow? The prosecutors or the police would call her any time now to testify. Then they would pick her up in Starkville and take her to Columbus. Everyone was being so careful to keep it a secret. So far, no one had any idea about her. She wanted to get it over with. Her breathing slowed. In a few minutes, she was asleep.

SIX

The trial resumed Friday under dark Columbus skies, with a threat of fierce rains and possible tornadoes. Undaunted by the forecast, a large crowd returned to the old courthouse. The room was jam-packed with spectators, and those too late to find a chair or window ledge were standing in the aisles and along the walls. Print journalists and the radio crew were set up at their established vantage points near the lawyers and the defendant.

Jonny Mattox seemed carefree throughout the day's proceedings and moved about during the breaks to visit with friends and supporters. Not included among them, however, were the overly zealous college girls. They had been banned from further attendance by M.S.C.W. president, Charles Hogarth.

That day, the jury heard testimony from over a half-dozen prosecution witnesses. The first to be called was the Tate's neighbor and friend, Jane

Hamilton, wife of Dr. Doug Hamilton. The Hamilton's had resided in the neighborhood for thirteen years, and their family included three young children. Jane and Gene Tate had been "very happy" in their friendship and had visited with each other on a daily basis. She had admired Gene as a mother: one who was fair, nurturing, and responsible - traits the women held in common. And Gene had been fun to be with - light-hearted. Jane, who taught voice lessons at home, possessed a beautiful singing voice. She had sung at Gene's funeral - until her voice broke with tearful emotion.

A pretty brunette in her thirties, Mrs. Hamilton was sworn in. Because of her grief over Gene's murder, Mrs. Hamilton had avoided reading news articles or listening to the radio broadcast of the proceedings. Her appearance that day was for her a sorrowful but necessary duty.

She spoke politely and softly in response to questions by prosecution team member Lowery Lucas who, as county attorney, had been part of the initial murder investigation. A tall gentleman with dark, wavy hair, Lucas was quieter than the other prosecutors, and often during the trial, he chewed on a pencil and carefully followed the proceedings.

"Let's say for the last year, have you had occasion to see the defendant playing with the Tate children in their yard?"

"Yes, sir, until sometime around Thanksgiving or Christmas, and thereafter I did not see him playing with the children."

"You don't know the reason he didn't play with them?"

"I do not know."

"Would you give the jury your best judgement about how frequently you saw the defendant in the yard of the deceased?"

"I would say two or three times a week, at least. I could say that until Thanksgiving or Christmas, sometime around there."

"Now were you at home on the morning of January 31, 1960?"

"Yes, sir."

"Do you recall that morning?"

"Yes, sir."

Mrs. Hamilton straightened the lapel of her black silk suit and steeled her composure against the memory.

"I was in a hurry getting my children ready for Sunday school . . . And Doctor took them to Sunday school, and our Sunday school at the Episcopal Church starts at 9:30 - whether they got there on time that morning or not, I can't remember - but I believe they did, and they left with him to go to church in the Pontiac, . . . and then it was agreed that they would walk from the church down to the clinic, and I would pick them up, . . . so I went back to the breakfast table."

"I sat down and ate breakfast with Doctor's mother, who was visiting us, and we sat there until 10:15 by my clock in the kitchen."

"I see," commented prosecutor Lucas.

"And at 10:15, I hopped up and was in a hurry to get through with the dishes so I could pick up the children. My children called on the telephone from the church at quarter to eleven by my clock, and I said, 'Just wait a few minutes until I get something on for dinner. You walk down to the clinic like I said, and I will pick you up.' "

"Well now, did you see Mrs. Baker? Mrs. Baker or her automobile?"

"I saw her automobile. I did not see her."

"That was at the home of the deceased?"

"Yes, sir."

"Do you know what time is was?"

"It was before . . . it was sometime when my . . . before . . . let me think a minute. It was when I sat back down at the table to eat breakfast, after my children had gone off. It was some time after that. I couldn't say when."

"All right. Now, you received a phone call from your children, I believe you said about fifteen till eleven by your clock. Then what did you do?"

"Doctor's mother and I got in the car, the little Ford, and we went down 12th Street North, and went down Military Road . . . I passed Dr. Hamilton. He was stopped at Reese's Drug Store. Then I went down 9th Street, and I passed Mr. Tate driving a Volkswagen, and the boys. I didn't see Mr. Montgomery at that point because I couldn't see the other side, and the only. . . and I beeped on the horn twice because I knew it was a new car, and Stan waved and smiled, and all the boys were just laughing. Then I went to the clinic, picked up my children, and then came back."

"When you arrived home, what, if anything, did you find?"

Mrs. Hamilton took a deep breath and continued.

"John Montgomery was running out the Tate's front door screaming, 'Is the doctor at home?' I started walking up the walk . . . and he started screaming to me, he said, 'Hurry, Mrs. Hamilton!' He said, 'It is an emergency! It is an emergency! . . . ' So I started running - and I was screaming when I ran in the house for Doug."

"I see, and what did Dr. Doug do then?"

"He was putting a box of candy in his mother's suitcase, and he came out . . . He started walking across the street in a hurry, and Mr. Montgomery was screaming to, 'Hurry Doctor! Hurry!' . . . and he ran across the street."

"Did you go into the garage?"

"No, sir. I made my children go in the house and help their grandmother in the house - in our house - and I did not go in our house at that time because I realized something was really wrong."

"Prior to the time that you went after your children, Mrs. Hamilton, did you see or hear any disturbance in the neighborhood?"

"No, sir."

"Did you see any strange cars in the neighborhood?"

"No, sir."

Having concluded the direct examination, Mr. Lucas turned to the defense table.

"Your witness."

Jesse Stennis rose from his table and, in a rolling walk, approached the witness stand.

"Ma'am, you spoke of Jon Mattox playing with the Tate children out on the front lawn there quite frequently. That was during the spring and summer and early fall that you had reference to was it not, ma'am, of last year?"

"Not only of last year, almost the entire time since the Tate's had moved up in that neighborhood, for several years."

"Now as a matter of fact, Mrs. Hamilton, I am sure that you saw Mrs. Mattox and Mrs. Gene Tate meeting out there and passing the time of day themselves, did you not, ma'am?"

"Yes, sir, until around Thanksgiving or Christmas."

"And you wouldn't say that she stopped going then would you? I mean it could have happened, and you not noticed it, couldn't it?"

"I wasn't there all day long, but I didn't notice either one going."

Mr. Stennis then led a series of questions about whether she had seen Mr. or Mrs. Mattox's cars at home, or Jon's car, and Mrs. Hamilton stated that she had seen none of the cars belonging to the Mattox family that morning and explained that she had not been looking for any cars.

"And you noticed Jon Mattox playing in the front yard of the Tate home with the children, and with the other children, and in other front yards. . . could you tell the court and jury approximately what time Mr. Martin Tate usually went to work in the morning?"

"When he was home, not traveling, I would say he left, he left in time to take the boys to Franklin Academy. It was around eight o'clock in the morning."

"And that was on occasions when he did not spend the night out of town?"

"Yes, sir."

"About how many nights a week did he spend out of town when he was traveling in 1959?"

"Let me think. May I take a moment?"

"Sure, sure. Take your time."

"I would say out of the week, Martin was in town on Wednesdays - Tuesday nights and Wednesday nights, and then Saturday and Sunday nights. . . And possibly the rest of the week, he was gone. Because Gene told me he was always in the office . . . "

"Wait, just a minute. We can't testify as to what someone else told you, Mrs. Hamilton. That violates the so-called hearsay rule. Now he was out of town on what nights?"

"On Mondays . . . "

Prosecutor Lucas then stood up. "May it please the court. I hesitate to interrupt . . . "

Mrs. Hamilton corrected herself: "I ought to say, 'in my opinion . . . ' "

Then Mr. Stennis, in agreement with the witness, stated, "Of course, you can just give your opinion about it."

Irritated, Mr. Lucas admonished him. "If you don't mind, Mr. Stennis, may I? It is obvious her testimony is based on hearsay evidence, and unless she can show that she knows of her own personal knowledge when he was out of town, we will have to object. Because she was about to say what Gene told her, the reason on which she was basing her answer."

Stennis addressed himself to Mrs. Hamilton - "You can't say what someone told you."

Judge Greene said, "If you bring it out on cross-examination - you can."

Mr. Stennis resumed with the question.

"But Monday nights, and did you say Tuesday nights?"

"He came in usually late Tuesday night because he spent Wednesday at the office."

"Yes ma'am. What about Thursday night and Friday?"

"Frequently, I would say he was out of town Thursday and Friday night. Or, he would come in late Friday night."

"I see. And it has been testified here that there was a strained relationship between Mr. and Mrs. Tate. I will ask you if you observed evidence of that?"

Mrs. Hamilton thought she must have misunderstood the attorney.

"You mean Gene and Martin Tate?"

"Yes, ma'am."

"No, sir," she slowly answered.

"You observed no evidence of that?"

"No, sir." She had no idea what Stennis was talking about.

"Now Mrs. Gene Tate was in your home, and you were in her home occasionally, were you not?"

"Almost every day."

A few more questions were posed by the defense regarding the day of the murder, rehashing previous testimony, and then Mrs. Hamilton was excused. To a few observers, she would prove to be a most interesting witness, especially in light of the prosecution's objection to a portion of her testimony. She was, after all, their witness.

The next witness for the state was Charles Clarkson, an attendant at Brown's Pan Am gas station. Clarkson described the shirt worn by the defendant when he stopped for gas sometime between ten and eleven o'clock on the morning of the murder. The Pan Am station was located about a mile from the Mattox home. It had been established that Gene Tate was killed within a few minutes after ten-thirty.

District Attorney Harvey Buck questioned the witness. A neatly dressed man of forty, with dark graying hair, Buck had only been a prosecutor for four months. He had been a former agriculture major turned law student.

Mr. Buck presented Mr. Clarkson with a blue-checked flannel shirt, and Clarkson identified it as "looking like" the shirt Mattox wore that morning. The witness said he remembered it because at the time, he was struck by the pretty blue color. Mr. Clarkson told the jury that the next day, on Monday, Jonny returned to the gas station and asked him whether or not the police had been around to ask about him.

"He said that - he asked me did I tell them what time he was in there, and I told him I didn't know what time he was in there, it was just between ten and eleven, and he said that he thought that he was in the station around ten-thirty . . . and I didn't know."

Mr. Stennis led a lengthy, sometimes confusingly, detailed cross-examination regarding the identification of the shirt and the time-line of the defendant's visit to the gas station. The witness, however, stuck by his previous testimony and added only that Jonny seemed like " his old self" when he saw him on Sunday morning. Clarkson had noticed nothing unusual about his demeanor.

When the witness left the stand, the jury was excused, and the judge heard motions by the defense - the first to exclude identification of the shirt, which was denied. Stennis also moved the court to take the testimony of the next witness, Police Chief Mahlon Vickery, in the absence of the jury to determine its admissibility. Mr. Stennis complained that he had been denied access to the shirt, coat hanger, and scarf, the latter two to be introduced during Vickery's testimony. Further, he moved the court to exclude the F.B.I. report regarding the fiber findings, because the defendant had not been allowed to examine the fibers.

Judge Greene puffed his cigar and again denied the motions of the defense. "Overruled. Let's proceed. Let the jury come out."

Police Chief Vickery, heavyset, but youthful in appearance, took the stand and identified the shirt as the one delivered to his office by the defendant's father on Tuesday, February 2nd, pursuant to the chief's request that he bring in the clothing worn by Jonny on the day of the murder. Mr. Mattox brought the shirt and a pair of slacks, neatly wrapped in an A&P grocery bag that was tied securely with a piece of brown twine. The shirt and slacks were damp, as Mr. Mattox had retrieved them from the washing machine. The chief described the procedure by which the clothing was tagged, stored, and accounted for by Lieutenant Louis Harper who subsequently delivered them, along with the victim's clothing, to the F.B.I. laboratory in Washington, D.C.

Special Prosecutor Burgin handed the chief the coat hanger, and then the black scarf - both of which he identified as the ones found near the body of Gene Tate. They were passed one at a time to the jury for examination. The jurors, however, handled the objects with their finger tips - as though they were reluctant to touch them. Some spectators leaned forward in their seats to watch their solemn reaction. Burgin adjusted his rimless glasses, then crossed his arms and waited.

When the items were passed back to the clerk, they were offered to the defense lawyers for their examination. Then Mr. Burgin moved to offer them into evidence, and predictably, Mr. Stennis rose to object.

"The defendant objects to the admission of the scarf and the coat hanger for the reason that it has not been properly identified and proved to be the ones testified to about - testified about by the witnesses," he studied his legal pad, " Hamilton, Montgomery, and Tate."

"Overruled at this time," responded the judge.

Stennis reserved the right to cross-examine Chief Vickery, and he was excused.

Lieutenant Louis Harper followed the chief to the stand. He was a nice-looking man with dark hair, about thirty years old, wearing a suit and tie. For the rest of the morning, the lieutenant testified about the collection, proper transport, and storage of evidence, particularly the defendant's clothing that Harper had taken to Washington, D.C. for F.B.I. analysis. He also confirmed that the crime scene photographs shown earlier to the jury did, in fact, accurately depict what he had personally witnessed at the Tate property the morning of January 31st.

Lastly, he was asked about a visit he made to the Tate house to search for blue clothing on February 6th, several days after he had returned from Washington with Mattox's shirt and pants. The officer said he looked in every area in the house where clothing could be found, and the only article that was blue, was a bath robe that belonged to the oldest child, Rob. The robe was also taken to Washington for analysis and comparison to the fibers found on Mrs. Tate's blouse and slacks.

Mr. Burgin asked that the bathrobe, along with Mrs. Tate's blouse and pedal pushers, be marked and entered as evidence.

"To which the defense objects, and assigns the same reasons assigned to his objection to the offering of all of the previous items offered by the state."

"Overruled, Mr. Stennis. All right, let's proceed."

Cross-examination followed with question after question that covered many details of the lieutenant's activities. At one point, the judge impatiently directed Mr. Stennis to move on.

"All right. Let's go on. We've been over that a dozen times."

Around noon, the defense concluded with the witness, but reserved the right to recall him for further cross-examination. The court then recessed for lunch. Several spectators remained in the courtroom, fearful that if they left for lunch they would lose their seats.

During the morning's testimony, rain pounded the courthouse roof, and witness testimony was interrupted from time to time with loud claps of thunder. The skies began to clear shortly after the court reconvened for the afternoon session.

Louis Harper had laid the groundwork for the first witness that afternoon, F.B.I. Special Agent C.G. McRight. McRight was an expert in hair and fiber analysis and had handled over a hundred such cases in the past four years. He had served as an F.B.I. agent for almost six years.

His fiber analysis report provided the first direct link between the murder victim and the defendant. Agent McRight had found seven blue cotton fibers on Mrs. Tate's white blouse, and one blue cotton fiber on her pedal pushers. The microscopic characteristics of all of the fibers matched in every detail the fibers taken for comparison from Mattox's blue-checked cotton flannel shirt.

Regarding Rob Tate's blue flannel bathrobe, the witness stated that fibers from the robe were slightly dissimilar in color to those found on the victim's clothing, but not sufficiently dissimilar to entirely eliminate the robe as a possible source. Later in the day, however, Martin Tate was recalled, and stated that his son Rob had not worn the bathrobe since Christmas. In addition, he said that it was his wife's habit to wear freshly laundered clothing every day.

When the defense attorney Stennis questioned Agent McRight, he explored with him many possibilities as to how the fibers from Mattox's shirt could have come in contact with the victim's clothing.

Working his hands in the pockets of his unbuttoned suit coat, he approached the witness.

"Mr. McRight, assuming that the person who lived - who owned and wore this blue cotton flannel shirt - lived in a residence on a lot adjacent to the lot upon which the residence in which the wearer of this ladies white blouse and checkered pedal pushers resided, and that the two residences were less than six feet apart," the attorney turned to face the jury box, "even the wind," Stennis dramatically emphasized the word by throwing up his hands, "could have blown some microscopic fibers from this shirt over to that house, couldn't it?"

Stennis was slightly deaf and failed to hear a spectator quip, "Those little boogers must've walked right through the front door!" Muffled laughter from the room followed, and the judge and jury suppressed their own amusement.

Sheriff Cricket Spruill, who was seated by the rail in front, turned his head and said, "Hush, or we'll have to tend to you!"

Judge Greene motioned, indulgently, to the witness to respond to the question.

"I would not say entirely that such a possibility does not exist . . . but I would consider that beyond any realm of the practical . . . And, as I pointed out before, there were seven fibers on the blouse and a single fiber on the pedal pushers, . . . and when such a number of fibers appear on one garment, to me, in my opinion, that indicates contact with a source of similar fibers - quite a number of similar fibers."

Other scenarios were suggested by the defense, such as the possibility of a dog transferring the fibers from the Mattox house to the Tate house. . . Finally, when finished with his questions, Mr. Stennis requested that he be allowed an opportunity to confer privately with Special Agent McRight. Judge Greene stated he had no authority to order the witness to comply, and then Mr. Burgin offered that he had no objection, so the judge ordered a recess to accommodate the defense.

Although Dr. Hamilton's previous testimony regarding the victim's cause of death added to reports that the prosecutors would not call the pathologist to the stand, after the brief recess prosecuting attorney, Lowery Lucas called Dr. James Beck to testify.

Dr. Beck, from Tuscaloosa, Alabama, was a silver-haired, bespectacled, older gentleman who had been engaged in the practice of pathology for almost thirty years. His impressive educational background included the universities of Alabama, Chicago, Pennsylvania, and Columbia.

He stated that the autopsy, on the body of Gene Tate, began at 6:00 p.m., the evening of January 31st. Dr. Doug Hamilton was present for the procedure. Mr. Lucas continued:

"Would you tell the jury what you found as a result of the postmortem?"

"Be glad to," responded Dr. Beck, and like an old professor fond of his subject, he did indeed seem comfortable making his presentation before the jury and crowded courtroom.

"The body was in the funeral parlor and had been embalmed. There was some hardening of the body tissues due to the embalmer's preserving fluid. But, in spite of this, there were the following changes: There was considerable blueness of the skin from the neck up, including the jaws, the face, the eyes, the eyelids, and the scalp. There was a deep groove in the neck of Gene Tate. The groove was three thirty-seconds of an inch in width, and it produced a deep furrow, forming a circle around the neck: Behind, it was about the midregion of the neck. In front, it was above the Adam's apple."

Jonny Mattox, seated against the rail with relatives, was fascinated by the description of death, but his face was without expression.

Dr. Beck then detailed for the jury the other changes he had found.

"There were small skin lesions that were oval, and about the size of lesions that could have been produced by nail injuries, as from the finger nails, as in scratching. They were on the sides of the neck, close to the grooving of the tissues. There were other changes: There were hemorrhages in various parts of the body, but in particular there were hemorrhages in the throat muscles, about the Adam's apple. Also in the lungs and in the heart. There were hemorrhages in the eyes, the whites of the eyes. These were the chief changes."

"Doctor, from your examination of the body, and based on your experience, which you have outlined, can you tell the jury your opinion as to cause of death?"

"This woman died of asphyxia because she couldn't get her breath - because she was choked to death with a wire-like thing tightly wound around her neck."

The pathologist had taken various measurements of the coat hanger, which had been provided to him by the police department, and the victim's neck and the tissue groove. He opined that the coat hanger dimensions perfectly matched those of the appropriate groove measurements.

Further, he stated that the victim's neck had been reduced in circumference by two and one-half inches . . . caused by the tightness of the hanger.

"Now this would have to be done with considerable speed in order to produce the curvature so indicated here," the doctor declared in reference to the hanger's curvature created by its application to the victim's neck. He held up the hanger to show it to the jury.

Lengthy and detailed cross-examination followed, but Mr. Stennis' time-consuming exploration of the testimony yielded no significant revelations. Dr. Beck was finally excused.

At the end of the day, Bill Burgin announced that the prosecution was about to rest. Mr. Stennis, aided by his co-counsel, state legislator Luther Sims, insisted that Burgin declare definitively whether or not he was calling more witnesses. Burgin stated that he had a few to recall, who were unavailable due to a funeral that afternoon.

The crux of the argument was based on a prior agreement that the defense could reserve its right to cross-examine witnesses prior to the time the state rested. So the defense wanted to know when, exactly, the state would rest its case. Judge Greene agreed with Mr. Burgin that the state was under no obligation to be precise about that, as it could be uncertain due to what may be developed by a witness or discovery of new information. He recessed for the day.

Reporters debated the issue as they left the courtroom. Was the state about to rest? Looked like it. And the circumstantial evidence against Mattox did not seem persuasive enough to get a conviction - much less the death penalty. On the other hand, stranger things had happened . . . And they thought they had seen it all.

SEVEN

The old wooden steps moaned as, one by one, she climbed the back stairs of the courthouse, accompanied by Lieutenant Louis Harper. She took a deep breath to calm herself. They entered through the back door of the second floor and, unnoticed amidst the loud hubbub of the crowded courtroom, she crossed in front of the lawyers' tables. Jon Mattox saw her and quickly whispered to attorney Stennis, who appeared to be quite confused. They whispered back and forth and stared in her direction. It was then that all eyes turned to the young, dark-haired woman in the simple blue dress, who was sworn in as the first witness Saturday afternoon.

Bill Burgin addressed the witness: "You are Miss Sarah Grayson?"

"Yes, I am." Sarah responded. Her high-pitched voice was almost inaudible. She had noticed Jon's reaction to her presence. All color had drained from his face, and there was the familiar scarlet blush around his neck.

"Where do you live Miss Grayson?"

"Bay Springs."

The court reporter asked her to speak louder.

"What does your father do?"

"My father, at present, is a school teacher. He has been County Superintendent of Education for eight years in Jaspar County."

"I see. Are you in school, Miss Grayson?"

"Yes, I am. I am a sophomore at Mississippi State University."

"I see. What is your major?"

"Right now, I am majoring in liberal arts. I have been in chemistry until this last semester."

Jesse Stennis interrupted:

"Your honor, I am going to ask the witness to speak a little more distinctly." He did not intend to miss a word. Who is this "liar?" as Mattox characterized her. And what the hell is she going to say?

"I think you must be hard of hearing, Mr. Stennis. I can hear her all right," answered Judge Greene.

"I am. That is the reason it is necessary that she speak a little louder."

Mr. Burgin continued. He was excited, keyed-up. Everything had to be just right. So many considerations: can she handle it - or will she fall apart? . . . In spite of the coming climax to his case, he maintained his poise. His voice was strong and smooth.

"Speak as distinctly as you can, Miss Grayson, so the court reporter, and the jury, and the counsel for the defendant may hear you. Do you know the defendant Jon Mattox?"

"Yes, I do."

"Is he in the courtroom?"

"Yes, he is."

"Would you point him out to us?"

"Right there." She pointed to Jon. During this exchange, Harley McNair carefully watched for any reaction from Mattox. But all he did was lean forward at the table and rest his chin in his fist, eyes fixed on Sarah. Harley, who covered the trial for the *Jackson Daily News*, was one of the very few people who knew what was coming - and knew both Sarah and Jon.

Sarah said that she and Jon had a class together, Qualitative Analysis, beginning in September of 1959, but did not get to know each other until later, on October 19th, during a make-up lab.

"I had been to Ole Miss to a ball game on the weekend before, and I had met Monday lab instead of my usual Friday lab on this particular occasion. This was the lab Jon had on Monday."

"Did you talk to him on that day?"

"Yes, for the first time, I talked to him. I was sitting there writing a lab report, and Jon walked in and looked at me and then came back in and sat down, and we started talking about our chemistry."

The defense then asked the judge to excuse the jury and have the testimony evaluated for its admissibility.

"Overruled. Go ahead."

Special Prosecutor Burgin resumed questioning.

"You say he came in and sat down?"

"Yes, he did. He sat down in the chair beside me. We introduced ourselves to each other. And then we talked for over an hour about several different things. I asked him what he was majoring in, and he told me it was physics, and I told him about my brother who was a nuclear physicist, and I told him . . . I told him about my brother, and then I got on the subject of how I had been in California all summer and the job I had."

"What job did you have, Miss Grayson?"

"I was a nurse's aid in a psychiatric clinic."

"I see. What did you tell Jon about that?"

"Well, I started off telling him a lot of things. We had been talking about physics theories, and we got into . . . At this time, I told him how interested I was in psychology, and I told him about the different cases I had seen in schizophrenia, paranoia, and various ones I had seen, and also the shock treatments of insulin shock."

"Where had you seen that?"

"In the Livermore Sanitarium and Psychiatric Clinic, in Livermore, California."

Again, Stennis told the judge that he could not understand what she was saying.

"Young lady, just take your time and talk a little slower and a little bit louder."

"I believe you were, you stated you told Jon about the different cases of paranoia, schizophrenia, and shock treatment that you . . . ," asked Burgin.

"Well, I was telling him about all the cases I had seen, how they had administered shock treatment, and this kind of thing, and Jon was very interested in psychology. He even suggested at one time that I try to psychoanalyze him because he didn't know what was wrong with him, and he also, also was drawing doodles on the paper, and he asked me if I could analyze that. He said, 'I don't know why, but I draw things symmetrically.' I told him of course I couldn't analyze that - I didn't know nearly enough about it."

"Did you discuss each other's families?"

"Yes, we did. I had told Jon about my brother who is a physicist and about how he would read a book at night, at least a book, every night before he would go to bed, and Jon said, 'My father is like that, too. He is such a brilliant man.' And I said, 'Well, that's nice Jon.' He says, 'Yes, if I could be half as smart a man as my father is, I would be very glad,' and he also told me about his brother and sister: how he felt that his father and his parents had loved his brother and sister, but never had really cared about him, and I said, 'Jon, surely you don't . . .' "

Attorney Stennis rose from his seat.

"Now, if Your Honor please, we are going to object to all this stuff here about this boy talking to this young lady here."

Burgin responded, "We will connect it up, Your Honor."

"Overruled."

Stennis continued, "And telling her that he felt that . . . "

"Overruled."

"It is highly prejudicial!" pleaded the defense attorney.

"Overruled. Go ahead," Judge Greene ordered firmly.

"I said, 'Jon, surely you don't mean that?' and he said. 'Yes, I do mean that.' I said, 'Don't you think that now that you are older that it is a change?' And he said, 'Well, maybe there is, maybe they care a little bit now, but they never cared anything about me,' and I said, 'Well, maybe that is just the way you felt as a child and that you have grown out of it.' And he said, 'No, they have never seemed to really care about me. They were always too interested in other things.' "

"I see. What else did you discuss on that occasion?"

"We discussed several things - I asked Jon was he living in the dormitory, and Jon said no, he wasn't living in the dormitory, and he hadn't since the Old Main fire, and I asked him why, and he said well, what he had at home in Columbus was much more important. And I said, 'Well, you know it has always been my theory that you get a lot more out of college life if you live in the dormitory and associate with people.' And he said no, he didn't mind riding back and forth every day, that what he had in Columbus was worth a lot more."

"What did you say?" asked Burgin.

"I said, 'Oh Jon, you must be dating somebody at the 'W,' and all those girls, you are kind of lucky, all the boys will be envious.' And he said, 'No, I am not dating anybody at the 'W.' The girl I'm going with works in Columbus.' "

Sarah stated that she and the defendant had talked well over an hour that day and had become well-acquainted. Beside the steady hum of the old fan overhead and her voice, there was no other sound in the courtroom.

She saw Mattox again the next Monday, when he invited her to come to the lab and talk with him.

"I don't remember anything we said that afternoon, except I remember walking, as we walked back toward the dormitory, he said he had to hurry home. And I said, well, what was so important that he had to get home in such a hurry, and he said, 'What I have in Columbus is worth a lot more. I have got to hurry on. It is that important.' "

"I see," commented Burgin. "Did you see him after that occasion?"

"Yes, I did. I saw him usually three times a week. I had two lectures with him on Tuesday and Thursday, and I also saw him Monday afternoon. I saw him next on the next Monday. However, I didn't go to lab, and I saw him on Tuesday, and he was fussing at me, and said, 'Why didn't you come to lab? I wanted to see you.' And I said, 'Well, I didn't know you wanted to see me, Jon,' and he said, 'Well, tomorrow,' which would be Wednesday, November the 4th, he said he was going to be there all afternoon, for the Junior Proficiency Exams, and that he wanted to see me - that I would have to entertain him and . . . "

"Did you meet him then, that day?"

"Yes, I did."

"What did you do?"

"Well, we didn't know what to do at first. We sat out in front of Lee Hall trying to decide what to do, and then Jon . . . There was a line, and we were going to eat. There was a long line, and we decided it was such a nice day we would have a picnic. And we didn't know where we would go on a picnic, however, because I hadn't been around long enough to know of any, of any lakes or anywhere nice to go, and . . . But we decided that was what we would do. And so we went to the A&M Dairy Bar and got sandwiches and got some gas, and he said he thought he knew of a lake not too far."

"We went out Highway 12 and turned off on the Louisville cut off. I am not sure what highway. I had never been there before, of course. And we went out to the lake, and when we went out there, at first, Jon was hungry - He hadn't eaten all morning. He said his mother hadn't fixed him any breakfast, and so we ate immediately. He was very hungry, and then after we got through eating . . . We had been talking all along because, by this time, I had seen him three or four times in a couple of weeks, and we had gotten to be pretty close friends. And we talked freely with each other, and after we finished and got through eating, I was sitting there by a tree, and

Jon leaned his head against the tree, and he started . . . he started making advances to me, and I was, I was surprised! I couldn't believe it, that Jon was. And I fussed at him. I said, 'Jon, don't you have any respect for me? Do you think this is very nice?' And after I fussed so much, he was sorry."

Mr. Stennis addressed the court:

"We are going to object, if Your Honor please - highly prejudicial, highly prejudicial, has no bearing on the charge. This young man here is charged with the crime of murder, and it's introduction of evidence which tends to show that he attempted to commit another crime. So, we therefore submit that it is highly prejudicial, incompetent, and for that reason we object and ask the court to declare a mistrial."

"Overruled. Go ahead."

"After that," began Mr. Burgin, "did you have any discussion with him?"

"Yes, we did. Jon and I talked for a long time, and Jon started telling me about, about his girlfriend and about the trouble they were having. And I said, 'Well, Jon, I will be glad for you to tell me because sometimes it helps to talk to people and to know . . . and to talk about it - you might feel better about it.' "

"Did he tell you whether or not it was over?"

"At the time, not at first, he didn't tell me it was over. Later, he told me that she had broken off with him on the Friday before. And something I couldn't understand was outwardly . . . "

"Now we are going to object to her remarks about something she couldn't understand, Your Honor." Stennis broke in.

"Overruled," responded the judge. Stennis slowly shook his head, sat down, and slightly shrugged his shoulders.

"You may continue," the prosecutor instructed. "You say that outwardly what?"

"Outwardly, he seemed calm - but yet, when he got started talking about it, he would be so upset. Jon was upset about his girlfriend. He didn't know what had happened, and things were messed up, and I said, 'Jon,' as I said before, I asked him again would he like to tell me about it: why was he so worried. And he said, 'I am just so much in love with her, Sarah, and she has left me, and I can't see her anymore.' And I said, 'Jon, I think I know what it is to love somebody,' and I tried to understand what he meant. He kept . . . He was so upset about the things that had gone wrong, and he loved her so much, and he says, ' Sarah, you . . .' "

"She is giving her opinion there, and she hasn't qualified as an expert." Stennis objected.

The judge told her to go ahead.

"He said he was so much in love. He said, 'Sarah, you will never understand what it is to love somebody the way I love her, because we loved each other more than, more than just . . . more than just usual.' He said, 'Our relationship had gone further than that.' And I was surprised. He said I wouldn't understand that. I said, 'You are right, I guess I don't. But, I understand what it is to love somebody.' And he said, 'But I loved her so completely, she was the kind you looked at her, and if you looked at her, you just made chills come all over you, and, and every time you touched her you could hardly stand it.' He says, 'You don't know what it is to love somebody, and just have them, and love them so completely.' "

"And I said, 'I probably don't Jon, but I see what you mean.' And I said, 'What's wrong now, Jon?' And he said, 'You will never understand, Sarah, it is so shocking.' And I said, 'Well, Jon, you have already shocked me to the fact that your relationship went so far.' And he said, 'Well, this will shock you more than anything has ever shocked you in all your life.' And I said,

'Well, Jon, I'm pretty broad-minded. I will try to understand.' And he said, while he was leaning back against this tree - he got this wild look in his eye - and he said, 'She loved her husband and four children more than she loved me.' "

"And I was shocked! And he jumped up right quick and, he was upset. He said, 'I know I should have never told you! I should never have let you know. I knew I would shock you, and I did shock you, didn't I shock you?' And he started walking off, just talking loudly, and I sat there. I was stunned because I had been so impressed with Jon because he was from a respectable family and because of his father.' "

"What did you do then?" asked Burgin.

"I knew I had to calm him down. He was so upset. He was blushing and talking loudly. And I walked over, and I tried to calm him down. I said, 'Jon, I will try to understand. I don't see how you could have gotten that serious.' Finally, I calmed him down enough to sit him down. And he sat back down by the tree, and he started telling me about it. And by this time, he was calm, and the things he was telling me - he . . . he knew what he was saying. He wasn't so wild as he had been before. And I said, 'Well, Jon, don't you know that something like this would be such a scandal for your parents?' And he said, 'Yes, I know, Sarah, I would die if my father ever found out.' "

Mattox sat at the defense table, expressionless, but focused. His mind raced between angry thoughts of revenge and practical strategy to discredit her.

"And the conversation went about . . . We kept discussing how bad it would be to create such a scandal, and he says, 'Yes, I know, I would hate to spread such a scandal for my family, and I am sorry. I would like to get out of this - I just don't know how to do it.' "

"He says, 'You will never know what pain we took to keep from being caught.' And I said, 'Jon, I don't see how somebody didn't know.' He said, 'Nobody ever suspected. Nobody ever had any idea.' And I said, 'Well, how long has this been going on, and he said, 'Oh, almost two years.' "

She continued, each word falling after the other in rapid succession. The entire audience, spectators, reporters, attorneys, and the jury, was captivated. The occasional pop of a flash bulb was a momentary distraction. Her revelations of the alleged affair was stunning news.

"He said, 'I moved home right after Old Main burned.' He told me that again, and he started . . . I asked him, I asked him, well, how long it had been since they had been so intimate, and he said, 'That's been going on for . . . well, two months after we started going together.' I said, 'Well, Jon, what did you do? You couldn't let people see you.' And he said, 'Oh, most of the time we just talked - we would go out and park somewhere, or we would go . . . or we would go to the drive-in.' And he says, 'You don't know how wonderful it is to have somebody to understand you, and to know and care about you, somebody that is really interested.' "

"And he said, 'From the very beginning, we understood each other.' He said also that when she came into a room, he felt her presence and that he knew she was there, and that she had told him after they started going together that she had felt the same way. And I said, 'Well, Jon, how did all this get started, and who started it?' And he said, 'Well, she started it.' He told me how he had been in her kitchen one day, and, all of a sudden, he was just kissing her. And it had gone from that. And that they . . . they went together from then on."

"Did he make any other statements with reference to that relationship at that time?"

"Yes, he did. He told me about how usually her husband traveled a lot, that he was a prominent businessman, and that when he was gone, she would call him to come over and stay with her at her house. I said, 'Well, Jon, how did, how did your parents not know?' And he said, 'I would leave as if I were going to a movie or somewhere.' And I said, 'Well, when did you come in, did you sneak in early in the morning?' And he said yes, he sneaked in early in the morning."

"Did he say where she lived?" asked Burgin.

"He said she lived close to him. I asked the question, 'Well, Jon, how did you keep from getting caught?' He said, 'The only person who could have caught us would have been her husband, and she knows something that would keep him from ever saying anything.' "

"What did you all do other than talk that afternoon?"

"Well, Jon had brought a pistol out there with him that day, and he said he was going to teach me how to shoot his pistol. He had a can, and we were trying to shoot a can, and I out-shot him more times out of five than he did, and he said something to the effect that, that, 'Well, I wouldn't ever try to kill you with a gun because you could out-shoot me.' And, at one time during the conversation about the gun, he had this wild look in his eyes - and I had eased over and taken the gun out of his hand because I was a little afraid . . . I didn't know why because I trusted him completely."

"Sarah, what were you wearing on that occasion? Do you recall?"

"Yes. I had on a bulky knit sweater and a scarf around my neck - a red scarf, a small scarf, and sometime during the day, Jon had taken the scarf off and was playing with it and doing it like this." Sarah pretended to be stretching the scarf taut. "And then one time, we were talking and laughing and acting silly, and he put the scarf around my neck and said, 'This would be so easy to kill somebody with a scarf around the . . . with a scarf.'"

"Did you see him after that occasion?"

"Yes, I saw him three times a week usually. I saw him the next day, and he had told me the day before that she wouldn't last - that she would call him again - he knew she would, and he would have a hard time ever giving in. But he was so determined he wouldn't. He would keep his family from having a scandal - and that he didn't want to give in."

"Did you encourage him not to see her?"

"Yes, I did. I told him I thought it was wrong. He told me on the next day - in the morning when we were walking to class. The next day was Thursday, and we had a class at nine o'clock. I saw him before class, and he said that she had called him that night, and that he had said he wouldn't go. And he said, 'You know, Sarah, because of talking to you - you gave me enough courage to say no - to what she wanted me to do.' "

"Not long after that, I wrote Jon a letter, and it was just a kind of an essay on how he was having such a hard time and how there would be so many things that would come up that would make him want to give in and go back to her, and the idea of it was to give him, to let him think that - not to go back, and to have the courage not to do it. I told him this was a test of his character to see if he were able not to go back to something that he wanted, and that is what the essay was on. And then, I mailed it to him."

"Did you all discuss this situation, as he described it to you, after that time?"

"Yes, on several occasions, he would tell me that she had called him and that he hadn't gone back to see her."

"Did the defendant ever say anything about Halloween?"

"Yes, he did, on the day of the picnic, on November 4th. He said that she and her four children had been over trick or treating at his house, and that she said . . . He had told her, 'Oh, you want another sucker? Haven't you already got one?' referring to himself."

During her testimony, the news reporters wrote furiously and had difficulty keeping up with Grayson's fast-paced account. However, Harley had not had to take notes. In his possession was a copy of the twelve page statement she had prepared for the police. He nudged the reporter next to him who scanned the document and registered surprise. It was almost as though Sarah was reciting, word for word, from her statement as she responded to prosecution questions.

Sarah then recounted to the jury that in late November, or early December, she and a friend had gone to Columbus to shop, and while there they had driven by Jon's house.

"The next Monday, when I saw him, we were sitting in the same classroom adjoining the lab, and I told him about it."

"I see," said Burgin, "and who was present?"

"There were several people there working on lab reports."

"Were any of them in the conversation, so to speak?"

"No, they weren't - Jon and I were sitting in the back of the room. He was working on a lab report. I told Jon I had been by his house, and I said, 'Jon, I wondered where she lived, since you said she lived close,'and he got angry with me. He said, 'What do you mean snooping around! What are you trying to find out? Don't you know that is the way people get caught! I shouldn't have trusted you! I should have never let you . . . I should have never told you anything!' And he was just so very upset that I said, 'Jon, I am perfectly innocent! I just went by your house thinking I might see you outside or something.' And he was still so angry."

"He became so angry with me. He was talking so loudly that people were beginning to turn around and look. And, 'Why was I sneaking on him trying to find out something! Why was I even that interested?' And, I told him I wasn't that interested - that I wasn't trying to sneak on him, that I had simply ridden by his house . . . "

"How did you know where his house was?" interrupted Mr. Burgin.

"Because I mailed the letter to him, if you remember, and when I mailed the letter to him, I looked the address up in the student directory."

"I see. Did he calm down?"

Sarah sighed, as though the telling of the incident had been as taxing as the actual event.

"I had to talk to Jon for about ten or fifteen minutes to get him calmed down - he was so angry. He thought I was trying to betray him and everything he had done. And I finally got him to calm down and talk about it. He was still so angry though. He had become flushed and was looking off into space . . . And, as I said before, people had turned around and looked. And after he had calmed down, he was just weak."

"And I asked him, I said, 'Jon, do you remember some of the things you said?' And I mentioned things he had said, and he said, 'I don't remember saying that. I wouldn't talk that way to you, Sarah.' And he was sorry."

"Did you see him subsequent to that occasion?"

Sarah answered that she had seen Mattox many times after that, and they had a habit of meeting at the "Grill" and walking to their nine o'clock class together. She remembered, however, a different time they met one afternoon, in December, sometime before Christmas, when they sat in front of Lee Hall to talk.

"And we were talking that day, and he seemed upset. He was cutting me short on everything I said, and I said, 'Jon, you have no reason to be angry with me, because I haven't done anything.' And he says, 'Yes, I know, Sarah. I am always sorry when I get angry with you because you have been so nice to me.' And then he said, 'But you know, Sarah, I lay awake at night worried - so afraid that you are going to tell if I ever kill her.' And I say, 'Jon, don't talk like that. You know you will never kill her.' And he said, 'Well, what would you . . .' "

"Slow down," the court reporter reminded the witness.

"He said, 'What would you do if I were to kill her?' And I said, 'Jon, I don't think I will ever be faced with a problem. I don't know what I'd do. But I know one thing - I would never let innocent people be hurt.' And he said, 'That's what I thought. I don't want to die. You are too conscientious, Sarah. You would tell.' And I said, 'Let's don't even talk about this, Jon, because you are not going to do it, and it is just silly to even discuss it.' And he was very upset that day, and by this time, it had gotten time for him to go to lab . . . "

Again, the court reporter interrupted and asked her to please slow down.

Mr. Burgin then asked if she had seen the defendant after that time.

"Yes, I did. I saw him a good many times. Right after Christmas, I remember one morning we were walking from class, and we were standing in front of Lee Hall, and he told me how he had been deer hunting and how he had shot a deer out of season, and how angry his father was at him. And he said, 'Whew! Was he . . .' "

Defense Attorney Stennis rose to object.

"That conversation tends to prove the defendant guilty of another, and separate, crime for which he is not on trial at this time, and such things is highly prejudicial, and it is elementary that the courts cannot permit the testimony about other crimes."

"Overruled."

"You say he said he shot a deer out of season, and his daddy was mad at him?" asked the prosecutor.

"Yes, he said his father was very angry with him. And I said, 'Well, Jon, you shouldn't have shot him out of season, but I know how much you like to hunt.' And he said, 'I didn't . . . I didn't kill him for any reason, except I just had to kill him - poor little thing. I just had to kill him.' "

"I said, 'Jon, you don't mean to say that.' And he says, 'Yes, I do. I had to kill the thing. We didn't need him. Mother has a freezer full of meat now - of things I have shot.' And I said, 'Well, Jon, you just like to hunt.' "

As she spoke, Sarah took notice of Mrs. Mattox's reaction to her testimony. She was puffing nervously on her cigarette, and Sarah, at that moment, knew Jon's mother realized she was telling the truth. Sarah felt sorry for her.

"Did you have occasion after Christmas to have any other conversation with the defendant, or to ride in his automobile?"

"Well, on one afternoon, we were coming from the lab, and I had gone from the lab to the library and came back over to, to . . . as I was walking to the dormitory, Magruder Hall, and he was out there in his car. And he said, 'Well, come on, you can drive my automobile.' And so we drove around the circle in front of Hull Hall and came right back to Magruder, and I got out and went in. And then another time, after Christmas, he has a physics lab from two to four on Tuesday."

"What kind of automobile does he have, Miss Grayson?"

"He has a gold and white Mercury with a Cadillac transmission."

"When was the next to last time you saw him before the end of the semester?"

"On this time, I saw him . . . it was four o'clock in the afternoon - this would have been January the 19th. It was two days before we went home for the end of the semester. And I went out, I saw Jon as he came out of the lab at four o'clock. He came down to the 'Grill', and I was sitting with a couple of friends talking, and we went outside. It was raining that day, and we went outside and sat in his car in front of the 'Grill.' "

"And all right, you sat in his car?"

"We were sitting in his car talking, and he was upset this day too. We talked about several things, and on this day, I had gotten in the car - it had been raining before we went out. And I took my scarf off and stuck it in my pocket and took my raincoat off. And while we were talking, Jon had gotten my scarf out, out of the car - and was doing it like this . . . " Sarah demonstrated with her hands how he stretched the scarf. "And he said, 'You know, that is pretty strong!' And he kept talking then about how he was . . . he was going to kill her, and what would I do if he killed her. And I said, 'Jon, don't even talk about that. It is not even something to discuss!' "

"And he said . . . he said, 'Well, I have figured out how to commit a perfect crime. The best way is to use a coat hanger - because you don't have any finger prints, and it is strong enough.' "

"What color was the scarf, Miss Grayson?"

"Black. A long, black scarf."

"Did you subsequently miss that scarf?" asked Mr. Burgin.

"Yes. I remember walking up the steps in front of Magruder, after I left Jon that day, thinking, 'Now, where did I leave my scarf? My hair is getting wet.' And when I got back to the dormitory, I looked in my raincoat pocket and everywhere I could think of, and it wasn't there. I remember thinking, 'Well, I will have to ask Jon did I leave my scarf in his car.' "

"Did you ever ask him that, Miss Grayson?"

"Yes, I think I did. I saw him the next Thursday, before we had our final quiz, and I asked him about it then. I do not remember his answer."

"What texture was that scarf, Miss Grayson?"

"It was a kind of chiffon."

"I hand you here a scarf that was marked Exhibit 2 to the testimony of Chief Mahlon Vickery, and ask you if you can identify it?" Burgin handed the scarf to Sarah.

"It is just like the one I had."

"Does it have the same texture fabric?"

"Yes, it does."

He took the scarf from her and placed it back on the table by the court reporter.

"On the occasion when you . . . after which you missed the scarf, was anything else said by the defendant relative to the . . . "

"No. The next time I saw him was before the quiz, as I said, and that day: the day he got angry for no reason . . . He had done that before on several occasions. I would say something that, you would never know why he would be angry. And he would get angry and just stalk off in class. And that day he got angry and just walked off into class. But before I left that day, he made a point of smiling at me. That was the last time I saw him - until after the murder."

"On the occasion when he mentioned that he had figured out a perfect way to kill somebody with a coat hanger, because it wouldn't leave any finger prints, did he make any other statements relative to killing?"

"Well, he just said he was going to kill her . . . and I said, 'Jon, you know you are not going to kill her. Don't even talk that way.' "

"Did you believe him?"

"No, I did not believe him! He said, 'You don't believe me, Sarah, but some day you are going to hear this on the radio, and you are going to know what has happened, and you can't say a word.' And he said, 'You have got to promise me that you will never say anything - no matter what happens.' And I wanted him to be quiet, so I said, ' Jon, all right, I won't say anything about it,' because I wanted . . . I said, 'I want you to know one thing though, and that is, if anything ever were to happen, I would expect you to have enough character to turn yourself in, that you wouldn't let anybody innocent be hurt.' "

"How did you learn of the death of Mrs. Tate, Miss Grayson?"

"I learned of the death on Sunday afternoon, somewhere around two o'clock. I was sitting in my room with two other friends, and I was sewing. I heard it on the radio, . . . and everything fit: the four children, the prominent business man."

"Did you see the defendant after that time?"

"Yes. I saw him on Wednesday after the murder on Sunday."

"Where were you?"

"I was in French class in Lee Hall. I had just had a French class, and I was going to change desks because I have German the next period in the same class room. And I picked up my books, to go move from one desk to the other, and just about the time I did, Jon walked in. We were both so startled to see each other . . . I had wondered how I would feel when I saw him - knowing what I did. And then, at the time, I did . . . He started stammering, and he was blushing, and he turned very red. And he said,

'Well, I didn't know we had a class together.' And I said, 'I didn't know either, Jon.'"

"What did he do then?"

"I started to walk off, and as he walked off, I saw the back of his neck, and I will never forget how he was blushing so much."

"What color was he?"

"He was scarlet."

"Miss Grayson, after that, did you have any discussions with the defendant?"

"I saw him, I didn't see him . . . Well, I saw him once before he was arrested the next day, but after his arrest, and when he came back to school, I had psychology class with him. And I saw him before class and around the "Grill," but I never talked to him for any length of time. I avoided Jon because I was afraid. At first, I was very much afraid because I knew - he knew I knew about it."

"Miss Grayson, did you know a reward had been offered for information leading to the solution of the death of Mrs. Gene Tate?"

"I knew of a reward of a thousand dollars, when I told a girlfriend, and when I decided. One night, I was sitting in the library, and I had a Sunday's paper, and the Sunday's paper said there was a reward of a thousand dollars - and that scared me because I knew Jon might think money would mean something to me, and he might think that I would care about money . . . and I became afraid. I knew - I had known all along - that I had to say something. I had . . . A friend had told me a rumor about a week . . . "

"Don't," reminded the prosecutor, "Don't say what anybody told you now."

"On this date, I decided that I had to do something, that, that . . . that I - I might be hurt, too and also . . . "

"What did you do?" Mr. Burgin inquired. He had learned a little late that the witness was never at a loss for words and required a bit of structure.

"Well, I went and called a friend. I was going to borrow his car and come over to the police station. My girlfriend was going to come with me, and we were going to just tell them. I was just going to go in and tell them all I knew about it and anything that might help. When, at the time . . . "

"Did you do that?"

"No, I went to talk to the friend to borrow his car, and he said, 'Sarah, you will be involving yourself in something you don't want to get into.' "

"Don't say what he said now. Did, as the result of that conversation, did you not then come to Columbus yourself?"

"No, I did not. That very same night, I told Harley McNair about the story. Harley is the editor of the *Reflector* at school."

"Do you work on the paper?"

"Yes, I do. On this particular . . . "

"Who contacted the police in Columbus?"

"Harley did. Harley and I tried . . . "

"At whose request?" asked Burgin.

"At my request. He came over on Saturday, after that Thursday night, and talked with Chief Vickery."

"As a result of that, did you subsequently have a conference with Chief Vickery?"

"Yes."

"And others?"

"Yes, but it was after spring holidays before I did that. Before this time, I had written a statement to the police."

"I see. You furnished them with a statement?"

"Yes, I furnished them with a twelve page statement of the same things I have said today."

"Miss Grayson, have you been offered a reward?"

"No, I have not."

"By anyone?"

"No, not by anyone, and if I were offered - I don't know whether I would take it."

"You may take the witness," Mr. Burgin said as he turned toward Mr. Stennis at the defense table.

Mr. Stennis made some last minute notes on his pad and considered his move. Lordy, Lordy. He was gonna have his hands full with this little ole gal. Boy, could she talk!

And it hurt him bad. Burgin's hurt 'em bad now. She was good. Sounded very earnest, truthful. Provided the jury with a motive - not that Burgin had to prove a motive, but it made the jury feel better to know why - a missing piece to the puzzle.

What he was gonna have to do is get her - under oath, to tell him as many facts as possible, no matter how trivial or insignificant. That way, over the weekend, he and his staff could do some research on her and trip her up later. That is, if they can't disprove her all together. After all, nobody's got perfect recall. It's just human nature to make a little mistake in recall about this or that. And he was gonna catch her! He was going to convince the jury, little by little and step by step, that she was not believable. Not beyond a reasonable doubt.

Aside from a last-minute confession from somebody else, or the discovery of evidence that cleared his client - and these things rarely happened -

this strategy was his most common weapon. Effective, dramatic, hard-hitting cross-examination, cushioned with appropriate finesse. It was the hallmark of any criminal defense attorney worth his salt.

"I believe you said your name was Miss Sarah Grayson. Is that right, ma'am?" The old lion fingered the change in his left pants pocket and slowly strolled toward the witness box.

He would lead her like a lamb to the slaughter.

EIGHT

Defense Attorneys Stennis, Sims, and their client Mattox, had made notes throughout Sarah's direct examination. Mr. Stennis referred to them as he questioned the young co-ed. For her part, Sarah remained poised and erect in the witness chair with her full attention focused on the attorney.

He asked her for detailed accounts of where she and her parents had resided, her mother's family background, and her father's professional history. Then he inquired as to whether either, or both, of them were present in the courtroom, to which she replied they were not.

Abruptly, Stennis launched into another area.

"Where was it that you said that you had had some practical experience , or some contact, with the subject of psychology?"

"Well, you see, sir, I have a brother who is a nuclear physicist, and he is with the University of California in Livermore, California. I went out to visit him this summer, and while I was there, I had this job in Livermore at the Livermore Sanitarium and Psychiatric Clinic. I worked there all summer."

"I see. And that is where you learned so much that Jon asked you to psychoanalyze him, wasn't it?"

"Well, I didn't learn so much. I saw a good many things along that line."

Then Stennis asked her to repeat the name and location of the clinic, her brother's name and address, the school where he earned his doctorate degree, and more details about her college attendance. From there, his questions changed to explore the chronology of her decision to inform the police about her knowledge of the murder. As she had during her previous testimony, Sarah once again explained the reasons for her decision, her meeting with Harley McNair, the editor of the school newspaper where she worked on staff, and their subsequent meeting in West Point with Columbus authorities.

"Now you tell the court and jury that young Mattox had told you that he was going to kill his lover?"

"Yes, he had told me more than once."

With sarcasm in his voice, Stennis continued.

"He had told you on innumerable times, had he not?"

"I would not say innumerable, but . . . "

"Well, how many then?" he demanded.

"I could not innumerate them, sir, but he had told me on at least two specific times, of which I have already mentioned."

"Now, two specific times that you have mentioned. Did he tell you on any time that you haven't mentioned?"

"Well, sometimes in conversation, in the hall, he would start talking about how much he loved her, and said, 'Well, now she has done me wrong and I am going to kill her,' and I would stop him immediately."

"And how many times did he tell you he was going to kill her, so many times you could not innumerate them? Is that correct?" Stennis swaggered back and forth in front of the jury box.

"He told me quite frequently."

"Yes, ma'am, practically every time he saw you, didn't he?" smirked the lawyer.

"No, not every time he saw me, " Sarah answered politely, but firmly.

"I said 'practically' every time!"

Burgin objected to the repetition of the questions, but Judge Greene overruled him.

"Would you say he told you practically every time he saw you?"

"No, I would not. I saw him many times in lab when he mentioned nothing about it." With his hands on his hips, he stood near the witness.

"I see, and then after the death of Mrs. Tate, he hunted you up the very first day he returned to school and told you he had killed her, didn't he?" The attorney leaned in so close to her, Sarah thought his bushy black and white eyebrows would brush against her face.

Sarah was unnerved by Stennis's combative tone and close physical proximity. She remembered Bill Burgin's advice to her: 'Just tell the truth and you will be all right.' Yes, she thought, he can't foul me up as long as I tell the truth.

"No, he did not, sir. He mentioned nothing to me about killing Mrs.Tate. I saw him Wednesday, after the murder on Sunday, and he did not mention anything about the murder."

"Did he talk with you about the murder after the murder?"

"I talked to Jon, but never about the murder."

"Could you give the jury an estimate about how many times, ma'am?"

Sarah's eyes shifted toward the jury box, and she smiled slightly, deferentially.

"Well, I saw him one day in the line - lunch line, and I introduced him to a friend of mine, and we talked a few minutes that day. And I saw him the day he first came back after he was released from jail, and I said something to him. And a couple of times in psychology class, he turned around and said something to me. Other than that, I had no intimate conversations with him."

"I see, and he never did tell you, after the death of the lady, that he had done it?"

"Never after the death. I avoided Jon, sir, because I, I realized what had happened."

"I see, and I believe you said you came, you looked in the student directory over at Mississippi State there, and got the address of the defendant here and wrote him a letter?"

"Yes, I did, sir. I have the letter."

"You do have the letter?" Stennis asked uncomfortably.

"Yes, I do." Sarah replied expectantly.

He nosily flipped through his notes at the defense table and ignored her.

"Now, what was the name of the party that you went to borrow a car from to come over here and tell the police what you knew?"

"The friend I went with was Judy Jenkins."

"Was who?" Stennis looked up from his pad.

"Judy Jenkins."

"Jewie?"

"Judy. J-U-D-Y."

"Where is she from?"

"Elgin, Illinois."

Mr. Stennis determined that Judy Jenkins was present in the courtroom, and asked Judge Greene to have her removed along with Harley McNair. He informed the judge that he intended to subpoena them both as witnesses.

"They will not be disqualified if they stay here all afternoon. I will let them testify," ruled the judge.

"Now," the defense attorney turned back to the witness, "do you read a daily newspaper, ma'am?"

"Yes, sir, I do - the *Clarion Ledger* in the morning and the *Jackson Daily News* at night."

"Do you read the *Commercial Dispatch* of Columbus?"

"No, sir, I do not."

Stennis questioned Sarah regarding her knowledge of the one thousand dollar reward.

"You remembered seeing in the paper the offering of this reward, when it was first published, didn't you?"

"I saw a thousand dollar reward on that Sunday. That was the only time I saw it."

"Did you know that it had subsequently been increased to more than five thousand dollars?"

"Since then, sir, I have heard that."

"Yes ma'am, and it was since you learned of the reward that you came over to West Point and told the District Attorney about it, was it not?"

"No, sir, it was not."

"It was before then?" Stennis winked conspiratorially at the jury foreman.

"That's right. When I decided, before the money was ever mentioned, that I had to do this."

"When is your birthday, Miss Grayson?"

"December 13th."

"Now, I will ask you if it isn't a fact that, on your birthday, you made a long distance phone call to Jon Mattox?"

"Sir, I made a long distance phone call to Jon and accidentally got his uncle, John Mattox, to which Mr. Mattox replied that, 'You must want the tall, good-looking one?' I replied, 'Yes, sir, I do.' After that, I got the right number, and I talked to Mrs. Mattox. Mrs. Mattox called Jon to the telephone for me, and I talked to Jon a few minutes."

"And you, of course, considered Jon the 'tall, good-looking' Mattox, didn't you?"

"Yes, I did."

"In fact, you thought he was extremely handsome, didn't you, young lady?"

The defendant amused, grinned at the other attorney at the defense table.

"Not extremely. I thought he was . . . I thought he was a good-looking boy, yes."

"And on that occasion, ma'am, I will ask if you didn't tell Jon that it was your birthday?"

"It is highly possible, sir. I do not remember the date."

"And isn't it a fact that you told him that you were over there by yourself, and were lonesome, and asked him if he wouldn't come over to see you?"

"No, I did not ask him to come see me. I told him I was in the dormitory by myself, which I was. I was sewing at the time."

"And that you were lonesome, didn't you?"

"I did not say that I was lonesome."

"You did not say that you were lonesome, and . . . "

"The dormitory full of girls is hardly the place to be lonesome."

"Beg pardon?"

"A dormitory full of girls is hardly the place to be lonesome."

"Well, the most lonesome time a man can be sometime is when he is around a whole lot of other men. I believe you tell this court and jury that you have had only one date with this defendant. Is that correct?"

"I have only had what could be called a date once, yes."

"I see."

"And that was November 4th, when we went on a picnic."

"And that was the first date that he ever had with you in his lifetime, wasn't it?"

"That is right."

"And it is the last date he has had, isn't it?"

"You are right."

"And that was the first time he ever asked you for a date, wasn't it?"

"Yes, sir. Jon made the statement that, 'I cannot date you, Sarah, because you know all about me, and you could never go with me because you understand all this situation, and you will never be able to forget it.'"

"Now why was he called upon to explain to you why he could not go with you, ma'am?"

"Well, sir, he was never really called upon to tell me that - he, why he could not go with me. He made such a statement. However, at one time, I had tried to get Jon to enter into things and be more active and get to know people, because he had told me that he didn't like people, and he had to stay away from people. And I tried to talk him into going to the Freshman-

Sophomore Prom at one time, hoping he would get with people and enjoy himself. He refused that, sir, because he said, 'I, I would go with you Sarah, I would love to go. However, I do not want to go around people.' And he told me repeatedly how he did not want to be with people, and it was my intention all along to try to get him interested in people and things."

"I see. What things?"

"Well, just, just - just in something besides going hunting all the time. That is the only pleasure he said he had. He told me one time that the only time he was ever happy was when he was in the woods alone, by himself."

"And you have on many occasions, when this young man would be starting away from campus, waved to him, and call him, and tell him to wait, would you not?"

"No, not on many occasions . . . "

"On several occasions?"

"Now, may it please the court, the witness is entitled to explain," said Mr. Burgin.

"Well, all right," agreed Judge Greene.

"She was interrupted by counsel again."

"Go ahead and explain," the judge instructed the witness.

"On one occasion, which I am sure you have reference to, I tried to talk to Jon. Jon was going to have to go home early, and I tried to talk him into letting me borrow a friend's car and carry him home so he wouldn't have to hitch-hike. He refused this, however. He said, 'I can't risk, I can't see you, Sarah.'"

"You wanted to borrow a car to bring him home?"

"Yes, sir, I would have. I would have borrowed a car to bring him home so he would not have to walk."

"And he refused to let you do that?"

"Yes, sir, and do you know why he refused?"

"Now, I didn't ask you that now. Now I will ask you . . . " The lawyer was drowned out by laughter in the courtroom. The spectators were beginning to enjoy this feisty young witness.

"Just a minute, Mr. Stennis. Now, if you can't keep quiet and not laugh, and show more discipline than this, I am going to have to clear the courtroom," the judge admonished the audience.

"I will ask you, ma'am, if you will state to these thirteen gentlemen over here, if it isn't the truth that on some occasions, when he and the young gentlemen who were in the car pool with him would be driving away from the campus, and you would hail them and ask them to wait, that you wanted to talk with Jon?"

"I have never, on any occasion, hailed Jon when he was with boys in his car pool and asked them to wait and let me talk to him. The boys in his car pool all know me because they remember the book I gave Jon to read, and the boys also know me, as they called me 'Jon's bird dog.' They kidded Jon about me."

"You are known on the campus, the Mississippi State campus, as 'Jon's bird dog!' Is that correct?" Stennis loudly asked with dramatic flair. Again, the crowded courtroom responded in thunderous laughter. This startled Sarah and apparently hurt her feelings, as she teared up and appeared shamed.

"All right! Mr. Sheriff, get the crowd out." Judge Greene would tolerate no more. However, even though the over-flow people: those seated on the window sills and those standing along the walls - were ushered and motioned out of the room - most of those seated looked stricken, and with pleading eyes, persuaded the sheriff to ignore their presence.

Mr. Stennis continued his inquiry.

"Now, you gave this young gentleman here a book, I believe?"

"Yes, sir, the name of the book is *The Prophet* by Gibran."

"And did you give him anything else?"

"Not to my recollection. Sir, maybe I would like to explain about the bird dog. The people on the Mississippi State campus did not know that - only the boys in his car pool. And the reason I heard about that was Jon told me that he just couldn't have people knowing about me. And his parents - it was killing him because I had called him."

"Now, young lady, I didn't, I didn't ask you about that."

"She has a right to explain," argued Burgin. The judge agreed.

"Sir, you have a way of misinterpreting what I said," added Grayson.

The judge told her to go ahead and continue her explanation.

"Well, this was only, this was only from the boys in Jon's car pool, and they kidded Jon. Jon was upset one day because he did not want people to know about me. He was afraid evidence would go back. He was afraid that a scandal would come out. At least, that is what I thought."

"We object!" declared Mr. Stennis. Then the lawyers and the judge all talked at once and shouted "Wait a minute!"

"She is making an explanation, Mr. Stennis." responded Judge Greene. He nodded for Sarah to continue her statement.

"I would also like to explain how Jon was angry one day because his parents knew about me. He had told them my name, and also his uncle knew about me, and he did not want people to kid him, and he did not want people to know. He did not want to date anybody on campus."

"And do you deny to this court and jury that the book is the only thing that you ever gave Jon?"

"I gave Jon, as I said before, I wrote Jon a letter, and a note that I wrote Jon when he returned my book. Would you like to read the letter that I wrote Jon?"

"I am not interested in any letter that you may have written him, young lady." Stennis silently read over his notes, and the judge took the opportunity to call for a brief recess for the benefit of the jury.

Suddenly, there was the scuffle of feet and the popping of camera flash bulbs. Photographs for the next day's papers. Reporters quickly left the room to phone in their reports. The sound of chatter in the courtroom grew louder, and Sarah, with a sigh of relief, exited the courtroom for the privacy of the witness room.

The defendant, after posing for a photo or two, became engaged in an animated and light-hearted chat with acquaintances, but he briefly glanced at her as she passed the defense table. She looked neither right nor left.

The parties, jury, and spectators took their places as the judge called the court back in session. Sarah Grayson took her seat in the witness box. Defense Attorney Stennis resumed the cross-examination.

"Miss Grayson, I believe you stated that you tried to get the defendant here to move over on the campus at Mississippi State, did you not, ma'am?"

"I did not try to get Jon to move over to the campus. I suggested it would be nice if he tried to get into things, and know people more, instead of letting people alone the way he was."

"Did you suggest that it would be nice for him to move over to the campus?"

"I did not suggest it would be nice for him to move over to the campus, no, sir. I was talking to him in reference to moving over for his own personal sake. Never at any time was I more interested in Jon than in helping him."

"I see . . . I would like for you to tell now, all the different people that you have told about Jonny saying that he was going to use a coat hanger on someone in Columbus."

"Well, sir, as I have already told you, I told Judy and Harley. I have told my parents, and I have told my brother and his wife."

"And those are the only people?"

"I almost told my roommate, but I didn't. I didn't tell her any details."

"You almost told your roommate, but you didn't?"

"Well, I started to tell her, sir. That was the day I was so upset from having heard that Jon could have committed two possible other murders. That is what scared me - because then was the first time I . . . "

"We object to that," Stennis roared, "if Your Honor please, and move that the jury be instructed to disregard it!"

"That part of it, gentlemen of the jury, you will disregard," instructed Judge Greene.

"And now we move for a mistrial!"

"That is overruled." Undaunted, Mr. Stennis continued the interrogation.

"I believe you said you rode in Jon's car?"

"Yes, I rode in his car around the circle of Lee Hall one day, and I rode in his car on the day we went on a picnic. Other than that, I have rode in his car not at all."

"You have been in his car only two times?"

"Well, let's see. The day I saw him at the 'Grill,' which was January 19th, he drove me back to the dormitory."

"And what kind of transmission did you say it had in it?"

"I thought it had a Cadillac transmission, because that is what he had told me at the time. All I remember is this: it doesn't have a Ford transmission because it is a Mercury, but yet, it has a General Motors transmission in it. The shift is different from ordinary transmissions."

"And it was what model?"

"I do not know, sir. I believe it was '52 or 3. I am not, I do not know."

"And, did he ever give you a present?"

"No, he did not."

"Did he ever write you a note?"

"No, he did not."

"Did he ever call you over the telephone?"

"No, he did not. He came to Magruder Hall several times and sat in the lobby - called me from the lobby. And he told me on numerous occasions how he wanted me to come to the lab."

"When you were working in the psychopathic ward, or psychology institution, in California, who was your immediate supervisor?"

"Well, Mrs. Bernhart, who was the Chief of Nurses. It was a psychiatric clinic."

"And what were your duties there?"

"As a general rule, I helped with such things as electric shock treatments, and I also helped with, with, well, just the general routine duties of a nurse."

"What is schizophrenia?"

"Schizophrenia is a mental illness, where a person has a dual personality. A schizophrenic person, usually, the only, it is usually hereditary, and it usually doesn't show up until about the age of twenty."

"And you talked with people who had schizophrenia and other forms of mental derangement, did you not, ma'am?"

"Yes, I did - psychotics, neurotics, alcoholics."

"Yes, ma'am. And you were there how long?"

"Not quite three months."

"This shock treatment, did you ever take any shock treatments yourself, ma'am?"

"Oh, no, sir."

"Did you ever take any psychiatric treatment?"

"No, I did not."

"Were you ever psychoanalyzed?"

"No, I was not."

"Did you have any dates in California?"

"Yes, sir, I dated a boy who was a chemist."

Special Prosecutor Burgin objected to the question as irrelevant, but was overruled.

"Go ahead. Tell him if you had any dates out there." The judge smiled at her.

"Yes, I dated one boy, the boy who sent me the book Jon read. I dated him all summer, and he was working with Bio-Rad Labs in California."

"Would you spell that for me, please, ma'am?"

"B-i-o, dash, R-a-d."

"Bio-Rag?"

"Biological Radiation Laboratory."

"And would you please, ma'am , spell his name out?"

"His name is Stan Gold. S-t-a-n G-o-l-d."

"T-a-n-g-o-l-d?"

"Stan, S-t-a-n." Mattox grinned at the exchange while he doodled on a pad.

Stennis asked for Gold's address and telephone number.

"Berkeley, California. 2431 Webster Street. I do not recall his phone number, but I have it."

"Unhuh. You called it many times while you were in California, didn't you?"

"No, sir, I did not. I had never called it while I was there." Sarah was insulted by the question.

"And who else did you date in California?"

"I dated a couple of other people. I dated a mathematician, and I dated a physicist from the lab, but I did not date them as much as Stan." Stennis asked for their names and how many times she had dated each of them.

"Now, of course, you are going steady on the Mississippi State campus at this time, are you not, ma'am?"

"No, sir, I have been going steady for the last four years, and I broke up with the boy I had been going with last summer."

"What was his name?"

"Henry McCrory." Again, the lawyer asked for his address and school status.

"And are you, if you are not going steady at this time, are you going steadily? There is a difference, is there not?"

"I have heard such. I had been until about two weeks ago."

"And you broke up with him?"

"Yes, well basically, it was mutual."

"Unhuh."

"I see no bearing on my personal life."

"Well now, would you mind telling us the name of the young gentleman with whom you had been going steadily up until about two weeks ago?"

"I will be glad to, sir. I, I don't, I do not see the necessity in it. However, his name is Robert Stone."

Stennis wanted to know his major and where he was from.

"Electrical engineering. He is from Greenwood."

Time to perambulate. Jesse Stennis strolled back and forth in front of the witness box. He ran his right hand over his slicked-back, graying dark hair and jiggled the change in his left pocket. The courtroom was attentive. The sounds of chirping birds and the start and stop of downtown traffic could be heard through the tall open windows. Many of the folks seated there prayed for the cooling breeze that would not come.

Sarah was weary and wished she were outside in the sunshine, on the cool campus grass at "State," and that none of this had ever happened to her. There were so many people in the courtroom. Earnest faces trying to size her up. Some smiled at her. One lady with mean eyes stared at Sarah and made her uncomfortable, like she would slap her if she could get close enough. It comforted her to see, among the strangers, her friends Harley, Judy, and Lamar Savely, her co-workers at the *Reflector.*

"Now," said Stennis, "this picnic you say you went on with Jon, that is the only one you've been on where just you and your boyfriend went. Is that correct?"

"Yes. However, Jon and I were not boyfriend and girlfriend. We were friends."

"Very dear friends, though, weren't you?"

"Yes. I thought a lot of Jon, I really did. I knew, I knew from the beginning that Jon was emotionally disturbed, but I did not know what his problem was. However, since that time, I, I, I believe Jon, quite seriously, to be mentally deficient, because I have seen him be angry one minute and not even be aware of things he said the other minute. It is my personal belief that Jon has schizophrenia."

"You have analyzed him as having sissiphrenia?" A few muffled giggles were heard. Mattox was irritated.

"Schizophrenia is the word, sir. I do not consider myself capable of judging. I know that from my experience, from my limited experience, which is very little, Jon has shown me symptoms of such a thing. I know I have seen him angry and just without control. I know that Jon has some illness because he would not be capable of doing what he did otherwise. I told Jon one time that he was one of the sweetest people I had ever known, and sir, he was that . . . "

"Frankly, you were in love with him, were you not?"

"No, sir, I was never in love with him."

"What type of schizophrenia do you think he has symptoms of?"

"Sir, all of my knowledge of schizophrenia, it was a dual personality, and everything that Jon had told me was an indication of this - like telling me about the deer he just had to kill."

The court reporter asked her to please speak a little slower.

"Like telling me of the deer he had to kill . . . He didn't know why he had to kill it - but he had to kill it."

"I see," said the defense attorney. "You came over here voluntarily for the purpose of testifying in this case, did you not?"

"Yes, sir, my intention in testifying in this case was more to help Jon than anything else, because I sincerely believe . . . "

"Well," responded Stennis, "you certainly are helping him!"

Mr. Burgin, who still looked as fresh as the morning in his crisp tailored suit, rose and objected.

"Now may it please the court, counsel has not once, not twice, not ten times, but twenty-five or fifty times interrupted!"

The judge agreed and told Sarah to go ahead and explain her answer, but again the defense attorney interrupted, which began a lengthy debate between the lawyers and the judge. Back and forth, for close to five minutes.

Finally resolved, the special prosecutor asked the court reporter to read the question back to the witness. The reporter responded.

"'You voluntarily came over for the purpose of testifying in this case, did you not?' and then she started to answer, and he interrupted."

"Did she answer the question, Miss Bessie Kate?" Stennis asked the court reporter.

Another dispute broke out between Stennis and Burgin, and Judge Greene settled it again by instructing the witness to explain her answer.

"Talk slow now, I am tired. All right?" asked Miss Bessie Kate.

"Jon didn't, Jon didn't want me to ever tell anything he had told me, and I, I, did not want to tell. But yet, I knew that it was the wrong thing from the standpoint of the law. It was the wrong thing from the standpoint of moral and civic duty, but that, that didn't have as much bearing on me as the fact that I had promised Jon I would not say anything about it, and I did not fully. I fully never intended to mention it, except for the fact . . . for two reasons: I didn't want innocent people to be hurt, and two, I did not want to see Jon convicted of a murder, when he could not have committed a premeditated murder, unless he did have a sick mind . . . "

"And so long as you were loyal to Jon, you did not tell anyone about what you claimed he told you, did you?"

"Sir, I never told anybody. I, I have kept a secret. I have kept a secret for two months, and the reason I finally told when I did, was the fact that it finally dawned on me, after the rumor I heard, which you have already extracted, that he could have committed two other murders. That scared me a lot . . . "

"Now we are going to object to that, if Your Honor please! And we make the same motion."

"I will, I will. Gentlemen," the judge was addressing the jury, "exclude what she stated about the two other murders." Then he told Sarah to "go on with the rest of it."

"That statement scared me. It scared me into realizing that Jon could do something when he got angry, that he would never do in his logical mind."

"We are going to object to what she realized, if Your Honor please, being not in response to the question propounded." Stennis was beginning to feel helpless.

"Let her talk herself to death, Jesse." offered his usually silent co-counsel, Luther Sims.

While he puffed his cigar, Judge Greene again instructed the jury to ignore the testimony:

"Now, gentlemen, in reference to . . . We have things that will come out sometimes, in a lawsuit with a witness, that the Supreme Court says shouldn't come out. Now, any reference to any other murder cases, which is just hearsay, what she said she heard, why, disregard it. Just leave that out of your mind. Will you do that, all of you? Hold up your hand on that."

Like schoolboys, the twelve jurors, and the alternate, all held up their hands.

"And now comes the defendant," announced Mr. Stennis, "and moves for a mistrial."

"For what reason?" ask Judge Greene.

"For the reason of the testimony of this witness here, that Your Honor had just admonished the jury about!"

"All right, it will be overruled. Gentlemen, let's move along."

The defense had a few more questions, with not much time left in the afternoon session. Even though many were repetitious, Mr. Stennis felt it was necessary to have the witness retell various events with the hope that she would contradict herself. However, this particular witness seemed to be leading the seasoned attorney blindfolded through a mine field.

"When did you first decide to come over here and try to 'help' Jon?"

"On the night of March 31st, I knew I had to do something. Before then, I had known I had to do something, and also the fact, sir, that I was afraid because I knew Jon knew, I knew, what I did. He had told me before that he lay awake at night, worried that I would ever tell something. As I said before, I got in touch with Harley, and Harley came over and talked to Chief Mahlon, and then I talked with the district attorney, and I had written, in the meantime, the twelve page essay of the things that went on. After that, sir, they carried me to Birmingham on April the 24th and . . . "

Alarmed, Mr. Stennis immediately objected to any further testimony about her trip to Birmingham, and asked Judge Greene to have her testimony developed outside the presence of the jury, in order for him to rule on its admissibility.

After the jury left, Stennis reminded the court that Grayson had taken a lie detector test in Birmingham, and that no testimony pertaining to it should be allowed before the jury according to the Mississippi Supreme Court. However, after hearing the usual protracted argument from both sides, the judge ruled that evidence of the test was admissible, but evidence of the test results was not admissible.

Quite satisfied with the judge's ruling, and feeling magnanimous, Mr. Burgin asked that the recess be extended a few minutes because the jury might like to have a Coca Cola.

"I want this in the record!" demanded Stennis, on the verge of a fit. "I made a motion at the beginning of this trial, and I want every bit of this in the record!"

"Well, Mr. Stennis, I took all that," replied Miss Bessie Kate, the court reporter.

"And about the proposed Coca Cola!" raged Stennis.

"Oh, things like that can't go in the record," said Judge Greene, in his most sympathetic voice, "certainly not about the Coca Cola."

NINE

Sarah was cross-examined for another half-hour before she and the jury were excused for the day and instructed to return to court Monday morning. She had been on the witness stand for over four hours. The defense attorney had avoided altogether the topic of the lie detector by questioning her about her relationship with Robert Stone, the young man she had recently dated. Sarah's answers were consistent with her previous testimony, and no new light was shed on the facts before the jury.

Harley McNair, Judy Jenkins, and Lamar Savely, shoulder to shoulder, slowly made it through the bottle-neck of spectators at the head of the second floor staircase. The heat was suffocating until finally, as part of the mass, they baby-stepped their way out the front door and into the fresh air.

Now, away from the others, they could talk while they walked past the barber shop and storefronts toward Main Street. Harley grabbed the tri-colored barber pole and swung himself around it. It was nearing the end of what had been a beautiful spring day, and the light fragrance of fresh cut grass wafted on a breeze.

"Sarah was really something! I can't believe how long she had to testify. I don't think I could have done it," remarked Lamar. Her long brown braid flicked back and forth as she walked briskly alongside Harley. Beside working together at the *Reflector*, they were boyfriend and girlfriend.

"I know," said Judy, frowning, "I mean, gol-lee! That Mr. Stennis was so hard on her, but she just kept answering . . . She was so good."

"You girls will have to look at that twelve page statement Sarah wrote for the police,"said Harley. "You won't believe it! She almost followed it verbatim when Mr. Burgin was questioning her . . . Hey, wait a minute!" He stopped dead in his tracks and leaned in the doorway of McLellan's dime store.

From inside the store, where a radio was tuned to the trial, they heard the voice of Jesse Stennis telling Judge Greene that he wanted subpoenas issued for "that Harley McNair fella, and those young ladies, Judy Jenkins and Lamar Savely." Their names broadcast on the radio!

After a brief discussion, the three decided to head back to the courthouse to see what was going on. Upon their arrival, the lawyers were in casual conversation, and Harley approached Mr. Stennis about the subpoena. The lawyer was delighted and asked if they were all available to answer a few questions at that time. Having agreed to stay at Stennis' request, Harley went first - and was led to the witness room where he found Jon Mattox seated at a table. Mr. Stennis muttered to himself about misplaced notes, as he took a seat opposite Harley at the far end of the table. Mattox sat on the side at Stennis' left. The two college friends greeted each other in the stark, old room. Mattox made a small joke about the circumstances. They both chuckled uncomfortably. After a moment of thought, Harley had to ask the big question:

"Did you do it, Jon?"

"No, Harley, I didn't," replied Mattox, matter-of-factly, without dropping his gaze.

Harley realized that he didn't know what he had expected Jon to say, but, at the time, his answer didn't impress Harley one way or another. Instead, it was as though the television screen suddenly went black, and he was struck by the enormity of the consequences faced by Mattox. What an incredible situation for Jon to have gotten himself into!

Stennis, alarmed by Harley's question, immediately took command of the meeting. He didn't trust this smart-aleck one bit! He'd have "heaven knows what"splashed across the newspaper. Stennis asked Harley a few questions, and Harley very quickly outlined his limited role in the case and corroborated Sarah's testimony in that regard. Wasting no time, Stennis thanked him and asked Judy to come in. Harley left her alone with them.

After about twenty minutes, Judy emerged from the witness room. The pretty brunette was quite shaken and told her friends that Stennis had bullied her, called her a liar, and told her she was going to be in big trouble!

"He just tried to get me to say bad things about Sarah, and that we were making this all up together, like she is out to get Jon, and I was helping her! . . . He's awful! I'm not going back in there, and Lamar you shouldn't either!"

"Why don't we go over to Mr. Burgin's office, and ask him about this? Or Mr. Buck's, or Lucas's - one of them." suggested Lamar. She led the way out of the building with Judy and Harley.

For her safety, Sarah was invited to stay over the weekend, in Columbus, at the home of Lieutenant Louis Harper and his family. There were rumors that attempts were made, by someone sympathetic to the defense, to bribe the jury. With so much at stake, whether the rumors were true was beside the point - desperate people could do desperate things, and the prosecution wasn't taking any chances with the life of their vulnerable, young, star witness.

They didn't want to frighten Sarah anymore than she was, but it was explained to her that she needed to continue to be vigilant about her comings and goings. As a side note of interest, Sarah was told that after she left the court that afternoon, Stennis was overheard saying, "I've either got a pathological killer or a pathological liar on my hands, and, right now, I don't know which one." Maybe Stennis didn't know, but Sarah certainly did.

Determined to find out more about her, Jesse Stennis marshaled his troops and sent a couple of scouts to Starkville, Sunday - basically, to dig up dirt on Grayson. Leave no stone unturned! They were to question anyone they could find who knew her, dated her, or had a class with her. At Magruder Hall, Sarah's dormitory, subpoenas were being handed out right and left. The joke being told at the dorm was, "pick up your date, and pick up a subpoena!"

In the meantime, Stennis was making his own inquiries. He telephoned Judy Jenkin's father in Elgin, Illinois and told him that he had better come to Mississippi and see about his daughter, that she was going to be in big trouble. Mr. Jenkins later told his daughter that Stennis also made reference to that "smarty," Harley McNair. She had reassured her father about the situation.

From Bay Springs, Mr. Curt Grayson, Sarah's father, telephoned her and told her that a John Mattox had telephoned him and wanted to meet with him, as one educator to another. Mattox, Jon's uncle, tried to persuade Mr. Grayson that Jon's father was a fine man, and so on. Mr. Grayson told Sarah he felt as though he were being solicited for a bribe. This was all very distressing for Sarah to hear. She had not wanted her parents to be burdened by her involvement in the famous trial.

Sunday newspapers across the nation, and particularly the South, ran headline stories, like "Shapely M.S.U. Co-ed Drops Bombshell!", and "Perfect Murder Plan!" The Columbus paper's account headed it "State Fires Big Gun! Grayson takes the stand." A full verbatim transcript of her testimony was printed with two pages of photographs. Other papers dramatically filed similar reports. The local radio station played tape recordings of Saturday's testimony for those who missed it live, or simply wanted to hear it again. Tapes were made available for neighboring states: Louisiana, Tennessee, Alabama, Florida.

The impact of Sarah's testimony was profound, and what she had told the jury that lazy Saturday afternoon had become the main topic of conversation of virtually every household in Mississippi. The murder plan, the alleged affair.

Back in the Tate's neighborhood, the topic was Sarah Grayson. Thank God for her! Surely, the state had proved its case. While there was some sympathy for James and Elizabeth Mattox, the grief over Gene Tate's tragic murder was palpable - as was the fear of young Mattox. The possibility of Jonny's acquittal and return to the neighborhood was simply unthinkable.

Many of the dwindling, but diehard, Mattox supporters cursed Sarah and were convinced that she was indeed a "woman scorned," a vicious, evil liar. And their hearts were heavy with worry about the fate of the young, attractive, Jonny Mattox. They prayed for his acquittal - that the men of the jury would be moved by the Almighty to know the truth of his innocence. Others were confident that the jury could see through Grayson's lies . . . as they had, and would free their wrongfully accused new friend.

The jury, sequestered in the Gilmer Hotel, was taken on a Sunday outing to visit with family members. A picnic had been arranged for them, and the whereabouts was kept strictly hush-hush. It was a lovely spring afternoon, and the men welcomed the pleasant outdoor gathering away from the pressure of the court proceedings.

Bill Burgin whistled, while he straightened his tie on the way to the courthouse. He could not have been more pleased with the testimony of his star witness - Now, he was even more confident of a conviction. There was no doubt that he had been a little worried about going head to head with the legendary Jesse Stennis. But as it turned out, the young Miss Grayson had given the old boy a run for his money!

All parties were present in the courtroom for the Monday morning session. Before the jury came out, Burgin told Judge Greene that he wanted to make an objection for the record. He asked the judge to refrain from the issuance of subpoenas, unless the court was in session at the time the person was ordered to appear.

Burgin charged that the defense team had subpoenaed witnesses after the court recessed Saturday afternoon, and that one of the witnesses had been "browbeaten and intimidated to such an extent that she was rendered highly nervous and upset." Further, he stated that the out of state father of the witness was telephoned and told that his daughter was in trouble, and that he should get on an airplane and fly down there. The prosecutor accused the defense of abusing the subpoena powers of the court.

Mr. Sims, co-counsel of Stennis, offered some weak explanation, and after a brief debate which was joined in by Mr. Stennis, the judge granted the motion proposed by Burgin.

The jurors were instructed to return to the courtroom. As the men filed in to take their seats in the box, the foreman handed the judge a note complaining that the old courtroom trembled from an overload of spectators. The previous Saturday, Judge Greene said that the east side of the courthouse had sunk two inches since the Mattox trial began. In response to the concern of the jury, Sheriff Spruill ordered spectators to stay out of the aisles and windows.

Having dispensed with the early business, the court was called to order, and once again Sarah Grayson was sworn in as a witness to continue her cross-examination by Jesse Stennis.

Sarah appeared refreshed by the weekend break in the trial, but she was nervous after hearing about Stennis's tactics with her friends. She didn't know what to expect from him. And she had been quite startled by the magnitude of the publicity about her testimony, and by the newspaper accounts which weren't always accurate. In order to control some of what would be printed about her, particularly if Stennis made false accusations, she provided Harley with a list of her accomplishments that he could hand out to other reporters. The list included: chemistry achievement award, President's List, jr. college; reporter with the *Reflector*, Miss Bay Springs High, drum majorette, president of the school honor society, president of the band, and other impressive achievements.

Stennis seemed almost cheerful as he approached the witness stand.

"Miss Grayson, when you were on the witness stand here Saturday, did you make the statement that you heard about Jonny's arrest on the radio?"

"I did not make such a statement. I made no mention of hearing of his arrest. The only mention I made of hearing something on the radio - was when I heard about the murder."

"Did you . . . where . . . when did you hear of Jon's arrest then?"

"I heard it on Friday morning about seven o'clock, when a friend came into my room and said, 'Sarah, Jon has been arrested for the murder of Mrs. Tate.' "

"Unhum. Came into your room over at Mississippi State University?"

"Yes, sir."

"Who was there?"

"That was a friend of mine. I do not care to mention her name."

"You wouldn't tell the jury who was present when you were told that? . . . "

"My roommate was in the room at the time."

"And who was this friend who told you that?"

"I prefer not to mention her name, because I am sure you would subpoena her."

"And I will ask you if on that occasion, when you were told this, you were very much surprised?"

"I expressed surprise, yes, sir. That was the first time I could outwardly show any emotion for something that I had known for a week. I did not know whether he would ever be suspected, and I did not know whether he would ever be arrested for what I had already known of . . . At the time it happened, I . . . I . . . I just fell back on the bed. I stood up when she told me, and I said, 'Oh, no, I can't believe it,' and I fell back on the bed, and that is the first time I had been able to express anything of the way I had felt for almost five days or more."

The lawyer continued to question her about when she had heard about the murder, who was present with her, when had she heard about the indictment, when did she contact Harley McNair, who said what to whom, on and on. He insinuated that Sarah wasn't truthful and attacked her character. He questioned her again about the reward money. But throughout, Sarah held her ground. Nothing she said was inconsistent with her previous testimony.

Finally, Stennis told the court he would like to reserve the right for further cross-examination, if necessary. Mr. Burgin began his re-direct exam.

"Miss Grayson, on cross-examination, I believe you stated that you would prefer not to name the names of certain parties. Why was that?" asked Bill Burgin. As one reporter would comment: his deep smooth voice overshadowed his youthful appearance.

"I did not want to bring other people into this. I see no reason for him having them subpoenaed because they are my friends, and I don't see any necessity in dragging them into this - something that I am in myself."

"All right. Miss Grayson, when you learned of the indictment of Jon Mattox, and when you went to the *Reflector* office, in the evening - after you had learned through the telephone conversation of Harley McNair, of the indictment of Jon Mattox - what instructions or request had been made of you?"

"Now, we are going to object to that, Your Honor, please. What instructions or requests could open this thing up to where this girl could talk from now until sundown," declared Stennis.

"By whom? By whom, Mr. Burgin?" Judge Greene inquired.

"Did anyone make any request of you, relative to, after your . . . during or after, Harley McNair contacted the police on your behalf?"

The special prosecutor then had her recount that, when she met with the district attorney and Chief Vickery in West Point on Thursday, April 21st, she was instructed by them not to make mention to anyone what she knew about the murder and Jon Mattox. The following night, officers came to see her in Starkville, and she discussed it with them further.

"All right. What did you do then?"

"The next day I went to Birmingham, where I underwent a lie detector test."

"Who went with you to Birmingham?" asked Burgin. Stennis objected but was overruled.

"On, on this day, on Saturday, we met Louis Harper at ten o'clock and went to Birmingham. I spent Saturday night with my aunt in Birmingham, and Sunday at one o'clock, we went to the police station where, from one o'clock until six-thirty, I was given a lie detector test on all the things I have said in my statement."

Mr. Stennis began a series of objections about the admission of the lie detector test before the jury, citing the supreme court. Judge Greene reminded him that he had already "passed" on the issue, and his motion was overruled. With that, Bill Burgin announced that he had concluded his redirect.

Stennis stood at the defense table and loudly cleared his throat.

"Miss Grayson, I believe you told this jury last week that you gave Jon Mattox, the defendant in this case, a book, the title of which was *The Prophet*, by . . . ," Stennis looked around on the table.

"Gibran," replied the witness.

"Gibran?"

"Yes. G-i-b-r-a-n."

"I will ask you if you will examine this, and state to the jury and court, whether or not that is the book you referred to?" He handed her a book, and Sarah looked it over.

"Sir, this is . . . The book is the same kind of book that I gave Jon - as the one that Stan had sent me from California."

"And when did you give him this book, ma'am?"

"I do not know when I gave Jon . . . It was sometime, I would say, after Christmas. That is only a guess, but it . . . I know what you are fixing to do. When I first gave the book to Jon, I opened the book at random and turned to page 19, and on page 19, the prophet said, 'Speak to us of giving.' "

Interested, several jurors leaned forward in their squeaky swivel chairs.

"And you quoted that to him, or read it to him?"

"Oh no, I had just gotten the book and had not read it myself. I did not quote it. I read it to him."

"You read it to him. I see. And what did the . . . that say about giving?"

"Well, you have it in front of you. Would you like to read it? I could not quote it . . . Since that time, I have read the book completely. I have heard Stan refer to it frequently as one of the things he thought was one of the great, greater prophecies. It has prophesy on faith, love, marriage, God, various topics."

"And on the front fly leaf here, that is the picture of the author, is it not?"

"That is supposedly Gibran, Kahil Gibran. K-a-h-i-l."

"Is he an American?"

"No, he is not. I do not remember his nationality. I remember being surprised at the fact that he was not."

"As a matter of fact, he is a Middle Eastern, is he not?" Stennis eyed a couple of jurors, as though they shared a secret.

"I do not know."

"And the part you read was this: 'Then said a rich man, "Speak to us of Giving."' And he answers, 'You give but little when you give of your possessions, it is when you give of yourself that you truly give.' That is it, isn't it?"

"I read further than that. I read the whole page to Jon. I had picked that page at random, and I do think it is quite poetic - it exemplifies so much truth in the reality of giving. A gift is useless if it is not given with thought and emotion."

"Did you read this part to him, ma'am? 'Like sheaves of corn, it gathers you unto himself. He threshes you to make you naked. He sifts you to free you from your husk. He grinds you to whiteness. He kneads you until you are pliant, and then he assigns you to his sacred fire that you may become sacred bread for God's sacred feast.' Did you read that to him?"

Mattox was thoroughly entertained by his lawyer's insinuation and was delighted to see Grayson squirm. She, on the other hand, was utterly incensed.

"No, sir. I did not read that to Jon."

"That is in the book though, isn't it?" challenged Jesse Stennis. He moved closer to her.

"I find it amusing that you are looking for the parts and making it into dirt, when the book is really written in the greatest style of the author."

"Would you mind stating whether that is in the book or not?"

"Sure, it is in the book."

"All right."

"But if you would like for me to show you what else I read to Jon, I would be glad to do it."

"That is what I asked you. Now, young lady, I am an old-fashioned man, and I am embarrassed myself, and I regret the necessity of asking you this question, but I will ask you . . . "

"Why don't you just show the people the pictures? All through this book . . . "

"I ask you . . . Would you mind letting me ask the questions now? . . . I will ask you, ma'am, if this book isn't replete with naked men and women?"

"Yes, sir."

"Pictures of them?"

"Yes, sir, the book is . . . You are making filth and dirt . . . " Sarah was shocked at the depths he would sink to attack her character! He was insinuating that she was a loose woman, a slut! How hard she had worked to preserve her virginity! This was too much.

"No, ma'am, I am not making anything. I am just stating facts, young lady, and I will appreciate it if you will just answer the questions without giving me a lecture . . . On page 17 here, I will ask you if that isn't a picture of a male and female completely naked, in a semi-embrace?"

"Semi, yes."

"And on the page opposite the page number 20 here, I will ask you if that isn't a picture of a naked male and female holding hands, and in the background, and in the foreground, a picture of a completely naked woman lying down in a reclining position on her side?"

"Not as you stated it, no."

"Well, what is it then? What is it a picture of then?" Stennis asked incredulously.

"These pictures are not . . . They are not distinguishable as to the shape and form. They are merely without clothes. This is the author's essence. He writes . . . he . . . the . . . An artist , if you will remember, speaks of the human form as the greatest creation of God."

"I, I, I didn't ask you about your interpretation of what an artist thinks, young lady."

"You are just trying to make it vulgar!"

"No, ma'am. I beg your pardon. I am truly embarrassed. I have the greatest respect for you, ma'am . . . I am the father of two young girls, myself."

Special Prosecutor Burgin objected that he had not had an opportunity to examine the book, and asked the judge to allow no further testimony about it until he could. At the direction of the court, Burgin was handed *The Prophet*, and after he looked at it, he told Judge Greene that he had no further objections to its use in the examination by Mr. Stennis. Stennis then asked that the book be marked as an exhibit for the defense. That particular subject exhausted, the defense lawyer continued his questions of the witness.

"Would you mind telling the court and the jury when it was, now, that you asked Jon to go with you to Memphis?"

"I know what you are referring to."

"Well, tell them when it was."

"I am trying to think about the date. I do not remember anything in relation to this, but I remember telling Jon one time that he, that he ought to . . . I was going to Memphis at the time, and I remember telling him that sometime he ought to go with me - it would do him good to go somewhere. Because Jon had told me on numerous occasions, how the only thing he did at night - he would watch television for a while and go to bed very early, and he never got out anywhere, and he never did anything but hunt. I tried on numerous occasions to suggest things to Jon that would get him interested. I was Jon's friend, and not Jon's lover, as you seem to be implying!"

"No, ma'am, I'm not . . . I, I, I'm not implying anything. I am simply trying to get the facts before the jury, ma'am. Would you give us the approximate date when you asked him to go to Memphis to spend the weekend with you?"

"My brother lives in Memphis, and I suggested he could go up there one time. I was leaving to go, and I said, 'Jon, would you like to go?' I do not know the date. I am reasonably certain it was last year - '59."

"As a matter of truth and fact, it was soon after you gave him this book to read, wasn't it?"

"Oh, no, sir. I gave him the book to read right before, right close to the last time I saw him, because I remember thinking it was the end of the semester, and I wondered if I would see him after then, and he still had my book, and I wanted my book back, and I wondered when I would get my book back."

"Was it before or after you gave this book to Jon Mattox that you asked him to go with you to Memphis for a weekend?"

"It was before."

"Before. And he declined to go with you, didn't he?"

"Yes, he did."

"Mr. Sims, you think of anything else we ought to ask?" Stennis had turned to address his co-counsel, the state legislator.

"I think you have covered the territory pretty good," replied the old gentleman.

After a few cursory follow-up questions on re-redirect, to Sarah's great relief, Mr. Burgin made the long awaited announcement:

"The state rests."

TEN

After the state rested, Judge Greene called a recess for the day, and the Mattox defense team stayed on to confer with their prospective witnesses and prepare for the next day. The big question on everyone's mind was whether or not the defendant would take the stand, particularly after Grayson's powerfully damaging testimony against him. For his part, Jonny was accustomed to getting away with certain things, and that personal history, coupled with his arrogance, caused him to view things more optimistically than might be expected. Also, his newly acquired supporters and fans reinforced his attitude.

But one thing - for sure- was, come hell or high water, Sarah Grayson was going to pay. He would make sure of it - once he was out. It was, without a doubt, the biggest mistake he had ever made when he told her about his murder plan. How could I be so STUPID? He'd never do that again - no matter how big a charge he got from it. No siree . . . And all that crap about an affair - she fell for it hook, line, and sinker. Stupid cow . . . 'Jonny's birddog!'. . . I'll kill her . . .

As he contemplated his revenge, he felt more relaxed. After a while, he startled a jailer passing his cell when he overheard Mattox singing "Sea of Love."

" . . . I wanna tell you how-ow much I lo-ove you . . . " Mattox was stretched out on his cot, in his boxers and t-shirt, singing to the ceiling.

"Man, that kid's back there singin'! Don't know that I'd be in the mood, if I was him," The jailer told a co-worker.

"Well, he's a pretty easy-going fella. Not like I'd heard, you know, before he got here," the man responded.

A block from the courthouse, the elementary school children at Franklin Academy were summoned by the bell, back to their classrooms after the lunch recess on the playground. Ten year old Rob Tate had stopped in the school yard, on his way inside, to pick up a brilliant blue cats-eye marble he had spotted, half hidden in a clump of grass.

Rob had never really hated school like some of his friends, and now he had even started looking forward to it - just to get out of the house. Everything had changed. Home didn't feel like home anymore. His little sister, Genie, and his grandmother still cried sometimes about his mother. But his father worked even more than he had and didn't talk about it when he was home, so neither did Rob and his brothers. He couldn't avoid going into the garage almost every day since the murder - the door to the patio and washer/dryer were in there, but he was getting use to it.

For the first few weeks, he dreaded going in there because it always reminded him of that morning, finding her there on the concrete floor . . . Mother. He could see her lying there, and it was like a big hand was squeezing his chest and throat. And his thoughts, that if he had only stayed home that morning, it wouldn't have happened - or he could have saved her.

As time passed, and nobody talked about it, he just tried to think about other things, but at night sometimes, he cried, alone in his bed. He thought his brothers did, too.

The one good thing that remained unchanged for him were his friends in the neighborhood and at school - baseball, football, night games of kick-the-can. He also had a pretty good marble collection, so he was pleased about his find in the school yard.

Rob noticed a few boys nearby, who whispered to each other while they watched him. He tucked the marble in his bluejean pocket, and continued toward the school's back entrance when one of the boys approached him.

"Hey, ain't your name Rob Tate?" Rob didn't really know this skinny boy in the dirty T-shirt, squinting with the sun in his face, or the others. He thought his name was Bobby something from another part of town.

"Yeah." Aw shoot, maybe it was his marble that he just put in his pocket. He'd have to give it back to him.

"You're the one whose mother got murdered, ain't ya?"

"Yeah." He answered the boy and turned to go inside.

"Well, my daddy said your mother was a whore with that guy who done it!" The other boys giggled at his daring and covered their mouths.

Rob was frozen in place, eyes slowly widened.

"You're crazy!" He thundered back in disgust - his voice bigger than he was. Rob didn't know what the word really meant, but he knew it was nasty and bad. He clenched his fists.

"It was on the radio, and my daddy heard it his self!" Bobby yelled as he took off running, his voice squeaky with fear. "He said whores are bad, and that's why she got killed!"

Rob looked like he'd had the wind knocked out of him. He couldn't believe anybody could say something like that about his mother. "Whore" . . . He turned back, and walked into the building. On the radio? Sorry little crazy liar . . . A melancholy anger fell over him.

Soon enough, the Tate children would learn of the sordid allegations about their mother that had been reported from the trial. It was not spoken of at home, or in the neighborhood, but from time to time, as the months and years would pass, other strangers would confront them with unkind, rude questions and remarks. With that, and the trauma of finding her body, it was not surprising that over time, the children's once joyful memories of their mother faded into the darkness of those days.

There was nothing familiar left of her.

Tuesday morning, May 10th, the Mattox trial resumed at nine o'clock without the presence of the jury. Before the defense would call its first witness, Mr. Stennis made a motion to delay the trial because he had not succeeded in serving a subpoena on Mr. Joe Douglas and his handyman, Mr. John Chambley. Douglas was a hunting acquaintance of Mattox, and future testimony would indicate that the defendant had driven out to Douglas' home, on the morning of the murder, to retrieve his transistor radio. In support of his motion, a deputy testified that he had been out to serve the men several times, but no one had been home.

"May it please the court, I would like to make a statement regarding this matter, as soon as Counsel finishes," said Special Prosecutor Bill Burgin.

The judge instructed him to proceed.

"On yesterday afternoon, after leaving the courtroom, I went down to the Columbus Smoke Shop. Shortly after entering the Smoke Shop, a mutual friend of mine and Joe Douglas called me aside and told me that the witness, Joe Douglas, had just called him on the phone, and that the witness, Joe Douglas was at home, that he had been at home all weekend, and that counsel for defendant, Mr. Stennis, had told him in a conference, the latter part of the week, to go on about his business, to make himself scarce, and he would get in touch with him if he needed him."

"All right," said Judge Greene. His eyes shifted toward Stennis.

"With reference to me having a conference with Joe Douglas, that is quite true. I have had one conference with Joe Douglas, and present was my son, Hardy Stennis. I never insinuated, or suggested, that Joe Douglas make himself scarce!" declared Stennis, indignantly.

Judge Greene overruled the defense motion for delay and ordered the sheriff to keep trying to serve the witnesses. The jury was ordered back to the crowded courtroom, and Mr. Stennis called his witness, Mrs. Hartwell Loftis, a neighbor and longtime friend of the Mattox family. She was the first of forty-four defense witnesses who would testify over the next day and a half.

Mrs. Loftis lived on 13th Avenue North, commonly called Park Circle Drive, which ran alongside the north side of the Mattox property, where it intersected 12th Street North on the west side. Both the Mattox and the Tate homes faced west on 12th Street North. Her house was located downhill from the defendant's and two lots over. She reported, in her testimony, that she had heard dogs barking around 10:45 the morning Gene Tate was murdered. She said the barking was unusual for a Sunday morning. It was revealed under cross-examination, however, that her home was "pretty well isolated" from the Mattox and Tate properties.

On redirect examination, Attorney Jesse Stennis asked the following:

"Now, I will ask you, ma'am, if you learned of the presence of three young Negroes in that neighborhood on the morning of this tragedy?"

The judge sustained Mr. Burgin's heated hearsay objection to the question - just as a huge Air Force jet roared overhead. The judge smiled and told the sheriff to instruct the jets to fly higher which helped break the tension in the courtroom.

But the defense had accomplished their objective of getting the insinuation before the jury. Stennis figured that a jury was hard-put to convict a man for first degree murder when the only evidence was circumstantial. So, if they were looking for some doubt, or just something, anything, to hang their hats on to justify an acquittal, well then, he had gladly offered them a possible alternative theory of the identity of the culprits. Never mind that the witness did not provide any evidence in that regard.

The next witness was another neighbor, Mr. Buck McKellar, who lived behind the Mattox's, his home faced north on Park Circle Drive. He testified that on the day of the murder, he had notified the police of some fresh "skid" marks and what looked like a half heel mark that he had discovered on a slope adjacent to the Mattox backyard property line and near the Tate backyard line. While initially of interest, it was later explained by another defense witness that the neighborhood children had been playing outside the night before in that vicinity. The children had long ago trampled down a wire fence in the same area.

Mr. Stennis then asked Mr. McKellar about his relationship to the defendant.

"How long have you known him, sir?"

"Twelve years this coming September. The Mattox family lived there when we built our house in '48."

"And I will ask you, sir, if you know the general reputation for peace and violence of this accused in the community in which he lives. Do you know what his reputation is, good or bad?"

"It is good, in my opinion."

Before he was excused, in response to an inquiry from Mr. Burgin, McKellar, who lived next door to the previous witness, stated that, although he was home reading his paper that morning, he had not heard any dogs barking.

After a short recess that was granted to give the defense time to confer with witnesses, Mr. Stennis called to the stand, Miss Patsy Johnston, a student at Mississippi State University. Miss Johnston, an attractive blonde, lived at Magruder Hall and had been acquainted with both Sarah Grayson and Jon Mattox since the previous September.

"After Jon was arrested the first time, before he was turned a loose, I will ask you if you heard a news report about his arrest?"

"Yes, sir," the young woman answered.

"And would you tell the court and jury what news report it was on, I mean, about the hour?"

"Well, I heard it the first time on the radio at 5:55 a.m. It was five minutes to six, and I heard it again at five minutes to seven."

"And after you heard it the second time, I will ask you, where did you go, Miss Patsy?"

"I went down to Sarah Grayson's room to tell her."

"I will ask you, ma'am, if Miss Sarah Grayson had been paying quite a bit of attention to young Mattox?"

Special Prosecutor Burgin launched a series of objections to the question, but was overruled on each, and the defense was instructed to proceed.

"I will ask you if, during this time that you knew Sarah and Jon, Sarah was doing quite a bit of chasing of this young man?"

Again, an objection from Bill Burgin which was overruled. Stennis tried once more.

"I will ask you if she didn't make the statement to you, one time, that she had been trying to get Jon, but so far, she didn't seem to be making any headway?"

"We object on the grounds that the proper predicate has not been laid, and on the further grounds that it is leading. The witness is competent to testify as to any conversation that took place without being . . . "

"The question is leading, but I remember some testimony in this case. I think it is proper," interrupted Judge Greene, while he puffed on his cigar.

"I will ask the question one more time, please, ma'am. If this young lady, Miss Sarah Grayson, did not make the statement to you, in substance, as follows: that she had been trying to get Jon, but she didn't seem to be making any headway?" Stennis awaited her answer and hoped Burgin would object again. Made him look like he was afraid of her answer.

"Yes, sir," Johnston answered at last.

"She said that. Now, I will ask you, ma'am, if when you went down to, or went to Sarah's room, after hearing the broadcast of Jonny's being arrested the first time, you told her what you had heard, did you not, ma'am?"

"Yes, sir."

"And I will ask you, ma'am, if when you told her, she didn't say at that time, 'He didn't do it, he couldn't have done it because he is so good and sweet'?"

Bill Burgin, quite irritated, stood up and faced the judge.

"Now, may it please the court, we object on the ground that it is leading and that the proper question is to ask the witness what she said, and let her testify to it, rather than have Counsel put words in her mouth!"

"Well," the judge offered, and brushed an ash from his black robe, "that's true, that's true, but I am going to overrule it and let her answer."

"Do you understand the question?" Mr. Stennis asked the bewildered Miss Johnston.

"All but the last - I mean, he didn't say . . . she didn't say the last part."

"All right. I will ask you, if when you told her about that, if she didn't register shock and surprise and say, 'He didn't do it, he couldn't have done it!'"

"Yes, sir."

Stennis exhibited a fatherly demeanor with this witness, and he positioned himself in close proximity to her.

"Now, Miss Patsy," he asked sweetly, "do you recall seeing Miss Grayson on the evening of April 25th, 1960, the day when this accused was indicted by the grand jury?"

"Yes, sir."

"Where did you see her, ma'am?"

"I was coming upstairs after 10:30 that night. I was coming in, and I heard somebody call 'Patsy' on second floor, as I was going up to third, but there is other Patsys in the dormitory, so I didn't turn around. I kept right on going, and I was on the landing between second and third floor when they hollered again, so I turned around, and it was Sarah."

"Now, did you have a conversation then?"

"Yes, sir."

"I will ask you, ma'am, if on that occasion, that is, Monday, April 25th, 1960, there in Magruder Hall, if Miss Sarah didn't say to you, 'I don't know what to believe now.'"

"Yes, sir."

"Nothing else," Mr. Stennis told the court and took his seat at the defense table, where he lightly patted Jon on the back.

Bill Burgin then questioned the witness about her relationship with Jon Mattox. She said they had become very good friends and had shared several classes together since the first semester.

"And you are interested in helping him in this situation, aren't you?"

"Yes, sir."

"All right. And now you say you had a discussion with Sarah Grayson on the landing, or on the stairs, at the dormitory on the night after his second arrest - after he was indicted that afternoon?"

"It was the . . . He was indicted that afternoon, and it was that night."

"And I believe you said that you and Sarah discussed it there, on the landing, for several minutes?"

"Yes, sir."

"I mean, it wasn't a one-sided conversation, was it?"

"Well, Sarah asked me some questions, in my opinion."

"I see, and as the result of that conversation, you both said that you didn't know whether he did it or not. Is that right?"

"Yes, sir."

"I see. That's all." Burgin was satisfied with his cross-examination. In the end, she had not contradicted the testimony of the prosecution's star witness.

Mr. Stennis had a few more questions regarding her relationship with Jon Mattox. Patsy said, in response, they had never dated and agreed that she thought highly of him.

Miss Lamar Savely, M.S.U. student and staff member on the school's newspaper, *Reflector*, reluctantly took the witness stand next. She made eye contact with Harley which helped calm her nervousness. She was questioned about Sarah Grayson's reaction of surprise about the defendant's arrest and subsequent indictment. Lamar confirmed that Sarah had acted surprised about it. But on cross-examination, Mr. Burgin was prepared:

"You don't know, Miss Savely, whether or not she had been instructed not to discuss the case, or not at that time, do you?"

"Well," Lamar answered very softly, "now I know that she knew this all along, but when she came into the *Reflector* office, she acted surprised because that is, of course, what she would do - because she . . . because no one knew, until this past Saturday, that she was even going to be here."

Miss Savely was excused by the judge, and a third defense witness was called to offer character testimony on prosecution witness, Sarah Grayson. Miss Mary Boswell, another student from Mississippi State took the stand.

Boswell stated that she was acquainted with Jon Mattox and Sarah Grayson. Approximately two weeks prior to the trial, she had observed Sarah Grayson, on campus, hugging a young man at lunch time. This was to imply that Grayson was a "loose " woman. Mr. Stennis then offered the witness for cross-exam.

Mr. Burgin asked Miss Boswell whether or not she knew the identity of the young man, and she said she did not. He asked her if she was a friend of Jon Mattox, and Boswell said yes - as of the previous Saturday, when she - for the first time - talked with him in court. Mr. Stennis had asked her to testify, she said. She also acknowledged that she had never talked with Sarah Grayson.

"Miss Boswell, have you ever hugged a young gentleman?"

"You mean out on campus?"

"Anywhere?"

"Well, yes, sir."

"I see. That's all." She was excused.

Some spectators in the courtroom shifted uneasily in their chairs and began to wonder when the defense was going to put on some evidence - not only that would help Mattox, but would keep them from going to sleep. They were hoping for a bombshell, but would settle for a small flare.

The pace of the defense case began to change: One by one, several witnesses were called to establish the whereabouts of Jon Mattox at various times on the morning of the murder. It had been shown that Gene Tate was murdered sometime between 10:30 a.m., when she was visited by her mother, and approximately 10:55 a.m., when her young sons discovered her body. That left a small window of opportunity for the killer to strike.

Bill Thompson was sworn in. He said he was out that morning and picked up Joe Douglas at his cabin out on Old Macon Road. They were going hunting. On their way to town, Thompson said he saw Mattox traveling down Old Macon Road in the opposite direction. Douglas had told him that Jonny was going to his cabin to pick up his radio. Thompson said he thought it was around 10 o'clock when he saw the defendant.

Then, Mr. Jesse Barry, an older black man, testified that he was on his way to church that morning, and he stated that he saw Jon Mattox driving toward Columbus on Old Macon Road about 3 miles out of town. Barry thought it was around 10:20 to 10:30 a.m., at the time, because that was the approximate time he usually went to church. On cross-exam, he acknowledged that he wasn't wearing a watch.

Mrs. Charles Clarkson next took the witness stand. Her husband had previously testified about the shirt Mattox was wearing that Sunday morning, when he came by Pat's Pan Am gas station. Mrs. Clarkson had been at the gas station that morning where she had made a phone call to her daughter, Mrs. Grady Partain. She told the court that after she hung up the phone, she saw the defendant drive into the station. She wasn't sure of the time - just sometime between 10 and 11 o'clock. But her daughter and son-in -law, each testified after her, clarified the approximate time of the phone call. It appeared to be between 10:20 a.m. and 10:30 a.m. that Mattox drove into the gas station.

Another time-line witness was called before the jury. Mr. Gene Edmonds, who lived next door to Otho McDaniel, outside of Columbus on Nashville Ferry Road, said that on Sunday morning, January 31st, he saw that it was 10:30 by the clock in his bedroom. So, he woke up his son and then went outside to feed his dogs. Some time, he guessed, before 11 o'clock, he saw Jon Mattox coming along the road there, up to Otho's house where Mattox got out of his car and stood at McDaniel's screen door a few seconds. Then, he saw Mattox leave, driving toward Hairston Bend club house.

In a series of questions, Mr. Burgin asked the witness to describe the layout of the two properties, and then asked Mr. Edmonds, given his testimony, how it was possible for him to observe the screen door area of McDaniel's house.

"You can see it yourself, Mr. Burgin, if you'll go out there and look."

"All right," Burgin said, unconvinced. "That's all, Mr. Edmonds. Thank you. Nothing further."

"All right, Mr. Stennis. Who will you have next?" asked Judge Greene.

"Mrs. James Mattox, the mother of the accused."

She took her seat on the witness stand. Nicely attired in a dress and heels, Elizabeth Mattox, an attractive brunette of forty-five, was nevertheless under tremendous strain, and it reflected on her face. She appeared tightly wound and frightened, even though she would testify before the still, packed courtroom as a woman of strong conviction regarding her son's innocence.

"Mrs. Mattox," Mr. Stennis began kindly, "you, of course, recall the morning when Mrs. Gene Tate lost her life, do you not?"

"That's correct."

"Mrs. Mattox, did you go to church that morning?"

"I went to Sunday school. I did not go to church."

"I see. Now on that Sunday morning, before you went to Sunday school, do you recall whether your son made any phone calls?"

"I know that he made one phone call. He had been out the night before and left a transitor radio that he had built, and the boy said he would bring it to his house so he could pick it up Sunday morning. Jon was calling this boy, as I left to go to Sunday school, to make sure the boy had brought the radio for him to pick up."

"Who did he call, ma'am?"

"Joe Douglas. He was talking on the telephone with him when I left to go to Sunday school."

"And, how old is Jon, Mrs. Mattox?"

"He'll be twenty-one in July."

"Mrs. Mattox, there has been some testimony here about you and your Jonny's relationship, as mother and son. I will ask you to tell the jury, please ma'am, if there has been a relationship of love and affection be-tween your son and you, or not. Just tell the jury, please ma'am?" The jury panel watched the witness respectfully.

"Yes, sir, there sure has," she replied emotionally, "I have older chil-dren, and Jon is the baby, and he has certainly been our pride and joy. We have been very close."

"Has that relationship existed between him and his father?"

"Yes, sir. It sure has."

"Mrs. Mattox, I will ask you, if you have ever, in Jon Mattox's lifetime, seen him get into a rage and have a wild-eyed expression in his eyes?"

"I have seen him upset a little bit, but everybody gets upset. But I have never seen him go into a rage. He is much calmer than most people."

Turning to the events of January 31st, the defense attorney asked her what time she had returned home from Sunday school that morning.

"At twenty one minutes to eleven o'clock."

"And where was your son when you first got home?"

"I parked our car in front of the house and walked up the brick walk leading to the front door. As I was going across, in front of the house, well, Jon was on the brick outside of the den door."

"The front of the den door. Do you recall what, if anything, he had in his hands at that time?"

"Well, he had a little radio and a gun - things that he was taking, going hunting to look for some dogs."

"And did he state where he was going then?"

"He just said they had been out the day before, and they had lost some dogs. Friday, I believe they had lost the dogs, and he checked to see if the dogs had been found. The man was still out, so he said he was going to help look for the dogs."

"And who was that man that he said he was going to help look for the dogs?"

"Mr. Otho McDaniel."

"Well now, did he leave your home after you got back from Sunday school?"

"He left later. He didn't leave then."

"I see. You say 'later.' Do you know what he did from the time that you saw him with his gun and his portable radio in his hands, standing on the brick there, near the outside den door? Just if you will, please ma'am, trace his steps from there."

"I went in the den door, in the den, and our bedroom joins the den. I took off my hat and jacket from Sunday school, and Jimmy, my husband, came out of the bath which is on the other side of the bedroom. He said, 'Well, you are early,' and we looked at his watch, and it said it was twenty-five minutes of eleven."

"Yes, ma'am."

"I stopped by the bathroom and went on to the kitchen to wash the breakfast dishes. And when I started washing dishes, well, Jon came out of his room, which is on the other side of our kitchen, with some boots or shoes, some heavy shoes, something in his hand, and he went on out, I presume, down the hall from the kitchen. I finished washing the dishes, and then Mr. Mattox got dressed, and he came on in the kitchen with the paper, and about that time, the sermon started on W.C.B.I."

"Now when you saw your son, Jon, on the brick with his gun and his portable radio in his hand, which way did he go from there?"

"He took those to his car, directly in front of the den, on the street in front of the house."

"Where did he go from there?"

"He put those in the car, and then he came back in the house to get his heavy shoes."

"And after he got his heavy shoes, where did he go?"

"He went back down the hall toward the den, from the kitchen. I think he spoke to his father as he went out through the den door."

"Do you know what he spoke to his father about?"

"No, I was in the kitchen at the other end of the house. But as our radio program was coming on at eleven o'clock, the sermon from W.C.B.I., Mr. Mattox looked at his watch, and he said, 'Well, you didn't get home as early as I thought you did. My watch is four minutes slow.' So that is where I knew I got home at twenty one minutes of eleven."

"And actually, it was twenty one minutes of eleven when you arrived there?"

"When I got in the den."

"Now, after Jon went into the den and said something to his father, where did he go?"

"Out to his car, and left."

"And did you see or hear your son when he left your home?"

"Yes, sir. I'm afraid we can hear his car when it starts off. Sometimes, the exhaust makes a little noise when he starts off."

"Yes, ma'am. Mrs. Mattox, when you saw your son there on the brick in front of, or near, the den door, was his demeanor, attitude, conduct, or actions, normal, as you have seen them, or seen him, for the past years, or was it abnormal?"

"Well, he certainly acted normal to me. I have had many a conversation on those steps with him, and I certainly couldn't tell any difference."

"And when he came into the house to get his hunting boots, I will ask you to state, please, ma'am, what his actions were, his attitude was, his conduct was, with reference to being normal or abnormal?"

"Well, he was just as normal as ever. He went on back to his room and got his boots, stopped by the refrigerator, I think, and drank some orange juice because the jar was still there where I had to wash it. And I guess he drank the orange juice while I was in the bathroom."

"Did he appear to be upset or excited?"

"No, sir. He did not. He was the normal, same old Jon I have known always: happy-go-lucky, very pleasant."

"Mrs. Mattox, what time did you see your son again on this fateful Sunday?"

"It was dark. It was just getting dusk when he came home that night. He called in and said that they had found the dogs, and that he would be home in a few minutes, and his father told him that he thought that he should come on in, as soon as he could, and I imagine it was six or seven-thirty. I don't know exactly the time."

"And when he came into your home that evening about dusk, did you notice anything unusual about his conduct?"

"No, sir. He was just like we all were - very shocked to find out what had happened in our neighborhood. We enjoyed her. She was a friend of mine."

"Did she visit in your home, ma'am?"

"Yes, sir. She certainly did."

"Did you visit in her home?"

"Yes."

"I will ask you, if she came over, Mrs. Tate came over, to have coffee with you on some occasions?"

"Quite frequent. They do not drink coffee, or Mr. Tate didn't particularly care for it, and she would not make it every morning, and after she would get her children off to school, quite often she would come over, and we would have a cup of coffee in the morning."

"Now, when she was in your home there, would you and she talk small talk?"

"Yes, just 'yak' mostly."

"And some husbands, when they refer to it, call it 'yakity-yaking,' don't they?"

"That's correct."

Then Mr. Stennis retrieved, from a table, the blue checked shirt that the prosecution had introduced as evidence. Mrs. Mattox examined it, and said that it was the shirt that she had made for her son, Jon. She said that it was made over a period of about a week, and during that time, Gene Tate had admired her work on it as she did not sew.

"Gene was quite fascinated with me making the shirt. She thought it was very pretty, and she handled the material and was impressed at how heavy it was. She did not sew, and she watched it grow very closely, and she was in and out a number of times while I was making the shirt."

Pursuant to defense questions, Mrs. Mattox testified that she normally dried the family's laundry on a backyard clothes line, but, from time to time, she would use the Tate's clothes dryer.

"I will ask you if a few weeks before Mrs. Tate's death, you had an occasion to use Mrs. Tate's home automatic dryer?"

"I did. It was awfully rainy weather, and I had two grandchildren I was keeping, and I couldn't get their clothes dry, so Gene said, 'Well bring them. I don't need the dryer now, put them in there.' In fact, Gene took the clothes home and put them in there."

"I see. Now did you go over to Mrs. Tate's, on that occasion, and get the clothes?"

"No, Jon picked the clothes up. I was fixing supper that night and realized I had not picked up the clothes, and he said, 'Mother, I will go get them while you finish supper.' So, he picked up the clothes."

"And this friendly relationship between you and Mrs. Tate, did it continue up until the time of Mrs. Tate's death?"

"Yes, sir."

"Did you consider Mrs. Tate one of your better friends, or just a mere acquaintance?"

"I think she was a pretty good friend."

"Yes, ma'am, and Mrs. Mattox, I'll ask you, ma'am, did you ever see any unseemly conduct on the part of Mrs. Gene Tate?"

"I did not. I admired her very much. I thoroughly enjoyed being with her."

"And I will ask you this now, did Mr. Martin Tate, at any time that you know of, indicate that he thought your son Jon and his wife were having a back-door romance?"

"No, sir. I was over at the Tate home on the Monday morning, after this tragedy happened, and Martin was just as nice to me as anyone could possibly be. When I left to go home to change my clothes, well, he thanked me for what I had . . . the help I had been that morning over there."

"I will ask you why you went over there that morning?"

"Well, I was pretty upset when I found out what had happened, and there were so many people there, so I thought I could be of more help if I got up and went early Monday morning and helped prepare the children's breakfast. So, that is what I did. I was over there by seven o'clock and stayed until after lunch."

"On that morning, did he have any workmen there, around his residence, any workmen, carpenters, and craftsmen of any kind, on that morning?"

"There was some man there that came to change some locks on the doors, and some men checking. There was some screens that didn't operate right - they couldn't get locked or something. I know I went around with them while they were trying to get a couple of windows up so they could fasten the screens."

"I see. I believe that he had some work done to make his residence more secure?"

"He was changing locks on the doors, and the man who was changing them asked me if I would go with him, you know, while he was in the house, and he went into the garage, and he said that he had to do a little work on the door that goes out of the back of the garage, that it would not close, and he had to do a little repair on the door and fix the lock, put a lock on that door."

Mrs. Mattox went on to say that she and her husband had slide locks installed on the inside of their doors also, those that opened to the outside.

Next, Stennis asked her about the times Mr. Tate spent the night out of town, on business. She stated that she was aware that he was gone most Monday nights, but was not allowed to testify as to what Gene had told her regarding any other nights.

"Mrs. Baker, Gene's mother, would come stay with Gene on the nights that I knew that Martin's car was not in the garage, in the driveway."

"Well, tell the jury, ma'am, what was this lady, Mrs. Gene Tate's, actions, insofar as you saw or knew of, with reference to her being a good and faithful wife to her husband?"

"I have known Gene since she moved next door to us, and there was never anyone that was more faithful to her children and family. Many times I have heard her say, 'I would like to go somewhere, but I cannot leave my family.'"

"I see. Thank you, ma'am. Nothing further, Your Honor."

"Mr. Burgin, your witness," said Judge Greene.

"Mrs. Mattox, I believe you identified this shirt and testified that you made it?" asked Bill Burgin, as he held up the blue checked shirt for the witness to see.

"Yes, sir."

"When did you make the shirt?"

"Either in December or January. It was bad both months, and I couldn't get out, and I sewed a good bit during both months. But I can't be positive which month it was."

"I believe Mary Dell Gardner visited in your home, on at least one occasion, when you were in the process of making the shirt, didn't she?"

"I imagine she did. She was in and out of my home quite frequent, too."

"As a matter of fact, you made the shirt early in December of 1959, did you not, Mrs. Mattox?"

"I just said I am not positive whether I made it in December or January."

"Yes, ma'am. Mrs. Mattox, I believe you testified that you saw your son when you returned from Sunday school, in the carport?"

"He was on the brick in front of the den door. It is not really the carport. The brick terrace comes on out in front of the house."

"I see. He had that shirt on at that time, didn't he?"

"I, he had on a plaid shirt. I do not know whether it was this one. He had on a khaki jacket and trousers, I am positive of."

"But you told your husband, did you not, that that was the shirt which your son had on, on the morning of January 31st, 1960, did you not?"

"I don't remember it, if I did."

"I see. If he said you did, then he was mistaken?"

"I do not know."

"You do not know? What time did you go to Sunday school on the morning of January 31st?"

"I usually leave home about 9:30. I have to pick up my husband's mother and her sister, who live together, three or four blocks from our house."

"I see. Did you arrive at Sunday school on time that morning?"

"Yes, I did. I am sure I did."

Prosecutor Burgin asked Mrs. Mattox about her statement that she and Mr. Mattox had noted the time on his watch when she returned home from Sunday school.

"Now, Mrs. Mattox, if you looked at Jimmy's watch, what time did it say?"

"Twenty five minutes to eleven."

"Why then, Mrs. Mattox, in your prior statement, taken two days after the murder, did you state that you arrived home . . . "

"We are going to object, if Your Honor please . . . "

"Overruled."

"I might help you understand your notes there a little bit better," offered the witness, "We found out at eleven o'clock that Jimmy's watch was four minutes slow. Therefore, I got home at twenty one minutes of eleven."

"And, of course when you got home, as you stated, you looked at his watch and you all discussed the time?"

"That's right."

"I see. Mrs. Mattox, I believe you said that you did give a statement to Mr. Lucas and to Chief Vickery. They asked you if you would mind answering some questions, and you did answer. They asked, and you answered some questions?"

"We tried our best."

"And when was that, Mrs. Mattox?"

"It was either Monday or Tuesday night after this accident. We were called at home and asked Mr. Mattox to bring me and come to Mr. Lucas's office. We got up there, and they put Jimmy in one office and me in the other, and then they started asking different questions, and it was recorded."

"I will ask you, Mrs. Mattox, if during that conversation, you did not make the statement, when asked about the time you returned, you arrived at your home after Sunday school, that 'They did not keep us as long as we usually stay, so I got back home, I guess, between twenty five minutes and a quarter of eleven'?"

"I could not tell you whether I said 'guess' or not, but we do know that I did look at the watch, and I do not feel like I said that."

"I see. And of course, you knew that you looked at, had looked at, his watch when you gave this statement to Mr. Lucas and Chief Vickery, did you not?"

"Yes. I know what time it was."

"I see, but you didn't advise them, in the course of that statement, that you looked at the watch, did you? As a matter of fact, Mrs. Mattox, didn't you tell them that your husband said to you that it was a certain time - that you didn't look at the watch?"

"I did look at his watch, Mr. Burgin. I just have repeated that to you."

"Were you not, during that conference, asked the question, 'Did you check your watch?' and your answer was, 'No, he did.'?"

"I did not have my watch on."

"You deny having answered that question in that manner?"

"I did not have my watch on," she responded in a mild, but exasperated tone.

"I don't believe there is anything further, Your Honor."

Mr. Stennis had some questions on redirect regarding whether the Mattox's owned a deep freeze at any time. He sought to discredit Grayson's testimony that Jonny had told her that he had killed a deer out of season - even though their freezer was full of meat.

"No, sir. I have never had one."

Mr. Burgin wished to explore this further:

"Mrs. Mattox, does your refrigerator have a freezing compartment?"

"It has one large tray of ice cubes and four smaller ones, and that is the extent of the freezing unit in my refrigerator, because in the summer I have trouble keeping enough ice for iced tea."

"I see. Is there room for frozen foods to be placed in that unit?"

"No, sir."

"Do you have a locker at the frozen food plant?"

"My son has, yes."

"I see. You have prepared meals from the food from the locker, have you not?"

"That is correct. I sure have."

"And that is true during the past, we will say four or five, maybe six months, prior to the tragedy, is it not?"

"I couldn't say how long, but I have had meat from the locker plant in my home this winter."

"I see. What kind of meat."

"Different kinds. We have had venison."

"Pork?"

"Wild pig. We have had squirrel."

He had made his point regarding the existence of the freezer. Burgin continued to question Mrs. Mattox in other areas pertinent to her previous testimony, but there was nothing of substance revealed nor any significant misstatements. She was excused as a witness, and as she passed by the defense table, she hesitated and warmly grasped her son's extended hand. It was a poignant moment to all - regardless of their opinion of the defendant's guilt.

There was still a battery of witnesses to be heard, and after a recess for lunch, the defense called its next witness, Mr. James Mattox, father of the defendant.

ELEVEN

The trial atmosphere had become charged with emotion, once again, with the testimony of Elizabeth Mattox. And now her husband, James, or "Jimmy" as she called him, took the witness stand on behalf of his youngest son, Jon. His son Jon - whose very life could be abruptly and prematurely ended by the state. A planned killing, strapped in a chair, forced to breath a lethal, foul gas - a moment in "Hell," to be witnessed by the righteous. James Mattox could not bear the thought, and yet, it could not be avoided. Not a restful sleep in months. Jonny, on the other hand, slept like a baby.

He was a quiet man, unassuming. Stoic. In suit and tie, he nervously adjusted his dark framed glasses and awaited Mr. Stennis. Jon, too, was tense and, unconsciously, repositioned his chair several times during his father's testimony.

"Your name is James Mattox, sir?"

"It is."

"How old are you, sir?"

"Not quite fifty."

Mr. Mattox went on to tell the court that he was born in Columbus, and had obtained a degree in Electrical Engineering at Mississippi State.

"Mr. Mattox, I will ask you to tell the jury and the court as to what has been your relationship between yourself and your son, Jon Mattox?"

"It has been very good. He has been a son of whom I have been proud."

"Has his relationship toward you, as his father, been an affectionate relationship, sir, and on a friendly basis?"

"It has, sir."

"And have you loved your son, sir, as a father should love his son?"

"I have."

"Now, when your son returned from his trip out to Joe Douglas' to get his portable radio, were you at home, sir?"

"I was."

"Could you tell this court and jury approximately how long he had been there before your wife returned from Sunday school?"

"He had been there several minutes. I was in the bath, shaving with an electric razor. I estimate that I completed my shaving approximately twenty-five minutes until eleven. Very shortly after I completed shaving, while I was still in the bath, I heard my son dial the telephone, which is immediately outside the bathroom door. A couple of minutes thereafter, two minutes, three minutes, minute and a half, more or less, I heard my son go through the hall in the direction of the bedroom and den, which is the normal door through which we go in and out of the house. Just a very few moments, a minute, more or less, after that, I came out of the bath and went into the bedroom. As I entered the bedroom, my wife came in, returning from Sunday school. I was a bit embarrassed, because I like to finish my shaving and dressing before she returns on those days on which I do not go to Sunday school."

"And after your wife returned, I will ask you if your son, Jon Mattox, left your home?"

"He did. I would estimate it to be five, six, or seven minutes. I finished my dressing, picked up the paper, and sat down in the den to read the paper. Immediately after I sat down, my son came through the den with a pair of boots or shoes in his hand and started out, and I asked him where he was going. He said he was going to help Otho, who is Otho McDaniel, I believe, find his dogs, and then I resumed reading my paper, and my son left. I, when my wife came in, as I entered the bedroom, I had looked at my watch and commented on her early return from Sunday school. I, at that time, my watch showed twenty-five minutes until eleven. I later learned that my watch was four minutes slow."

"Now, on that occasion when you saw your son, Jon, there in your home, did he appear to be excited, upset, nervous, or in any strange or strained condition, sir?"

"He appeared perfectly normal."

"Uh. And who is Norman, sir?" asked Mr. Stennis, a little confused.

"Sir?" asked the witness. The judge frowned and scratched his head, while a few muffled giggles sounded around the room.

"Mr. Stennis, sir, you misunderstand me. I said 'He appeared perfectly normal,' " Mr. Mattox politely instructed the attorney.

"Of course, sir," said Mr. Stennis, unruffled, "My apologies to you. Now, Mr. Mattox, sir, did you see, did Mrs. Gene Tate visit your wife in your home, and did she visit her in her home on occasions?"

"They did."

"And were they on friendly terms?"

"Yes."

"Were you and Mr. Martin Tate on friendly terms, sir?"

"In a very casual way, yes."

"And I will ask you to tell the jury and this court, whether or not, in your observation there of the deceased, if she ever indicated anything in your presence that led you to believe that she was not a perfect lady, a good wife, and an affectionate, interested mother?"

"I saw nothing," he responded emphatically, "to indicate in any way that she was not a person of the very finest type. I had, and have, the opinion that she was a perfect lady."

Then Mr. Stennis asked Mr. Mattox about his employment history in Columbus, that he had worked for the city as general manager for the light and water department, and went on to be employed by Hooker Chemical Company where he continued to work as chief engineer. This history was followed by his telling the court the names of his children, his close relatives in town, and he and his family's church affiliation at the First Methodist Church.

"Mr. Mattox, after Jon left to go on this hunt for dogs, when did you see him next, sir?"

"On that Sunday evening, I would estimate between six and seven o'clock."

"I see, and he had learned of this tragedy, in your neighborhood there, before he returned, had he not?"

"I told him about it on the telephone shortly before his return."

"And did he come home immediately from there?"

"Within a very short while."

"Where did you locate him on the telephone?"

"Mr. Otho McDaniel's."

"Mr. Mattox, did you remain at your home all day this Sunday?"

"I was at home all day, or in the neighborhood."

"When did you first learn of this tragedy, sir?"

"A short while after eleven a.m. I would estimate ten to fifteen minutes after, when one of the policemen knocked on the door. I answered the door, and he told me of the tragedy and asked if I had seen any strangers or unusual happenings in the neighborhood."

"I see. I believe that's all, sir."

"What says the state, Mr. Burgin? Cross-exam?"

"Yes, Your Honor." Bill Burgin rose to greet the witness.

"Mr. Mattox, it is true, is it not, that your son, Jon, has his own private entrance to his bedroom that is accessed from your backyard area?"

"Yes, however, his room is on the far rear of the house, and you would have to climb up a bank or cross the entire backyard to get to his bedroom."

"I see. But there is a set of steps up to his private entrance?"

"Yes."

"Now, your carport is less than six feet from the Tate's garage, is it not?"

"Yes, approximately."

"And behind their garage, there is a gate, along the property line there, between your backyard and theirs, that opens into the Tate's backyard?"

"Yes, there is."

"I see. Mr. Mattox, I believe you testified that you had a very pleasant relationship with your son?"

"Yes."

"I believe you testified that he had been a very good son, and you never had any trouble with him?"

"Yes."

"And that he was the son of whom you had been proud?"

"Of whom I am proud," Mr. Mattox corrected him.

"I see. Were you proud of him when he was kicked out of the Scouts in the City of Columbus?"

"We are going to object to that, and ask the court to instruct the jury to disregard it," said the defense attorney, "It's too remote."

"Too remote? Four or five years ago? The witness has testified that his son was the perfect gentleman," retorted the special prosecutor.

"Overruled. I'm going to let him answer."

"I have no knowledge of his being kicked out of the Scouts. I was told he was dropped from the rolls for nonattendance."

"As a matter of fact, Mr. Mattox, were you not told that he was asked to leave a meeting of his Scout troop, at the Scout Hut in the City of Columbus, for brutally mistreating a much younger boy?"

"I have no knowledge of such a thing."

"You deny that then?"

"I deny it absolutely."

"And you haven't heard of it at all?"

"No."

"And it didn't happen?"

"I do not know that it didn't happen, but I have no knowledge of such a thing."

"I see. Were you proud of him when he shot a younger boy with a pellet gun, when he was running away from him, in a fit of anger?"

"I have no knowledge of such an incident. If it happened it must have been an awful long time ago."

"In the summer of '55 or '56, Mr. Mattox?"

"I had no knowledge of such an incident."

"You don't deny that it took place?" Mr. Burgin persisted.

"I don't know that it did or did not."

"Mr. Mattox, isn't it true that on three consecutive months during Jon Mattox's senior year in high school that you received, from the principal of Lee High School, notices that he was failing in his grades, and that there was a chance that he would not graduate, and that neither you, nor his mother, went down to check with the school authorities, pursuant to that request, after receiving those notices?"

"Just a moment, Mr. Mattox," said Mr. Stennis and held up his hand to caution the witness. "We object to that. If you are going to send a man to the gas chamber because he failed, I will lead the parade! I failed two years in high school." There was laughter in the courtroom.

"Objection sustained. Let's have order now," Judge Greene warned. "One of you bailiffs go back there and keep order now."

"Crucify him because he failed!" snorted the defense attorney. More laughter followed.

"We have to have order now. We hate to have to ask you to leave," announced Sheriff Spruill.

"I believe you testified, Mr. Mattox, that you always gave him fatherly advice and assistance where it was needed?"

"I testified that I tried to do so."

"Now, what have been his grades at Mississippi State?"

Again, a round of dramatic objections by Mr. Stennis which were sustained.

"Mr. Mattox, are you paying your son's expenses at 'State'?" The next objection was also sustained.

"Now, Mr. Mattox, on Tuesday, February 2nd, Chief Mahlon Vickery asked you to furnish him with the clothes that your son wore on the morning of Sunday, January 31st, 1960, did he not?"

"Yes, sir."

"This is the shirt your son was wearing on Sunday morning, January 31st, 1960, isn't it?" Mr. Burgin held up the shirt for the witness to see.

"I cannot swear to that."

"You saw him, didn't you?"

"I saw him."

"You furnished him with this shirt, as being that shirt, didn't you? Furnish Vickery with it?"

"To the best of my knowledge at that time."

"Yes, sir, and then you know this is the shirt he was wearing that Sunday morning, don't you, Mr. Mattox?"

"No, I do not know."

"That shirt was freshly laundered, wrapped, and in the package when you delivered it to Chief Vickery, wasn't it, Mr. Mattox?"

"When I arrived home after Mr. Vickery requested those articles of wearing apparel, I asked my wife where the clothes were that Jonny had been wearing. She said they were in the washing machine. I called Chief Vickery. I told him that they were in the washing machine, within ten to fifteen minutes after I arrived home, that they had been washed, they had not been dried. I asked him if he wanted them wet. He told me he did, and a short while later, I took them to him."

"You do know, don't you, Mr. Mattox, that that is the shirt that your son was wearing on the morning of January 31st?"

"I do not know it positive. I think it may have been."

"You think it may have been?"

"Yes. I asked my wife where the clothes were that Jonny was wearing Sunday. She said they were in the washing machine, and they were wet. I am not even sure that the washing machine wasn't running when I asked her. I called Mr. Vickery. He said he would like to have them wet or dry. I asked my wife which ones Jonny wore on Sunday. My memory for things of that sort is not much good. She said she thought it was the heavy plaid shirt. I went and pulled the heavy plaid shirt and the trousers and delivered them to Mr. Vickery."

"Now, Mr. Mattox, after your son left to go to Joe Douglas's to get his radio, and before he returned, you went in the bathroom to shave, didn't you?"

"Yes, sir."

"You have an electric razor?"

"Yes."

"I believe it is a noisy one, isn't it?"

"Yes."

"Can't hear very much when it is running, can you?"

"No."

"I believe you testified that after your wife's return from Sunday school, you saw your boy leaving to go look for some dogs, or go hunting or something, didn't you?"

"I saw him go out the door, yes."

"And that was prior to the time when you learned of the murder of Mrs. Tate, wasn't it?"

"It was."

"Did you hear his car start up after he went out the door?"

"Yes."

"Did you hear it drive away?"

"I heard it go around the corner and down the hill, yes."

"I see. And that was after your wife returned from Sunday school, but before you learned of Mrs. Tate's murder?"

"That's right."

"And you knew he had left the house?"

"That's right."

"Mr. Mattox, George Graves came to your den door and informed you of the death of Mrs. Tate, didn't he?"

"No, sir. He came to the front door and rang the doorbell."

"To the front door. And he informed you of the murder, did he not?"

"Yes."

"What time was it approximately?"

"I estimate it between eleven . . . ten minutes after eleven, and fifteen minutes after eleven."

"I see. Mr. Graves asked you, on that occasion, did he not, sir, if you had heard anything or seen anything unusual in the neighborhood, didn't he?"

"Yes, sir."

"And you answered Mr. Graves, when he asked you that question, that you hadn't heard a thing unusual, and told him to wait a minute and let you go ask your son, Jon - he had been there all morning? And you went back to ask him, didn't you?"

"I did not say such a thing. I did not say that my son had been there all morning, because he was not."

"You deny saying that your son 'Jon is here, wait a minute, let me go ask him.'?"

"I deny that absolutely."

"I see. Now, Mr. Mattox, you saw Mr. Billy Furr about one o'clock on Sunday, January 31st, did you not?"

"I saw Mr. Furr and two or three hundred other people."

"I see, and Mr. Furr asked you where you were at the time of the murder, didn't he?"

The defense objected, and was overruled by the judge.

"Since you are laying a predicate, Mr. Burgin, you better repeat it."

"I said that you saw Mr. Furr, while you were standing in your driveway, about one o'clock on Sunday, January 31st, 1960, and, at that time, he asked you where you were at the time of the murder, didn't he?"

"I do not know that it was approximately one o'clock. I saw Mr. Furr in that general area. He may have asked me where I was. I do not remember the specific instance. If so, I probably told him that I was in the house, because I told several people that."

"As a matter of fact, Mr. Mattox, didn't you tell Mr. Furr that you were in the den, and Jonny was in the backyard?"

"At the time of the murder? I did not tell Mr. Furr . . . I did not make that statement exactly to Mr. Furr. I may have told Mr. Furr, as I told several other people, that my son Jon was there during that period."

"You deny telling Mr. Furr that you were in the den at the time it happened, and that Jonny, referring to the defendant, was in the backyard?"

"I deny that, as stated."

"Mr. Mattox, your son, Jon, has several pairs of gloves, does he not?"

"I am sure he has at least one. I don't know how many."

"He wears those gloves quite frequently when he goes hunting, does he not?"

"I am sure he usually carries a pair with him."

"Yes, sir. As a matter of fact, at the time he was arrested, the first time, in the office of Mr. Lowery Lucas, on Thursday night after the murder, he had a pair of gloves in his pocket, didn't he?"

"I do not remember specifically, but he may have. It was a rather raw, rainy night."

"All right. I have nothing further."

The defense attorney approached the witness for some follow-up questions.

"I will ask you, sir, if your son, Jon, has been a regular courter - that is - dating young ladies with a lot of regularity?"

"Well, with no regularity, really. He has had occasional dates. I believe there was, about the last of his high school, one girl he dated a number of times. There are other girls he has had dates with, but very few girls, more than just a very, very, occasional date. He has, in my experience, had less dates, a good bit less dates, than normal, for a boy of that age."

"Mr. Mattox, was Jonny ambitious to improve his mind and get an education?"

"He has shown himself ambitious to get an education, and to improve himself, yes."

"And in so doing that, would a person have as much time for girls, as he would have if he wasn't trying to improve his mind and get an education?"

Burgin objected to that question because it called for a conclusion by the witness. The judge agreed and sustained it. With that, Mr. Stennis thanked the witness, and Mr. Mattox was excused from further testimony.

The defense then called Mrs. Otho McDaniel to testify. She stated that Jon had called their house Sunday morning around 9:45 a.m., and she had told him that Otho was out looking for his lost dogs. Later that day, she cooked a late lunch for Jon and Otho, and at supper time, about six to eight hunting acquaintances, including Jon, came for supper.

Mrs. McDaniel said that Jon had hunted with her husband since he was about 12 years old, and she had never noticed any "abnormal" behavior, nor did she on that Sunday, the day Gene Tate was murdered. She stated that she believed Jon had a good reputation for peace in the community.

She was followed by her husband, Otho McDaniel. He said Jon came out to Hairston Bend on that Sunday and helped him look for the dogs. Cecil Gibson and Joe Gentry had come out there, too. Mr. McDaniel was with Jon the rest of the day and at supper, and said he didn't notice anything unusual about his behavior. McDaniel said that Jon had his radio with him out at the Bend that morning, but "it wouldn't play."

Like his wife, the witness reported that he had hunted with Jon since he was 12 years old, when Mr. Mattox had brought him out there. The witness said that he had trained the young Mattox as a hunter, and he had become a "pretty fair" one. They had hunted together frequently during "season" over the years. McDaniel said he didn't know Jon's reputation for peace or violence in the community, but when pressed by Mr. Stennis, he said, "It be good, I reckon." On cross-examination, he admitted that he had expressed concern that Jon "got blood on him more than anybody I seen." He acknowledged that he had once said that Mattox seemed to enjoy getting the blood all over him. McDaniel shrugged, and said he had just told Mattox that he should try not to do that.

Joe Gentry, who had hunted and fished with the defendant for the past two years, said he saw Mattox out at Hairston Bend, with Otho, on the morning and afternoon the day of the murder. He testified that he noted nothing unusual about his behavior, that Jon had acted like "the same old Jonny."

Cecil Gibson had been with Gentry that day, out at Hairston Bend, and also testified that he had noticed nothing unusual about the defendant's behavior either that morning or that afternoon.

A number of defense witnesses, well over a dozen, were called to testify about the reputation of the defendant, whether or not he was known for peace or violence in the community. Several of them were students at Mississippi State who had not known Mattox more than a few months - since the time he had moved back on campus in February. They testified that they had not observed any abnormal or antisocial behavior by him. But his former roommate, James "Ricky" Pierce, had lived with Mattox in the Old Main dormitory during their freshman school year, from approximately October '57 until March '58, when Ricky joined a fraternity and moved to the frat' house.

Pierce was from Amory, Mississippi, and said he had known Jonny since his senior year in high school. He said that while they had lived together at Old Main, and in the last couple of years around campus, he had not observed any "antisocial" behavior by the defendant. In fact, Ricky stated that Jon had gone home with him one weekend to Boston, Massachusetts, where his family lived at the time, and he had gotten Jon a date with a girl there. Pierce stated that the two had liked each other quite a bit.

Mr. Burgin, then, had a few questions for the witness:

"Mr. Pierce, isn't it true that the defendant told you on one occasion about strangling a dog with a coat hanger?"

"I am under oath? Is that right?"

"Yes, sir."

"Well, I couldn't swear to that at all. I am uncertain."

"You deny that he told you anything about killing a dog with a coat hanger?"

"With a coat hanger, yes, sir."

"All right, what did he tell you about killing a dog?"

"Well, I seem to remember that because, I guess that is funny, but I am under oath now. This has been a long time, but I think he told me once about killing a dog, that he had an old dog, I believe. His name was Mitzi, or something like that, because it was real old. He killed it with a rifle, like anyone else would kill an old dog."

"I see. You deny having made the statement that the defendant told you of killing a dog by choking it to death with a coat hanger?"

"I may have made that statement at one time, but then, sir, I wasn't under oath, and I was saying what I thought, and I can't say what I thought here, I can see right now."

"I see. All right, when did you make that statement?"

"I believe it was . . . I don't know. I may have said that to my mother along about the time Jon was arrested."

"I see. And that was your recollection of it at that time, wasn't it?"

"Yes, sir."

"I see, and when you told your mother that Jon had told you he had strangled a dog with a coat hanger, you were giving her your best recollection of what Jon told you, wasn't you?"

"Yes, sir. But, again, I wasn't under oath."

The witness answered a few unrelated questions by Mr. Stennis and was excused. However later, Stennis recalled Ricky to the stand, and he told the court that he wanted to clear up his previous testimony, that what he had told his mother were just rumors he had heard after the murder - about Jon killing everything from dogs to cats with coat hangers. So that, even though Jon had told him about killing a dog, Pierce said he just told his mother "maybe it was with a coat hanger" because of the rumors he had heard.

Mr. Burgin questioned him about his change in testimony, but Pierce insisted that he had not been able to explain himself previously.

"I see," said Burgin, "and so now, after conferring with counsel for the defendant, you say that Jon told you about killing a dog?"

"Well, by conferring, I just told him I wanted to come back on the stand and try to clear that up."

"I see. Well, what did he tell you about killing a dog?"

"Sir, that has been a while. We were rooming together. He told me that, and I couldn't remember that any more than you could - remember what somebody said to you two years ago, one morning just in passing."

"You said now that you told your mother that that is what he killed everything else with?"

"No, sir. I said that is what all the rumors were."

"I see. Of course, you didn't mention any rumors in your testimony yesterday."

"No, sir, because everything you asked me had to be answered yes or no."

"I see. That's all."

Ricky's testimony was a real curiosity to most observers, and quite a few thought, that with all that "hemming and hawing," he seemed to be trying to skirt around the whole coat hanger issue, like maybe he was scared to death to do damage to the defendant. Others thought he was simply trying to be completely honest about his recollection . . .

Another of the reputation witnesses was a dairy farmer, John Christopher, from Adaton, west of Starkville, who had known Jon since he was a youngster. Christopher had been a business associate of the defendant's father. He testified that he had hunted and target practiced with Jon, since he was thirteen, and thought of him as a good shot, "professional." Later, in high school, Jon worked for him on a construction crew. He stated that during Jon's college years, he would come out and horseback ride from time to time, but since his arrest, he had been a frequent visitor in his home - four times, or so, a week.

Mr. Christopher testified that in his opinion Jon had a good reputation for peace, and that he had visited the Mattox's, for the first time recently to convey to them his sympathy,

" . . . to tell them, knowing Jon as I did, I couldn't see how it was possible a boy of that character, strong and level-headed, could possibly have committed a murder like that."

Several other witnesses from Columbus, who had known Jon casually for many years, also testified that they thought he had a good reputation for peace in the community. They also stated, when asked, that they were not aware of Jon having dated any girls.

However, Rosalee Webb, a college girl, whose family had lived across the street from the Mattox's for fourteen years, came to testify that she had "dated" Jon, and that he had behaved "like a perfect gentleman." She thought his reputation in Columbus was a good one. She said that she and her parents were good friends of the Mattox's, and that she wanted to help Jon.

Miss Webb also stated that she had been in the Tate's home several times, and that Mrs. Gene Tate always conducted herself as a perfect lady. She agreed that she had seen Jonny outside playing with the children, often in the Tate's yard. Mr. Burgin asked her if it wasn't true that the children he played with were always much younger than the defendant, and she agreed.

More witnesses, all good friends of Mr. and Mrs. Mattox, were called to the witness stand to give their opinions about Jonny's reputation in Columbus. They all said they thought he had a good reputation. One in particular, Mrs. Hilda Miller, broke the monotony with the following exchange with the older Mr. Luther Sims, co-counsel for the defense:

"Mr. Burgin asked you if you were interested in helping Jonny Mattox, and I believe you stated that you were?"

"Yes, sir."

"Why are you?"

"Well, I am interested in helping Jonny because he is my friend, and I feel like he is innocent of what he has done." Laughter erupted in the courtroom.

"That's all," said the chagrinned Mr. Sims.

The defense had presented over forty witnesses on behalf of the defendant since they began on Tuesday morning, many of whom gave testimony regarding the reputation or character of the accused. But of all of the witnesses, not one had developed a close friendship with Jon Mattox. Not one could claim any more than the most casual relationship with him.

Now at mid-day Wednesday, the last three witnesses were called to testify. They would give their opinion regarding the reputation of the deceased, Mrs. Gene Tate. All three women had been good friends of Gene Tate's, and typical of their testimony was that given by Mrs. Fred Harrison, questioned by Mr. Stennis:

"How long have you lived in Columbus, ma'am?"

"Ten years in June."

"You have children, ma'am?"

"Yes, sir."

"Mrs. Harrison, it has been said in this courtroom by Mr. Martin Tate and a young college student named Sarah Grayson, that Mrs. Martin Tate, during her lifetime, was - or it has been inferred, I will say - was not a woman of good moral character. I will ask you, if you knew Mrs.Tate during her lifetime?"

"Now may it please the court," interrupted Mr. Burgin, "we object to that as not being a correct statement of the testimony. Mr. Martin Tate made no such statement, Your Honor."

"I don't believe Mr. Tate did, but the testimony of the young lady did reveal that. Leave Mr. Tate out, and I think it will be all right," opined the judge.

"All right," Mr. Stennis relented.

"Well, leaving out the names of the parties who said it, I will ask you, ma'am, how long you knew Mrs. Gene Tate?"

"Approximately, seven or eight years."

"Mrs. Harrison, were you in her home on occasions?"

"Yes, sir."

"Was she in your home, ma'am, on occasions?"

"Yes, sir."

"Were you in the homes of mutual friends, both at the same times, on occasions?"

"Yes, sir."

"Do you belong to any of the clubs that she belonged to?"

"Yes, sir. A garden club, the Junior Auxiliary, and a bridge club."

"I will ask you, ma'am, if, during your contacts with Mrs. Gene Tate, there was anything, anything in her conduct, that indicated to your mind that she was anything except a faithful wife and an affectionate mother?"

"No, sir." There were no questions by Mr. Burgin.

Mr. Stennis announced that the defense had no more witnesses to call and requested that the judge excuse the jury in order for him to make a motion out of their presence. The jury was excused. Mr. Stennis then began a long statement to the court about his many repeated, but unsuccessful, attempts to subpoena Joe Douglas and John Chambley. He stated that because these witnesses were critical to his defense, he wanted to move the court for a delay in the trial until he could have the two men subpoenaed. He related to the judge that there had been numerous problems with the service of process, and that the sheriff had even told him that neither he, nor his deputies, knew Joe Douglas, and wouldn't recognize him.

Mr. Burgin challenged Mr. Stennis's contentions and told the court that Joe Douglas had informed a mutual friend that he had met with Mr. Stennis several times, including in the courtroom, and that Mr. Stennis had told him to make himself scarce and that he would get a hold of him, if he wanted him. Burgin said further that Douglas had a friend get in touch with Mr. Lucas, the county attorney, to let him know of his contacts with Mr. Stennis, and that he, Joe Douglas, was worried that he could get into trouble for evading process, and that he was not evading process.

Then Mr. Burgin told Judge Greene that he would like for Mr. Stennis to take the witness stand so that he could cross-exam him. The judge said he couldn't force Mr. Stennis to take the stand, but he would ask him if he would do so.

"I do not desire to take the stand, no, sir," responded Stennis.

The sheriff then asked Judge Greene if he could be sworn in, because he wanted to make a statement. The judge agreed and had him sworn in. Sheriff Spruill testified that he never, on any occasion, told the defense attorney that his deputies did not know Joe Douglas.

With all of that, Judge Greene stated that he had been very liberal in giving the defense time to confer with witnesses, and therefore, he was overruling his motion for delay.

Then Mr. Stennis made several more motions, including one for a mistrial, and one for a directed verdict in favor of the defendant. His reasoning was based on portions of Sarah Grayson's testimony and the judge's denial of his motion for delay. He asserted that his client's rights under the U.S. Constitution, and the Constitution of the State of Mississippi had been violated. All of his motions were denied. As a result, Mr. Stennis announced that the defense refused to rest.

"This is all repetition - been motions made every day on that. It is just repetition, over and over, like playing a record - same song. Overruled." said Judge Greene. He instructed Mr. Burgin to begin his case in rebuttal.

"You gentlemen ready?," he asked the prosecution.

"Yes, sir . . . Mr. Si Thompson," replied Mr. Burgin and announced the name of his first rebuttal witness.

"All right. Call the jury back in."

TWELVE

The spectators were getting somewhat trial-weary, as yet another witness took the stand. But this was the prosecution's rebuttal case: people who were called to give evidence intended to contradict or dilute the testimony of the defense witnesses. Si Thompson was sworn in.

Thompson was a young man who stated that he had known Jonny Mattox since they were both about six years old. The two had graduated together from Lee High School and had been on camping trips together "very often."

"Si, I will ask you, if in your association with the defendant, you have had an opportunity to observe whether or not he had a temper?"

"Yes, sir. He has a pretty mean, violent temper."

The witness also reported that Jonny's reputation in the community for peace or violence was "bad." There were no questions on cross-examination by the defense.

Mrs. Dick Christopher was the next rebuttal witness. She and her husband had been present for supper at Otho McDaniel's home on the late afternoon of January 31st. Contrary to Mr. and Mrs. McDaniel, Mrs. Christopher said that Mattox was behaving peculiarly that day.

"He seemed rather unsettled to me - moving around from one place to another." She said he didn't do that normally, and he seemed nervous and upset.

"He was not the same old Jon that had visited in my home before."

"Had he visited in your home on many occasions?" asked Mr. Burgin.

"Oh, not many. I would say several."

"I see, and on those occasions, you had an opportunity to observe his . . . "

"Yes, because . . . Oh, I would say a couple of times they, the hunters, had come to my house for supper because we were newlyweds, and they came to eat, and I cooked supper for them."

The defense then questioned Mrs. Christopher about the seating arrangement that evening at the supper, and she explained that the main dining table seats were taken, so she was eating in the kitchen with others.

"I see, and that was why Jon was moving from one room to another?" asked Stennis.

"No, sir. This lady got me a chair, and before I could sit down, he was in my chair. I thought nothing of that, but he just seemed unsettled to me."

Her husband, Dick Christopher, was next to take the stand for the prosecution. Like his wife, Christopher was well-groomed and in his mid-twenties. He stated that he had known the defendant for four or five years, and that Mattox had visited in his home several times. The afternoon of the murder, he and his wife had supper at the McDaniel's, along with several others, including Jon Mattox.

"When I first came in the door, I noticed him. He didn't look quite like the same old Jon. Mrs. McDaniel said there wasn't enough room for us to eat in the dining room. She got a chair for my wife to sit down and told my wife to sit down - and Jon sat down in the chair with his plate. We didn't say anything. It didn't really matter. And in about two minutes, he jumped up and went in the other room, and he just seemed nervous and upset to me, and I asked Mr. McDaniel what was wrong with Jon, and he said, 'Well, he just . . . '"

Stennis objected to the hearsay of McDaniel's statement. The judge agreed and sustained his objection.

"You say he was nervous and upset on that occasion?" asked Burgin.

"Yes, sir, he was."

"I believe you said he wasn't the same old Jon?"

"No, sir, he wasn't."

"What was Mr. McDaniel's condition on that occasion with respect to the use of alcohol, Dick?"

"He had had some."

"Was he . . . Was it noticeable that he had had some?"

"Yes, sir."

"Did he drink after you arrived there?"

"Yes, sir, he did."

On cross-exam, Mr. Stennis asked the witness about his own alcohol consumption that day.

"You took a drink with Mr. McDaniel, didn't you?"

"No, sir. I did not."

"You didn't drink any that afternoon at all?"

"No, sir."

"You are known as a drinking man, aren't you?"

"That is approximately so."

"And was there anyone else that had any alcohol there that afternoon?"

"Yes, sir. Joe Douglas had some."

Then the witness agreed that it was possible that the defendant's "upset" behavior that afternoon might have been due to the news about the murder of Gene Tate. Christopher said everyone, including himself and his wife, was upset about the news. He said he felt sure that Jon must have known about it. There were no further questions.

Before the next witness could take the stand, a bumblebee had flown in one of the back open windows and created quite a mini-drama. With squeals of alarm, several ladies swatted it away from their area with their Baptist Church cardboard fans-on-a-stick, which they had brought to help with the discomfort of the late spring heat. Proudly, one of them was able to quickly dispatch the hapless creature. With a deft flick of her wrist, she struck the bee with her fan, and that was the end of that. It was over before the sheriff was half way down the aisle. Judge Greene then asked the prosecution to call its next witness.

Mr. Joe McHarg exited the witness room and was sworn in. Mr. McHarg lived on Park Circle Drive, several houses away from the immediate Tate neighborhood. He was the father of four and the manager of a local J.C. Penney store.

"Do you know the defendant, Jon Mattox?"

"Yes."

"How long have you known him?" asked the prosecutor.

"About nine or ten years," replied Mr. McHarg.

"Do you know of his reputation in the community, in which he lives, for peace and violence?"

"I know of it, yes. It is bad."

On cross-exam, Mr. Stennis questioned McHarg as to whether his opinion had been influenced by the murder charge brought against the defendant. The witness stated that had not entered into his opinion of Mattox. He said his opinion was based on what he had heard prior to the murder, including what he had heard the children say.

Mrs. Warren Gardner followed him to the stand. Mary Dell and her family lived next door to the Tate's. She said she had known Jon Mattox for almost ten years. Like Mr. McHarg, Mrs. Gardner said that his reputation in the community was bad.

"Mrs. Gardner, did you know Mrs. Gene Tate during her lifetime?" asked Mr. Stennis on cross.

She answered that Gene had been living next door to her for several years, that they visited back and forth in each other's homes and also the homes of mutual friends. They had both belonged to the Columbus Junior Auxiliary until Mrs. Gardner resigned when her third son was born.

"I will ask you to tell this court and jury if, during the last two years of Mrs.Tate's life, when she was visiting in your home occasionally, and you were visiting in hers, and when you were living right next door to her, if you saw anything in this deceased lady's conduct that indicated that she was anything except a faithful, loving wife and an affectionate mother?"

"No, sir, I didn't," Mrs. Gardner responded sadly, as she recalled her good friend. Anytime she pictured Gene, it was a smiling or laughing Gene she saw. It was painful to think about her brutal murder and the suffering she must have endured in those final moments.

"During the time that you and the Mattox family have lived just one house removed from each other, I will ask you if you ever came by the Tate home and saw this accused in or out of the home, going in or going out of, or inside, of the home?"

"No, sir."

"And I will ask you, ma'am, if it isn't a fact that up until this young man was first accused in this case, you and his mother were very good friends?"

"Yes, sir."

"And since that time, you do not speak to his mother, do you?"

"Oh, I wave, in passing," said the witness, uncomfortably. The murder had destroyed much.

"And you do not visit there now?"

"No, sir."

"Now you are, of course, frankly giving your honest opinion about what you believe about this young man, are you not?"

"Yes, sir."

"You are basing your opinion of this young man partly on what you heard after the death of Mrs. Tate and partly about what you heard before?"

"No, sir," replied Mrs. Gardner.

"I see . . . I believe that's all," said Mr. Stennis.

"You may step down now," said Judge Greene.

Over in the press section, reporters Reed and Shea had busily scribbled their notes and ran to the phone, from time to time, with story updates to their editors. Reed nudged Shea and leaned toward him.

"Wait till I tell you what I've been hearing."

"Okay," Shea said with great curiosity. "After we get out of here?" he whispered.

"Yeah . . . and man, I can't wait to get outta here. We've been jammed like sardines in this heat for over a week!"

The two men got quiet when Mr. Burgin called Mrs. Dexter Higgins to the witness stand. Kitty Higgins was a plump, attractive woman, who was known in town for her generosity and friendly disposition. She and her husband owned a jewelry store.

Mrs. Higgins stated that, in her opinion, Jon Mattox, whom she had known for ten or eleven years, possessed a bad reputation in the community. On cross-exam, Mr. Stennis asked her about the reputation of Mrs.Gene Tate.

"I was never around Mrs.Tate that much, but I have never . . . I knew her as a little girl, and she was a sweet girl, and I knew her in her young married life, and she was also sweet."

Her real purpose as a witness, to discredit the testimony of Mr. Mattox, was heard on Burgin's redirect exam:

"Mrs. Higgins, I will ask you if you have had occasion to have a discussion with Mr. James Mattox - relative to your son?"

"Right, I have."

Stennis jumped up to object and demanded that the time, place, and persons were named.

"When was that?" asked Mr. Burgin.

"My son was eleven years old then, and he was just seventeen this March."

"Was your son in the Boy Scouts, here in Columbus, at that time?"

"Yes, he was."

"Where did you have the discussion with Mr. James Mattox?"

"In front of Mr. Mattox's house."

"Who was present?"

"Mr. and Mrs. Mattox, myself, and my son."

"What did you do at the time?"

"I showed them my son's seat."

"What was the condition of his seat?"

"It was brutally beaten."

Stennis again objected, but Judge Greene agreed with the prosecution, that the testimony was submitted on the question of credibility of the witness, James Mattox.

"I believe Mr. Mattox denied knowing anything about it. All right, go ahead."

"What did you say to him at that time?" Burgin asked her.

"I asked him if he knew that his son had whipped my son . . . his son, Jon."

"You say you showed Mr. and Mrs. Mattox the boy's seat?"

"I did."

"What was the condition of his seat?"

"As I quoted, it was brutally beaten."

"Were there any marks on it?"

"There were. They were about . . . He had been whipped with a stick, and they were . . . I could put my finger in some of the places."

"Did you advise Mr. Mattox that his son, Jon, had inflicted those bruises?"

"I did, both parents, Mr. and Mrs. Mattox."

"You may take the witness, Mr. Stennis."

"You, of course, were not present when anything came up between your young son and young Mattox, were you?" asked the defense attorney.

"I was not at the Boy Scout meeting, no."

"And you, of course, know of no act, of your own personal knowledge, on the part of this accused, that took place between your son and him at the Scout meeting, do you?"

"My son had no reason to tell me a story."

"I didn't ask you that. I said, pardon me, please ma'am, you do not know of your own personal knowledge what happened between your son and young Mattox at the time that you state that your son received the whipping that you refer to?"

"I wouldn't call it a whipping. I would call it a beating . . . I did not see it happen. I heard my son cry at home about it."

"Please ma'am, this is something that you stated, I believe, happened about seven years ago?"

"It was six years ago. My son was eleven, and was a Cub Scout. Jonny Mattox was an upper scoutsman."

"Yes ma'am, but he was an assistant leader, was he not?"

"I wouldn't call that a very good leader - if you want to term him a leader."

Mr. Stennis had no further questions of Mrs. Higgins. It was powerful and very damaging testimony against the defendant and a blow to the credibility of his parents. But after a brief recess called by the judge, there would be more such witnesses.

The crowd had enough time to stand up and stretch and exchange comments about the trial. There were still too many people eager to watch the testimony, for those lucky enough to have a seat, to risk leaving the courtroom. The worry about the stability of the floor was reported again, in the newspaper, in an article about Chancery Clerk Morris Smith. On behalf of himself and his employees, who worked on the first floor of the courthouse directly below the circuit court, a local contractor, Mr. Harris McClanahan, was asked to inspect the building. Mr. McClanahan had cautioned Mr. Smith that there should not be more occupants than the floor was designed to withstand. Nevertheless, the trial went on with the usual jam-packed attendees. The radio stations around the region continued their daily coverage of the proceedings for those who could not, or would not, hear the proceedings in person.

"Lord have mercy! When's this thing gonna be over? My girdle's killin' me, and I'm not gonna have time to get home and fix supper at this rate," complained one lady, who stood with her friend and glanced around the room to look for familiar faces.

"Should be pretty soon," her friend responded, as she checked her watch. "Oh. Sure enough, there's Judge Greene. We better sit down."

The court was called to order, and everyone took their seats. The clerk then called Mr. Billy Furr as the next rebuttal witness. Mr. Furr lived on Park Circle Drive, diagonally across the street from the Mattox home. On the afternoon of the murder, around one o'clock, Mr. Furr said that he had talked with James Mattox in the driveway of the Tate home.

"Jimmy walked over, and I asked him where he was at the time the tragedy happened."

"And what did he say?" asked Mr. Burgin.

"He said that he was in the den reading and that Jonny was in the backyard, and that he came in the house and got his gun, and when his wife returned from Sunday school, said Jonny got in the car and left."

"I see. He said that he was in the den reading and Jonny was in the backyard, and that after his wife got back from Sunday school, Jonny got his gun and left? Is that right?"

"That's right. Said Jonny came in the house and got his gun, and when his wife came back from Sunday school, he left."

"I see. That's all."

Mr. Stennis unsuccessfully tried to challenge the statements of the witness, and then Mr. Furr was excused.

Police Officer George Graves took the stand next, and stated that be-tween eleven-fifteen and eleven-thirty, on the morning of the murder, he left the Tate home and went next door to the Mattox home.

"All right, sir, would you tell the court and the jury what you did?"

"I went there and knocked on Mr. James Mattox's front door, and Mr. Mattox came to the door. I told him who I was and what happened next door, and I asked Mr. Mattox had he seen anything unusual or heard any-thing unusual in the neighborhood that morning."

"What did he say?"

"He said, 'No, sir,' he did not - that he had been in the den most of the morning reading. And he said, 'Let me get Jon,' that 'he was here this morning, too.' And he invited me in the house, and I sat down in the den, and he went back in the back part of the house, and a few seconds later, came out with his wife, and said that Jon wasn't there, that he had gone."

After a short, unfruitful cross-exam by the defense, the witness was ex-cused.

The prosecution tried to introduce the testimony of one final witness. The witness was to testify that he recalled a vague statement by the defen-dant, made the previous summer, to the effect that a neighbor lady of his, who had several children and a husband who was a traveling salesman, was very attractive. He said, out of the hearing of the jury, that he had the impression, at the time, that Mattox felt sorry for the unnamed lady. Burgin argued that this was rebuttal evidence to show a relationship between the defendant and the murder victim.

Mr. Sims protested that the witness's recollection was "vague," as the witness had said, and that the information did not prove any relationship between Mrs.Tate and Jon Mattox. Only a possible infatuation on the part of Mattox - at best, ruled the judge, and he sustained the defense's objection to the testimony.

The jury returned, and Mr. Burgin announced to the court and the jury - that the state rested its case. Judge Greene turned to the jury and told them that all of the arguments were over, no more evidence would be presented, and that final arguments would begin the next morning, Friday, at 8:30.

He blew out a stream of smoke from a cigarette, cracked the gavel, and proclaimed the court was adjourned for the day. As the judge stood up in his black robes, the jury and spectators began filing out of the room. The reporters made a quick dash for the pay phones, and the radio crew continued their monologues of explanation to their large, faithful, listening audiences. The lawyers gathered their papers, and a cooperative deputy stood by while the smiling, friendly, defendant thanked his well-wishers and said goodby to his worried relatives.

The reporters, Reed and Shea, decided to grab a cheeseburger that night at Steve's Cafe, a small, comfortable place a couple of blocks from their hotel. There was a little activity at the Princess Theater next door. Lauren Bacall was starring in "Flame Over India." But the cafe was quiet, with only several other diners seated a few booths away. The two men were as different in appearance as they were in disposition. Reed was a large, hulk of a man, with a big heart and very inquisitive mind: a natural-born investigator. Shea was small and thin, an intellectual who preferred writing feature articles, and was uncomfortable with reaching beyond the obvious. But both were men of integrity - smart, talented writers, who shared a mutual respect for each other.

"Okay, so here's the deal," Reed told his colleague, "First, tell me something - and you have to pay attention: if you found out that your next door neighbor was really an escaped rapist, from somewhere else, who had changed his name and everything, before he moved to your neighborhood, years ago, or whatever - are there things about him that, on reflection now, you could see that could, theoretically, fit with his being an escaped rapist?"

"What! . . . Where's all this going?"

"Just tell me," Reed said impatiently.

"Okay, okay. Hm-m-m," Shea thought about it. "You mean like, because he subscribes to 'Playboy,' . . . or hates lawyers? Stuff like that? . . . Oh - he actually did tell me one time that he saw one of our neighbors naked through her window. He was just walking past there one day." Shea grinned.

"Yeah, basically. Stuff that's not uncommon, or you don't think twice about, that can be reinterpreted later to fit a certain situation . . . Like, just those few things you just mentioned could make you say 'Yeah, maybe those were signs,' or something."

"Yeah, I understand. So, who are you thinking about, Mattox?" Reed had his attention.

"Uh-uh," Reed said. "Gene Tate. Remember how you and I talked about the fact that her husband said he suspected her and Mattox, or insinuated it anyway, but he didn't do anything about it? And we thought that was sort of strange?" Shea nodded in agreement. Reed continued:

"Well, I heard something that really bothered me. I don't know if you heard it, too, but I heard that this week, some kid at school told her oldest son that she was a whore. And I'm thinkin' 'Jeez, this poor little boy - first he finds his mother's body, and now this.'"

"Ah, man . . . that's bad . . . God," commented Shea, sympathetically. "You know, I overheard some old geezer in court this week say that if she had been his wife, he'd have killed her for cheatin', if Mattox hadn't. Like she deserved it. Can you believe it? . . . But, anyway, you were saying?"

"Well, it dawned on me that there isn't really any evidence that she was even having an affair with Mattox," Reed said emotionally. "I mean, think about it . . . So I started asking a few questions here and there, and guess what? I don't think there was an affair. Period."

"Why would the prosecution present it at the trial, if it wasn't so? Everybody loved her."

"Exactly! . . . Everybody did love her, for good reason, but it backed up Grayson's testimony and gave the jury a familiar motive. Pure and simple . . . Just think about it - if they hadn't backed Sarah up: Here she comes, the little scorned college girl who nobody knows, with this affair story Mattox is supposed to have told her, and then Martin Tate and everybody else, like Gene's friends and neighbors, get on the stand and say 'Absolutely not. Gene Tate was not that kind of woman.' That leaves nothing to back up the idea of an affair, so the defense tears little Sarah to shreds for defaming this poor lady - and Grayson looks like a silly liar . . . And Mattox gets away with murder."

"So, are you saying that Martin Tate lied?" Shea was incredulous.

"No. I think he believes it. I think that, after the fact, after he found out about Grayson's statement to the police, that he reinterpreted things - things that he hadn't thought twice about before. Sort of like you and your rapist neighbor. Tate's a traveling salesman, gone a lot . . . He's completely torn up . . . in shock . . . you know. And, by the way, did you notice how the prosecution tried to hush up their own witness, Mrs. Hamilton, when she was testifying that she thought Tate was out of town several nights a week, including Friday night? Remember, Tate had said he was home on Friday nights and watched Mattox's car leave after his wife's, when she was chaperoning those dances - the whole affair thing's just based on Mattox's story to Grayson. That's all, just his story to her."

"Yeah, well, unfortunately, maybe it happens to be true. He sho' wasn't lying about his plan to kill her."

"But there's a lot that just doesn't add up: like the fact that, according to Mattox, he's sneaking over there to spend the night - when she's got four little children in the house, two downstairs - and one of them had asthma. Her mother testified that she was in and out of there several times every day. In fact, I heard that her mother stayed overnight there when Martin was out of town.

"Or, how 'bout the fact that Mattox has one telephone at his house, on the opposite side of the house from his bedroom, but Mrs. Tate's supposed to be calling Jonny all the time - with Mrs. Mattox answering the phone, no doubt? Ridiculous."

"But let me tell you what I found out: I was talking to one of the investigators, off the record naturally, and I asked him how come the cops were on to Mattox so fast? I mean, they had arrested him four days after the murder. So I asked him, 'Was it because Mr. Tate told you about the affair?' You know - is that what made them suspect Mattox so soon? And the investigator says, 'Oh, no - Mr. Tate didn't believe it, at first. We were on to Mattox because he demanded a lawyer at the interview. He said, 'I want me a lawyer right now!' and he had lied about a few things that we already knew about.'"

"No shit?" whispered Shea, wide-eyed.

"No shit." replied Reed. "So I asked him: 'When did Tate start to believe it, about the affair?', and he said it wasn't until later, when Tate started thinking about things . . . which just proves my point. So, not only is this poor lady murdered by this warped animal, but now her reputation is completely destroyed . . . and her children have to live with all of it . . . Makes me sick," said Reed. He had been talking so much, his dinner was still untouched.

"The kids have to live with grief and shame, all at once." Shea observed.

Reed nodded in agreement and continued, "I didn't stop there. I thought that I should check it out some more. So I talked to one of the fellas that hunted with Jonny. I figured if Mattox was involved with Gene Tate, the other hunters would know about it - like maybe he had bragged about it - you know how teenagers are. Or maybe he used one of the hunting cabins for rendezvous, etcetera. And I also thought that maybe, if the hunting buddies didn't know about it before the murder, that after they heard about it at the trial, they would have thought about odd incidents with Mattox and her that, all of a sudden, made sense . . . Anyway, the hunter said there had been absolutely no talk like that before or after the murder. In fact, he said that he figured that Jonny maybe had a big crush on her, but that she just looked at Jonny like he was a baby. He said that Gene Tate was just in the wrong place at the wrong time. Said she was just a nice person, and this boy killed her, for kicks, more or less. He said he didn't know anybody who believed Jonny had an affair with her. Said he didn't recall Jonny ever having a date with anybody, anyway."

Shea had a startling thought and furtively leaned across the table, "You don't think he's homosexual, do you?"

"Hell," Reed threw up his hands and laughed. "How would I know? . . . Jeez, man . . . He doesn't seem sissified to me, but I don't know . . . Wasn't it Stennis who called him 'sissiphrenic,' or something?" They both laughed.

"Brother . . . Well, if it wasn't because of an affair, why do you think he killed her?"

"Because he's mean as a snake. I think it's just like the *Jackson Daily News* reported it a few days after the murder. Their article said 'Thrill Killer Suspect,' that the police thought the murderer was a 'thrill killer, who the victim knew and trusted,'" explained Reed. "That's two months before Grayson came forward and gave them a different motive . . . Plus, if you look at how he killed her - that was very cold and calculating, not like any so-called crime of passion I ever heard of. They're usually pretty bloody."

The two men fell silent for a few moments and thought about it while they ate.

"You know, I talked to a criminologist friend of mine down at Tulane about this: this whole question about what makes a guy like Mattox tick."

"Really? You're really interested in all of this, aren't you?"

"Yeah. I guess. So my friend, Barry, he says these guys are wired differently. He said it sounded like Mattox could not accept rejection in any form, and probably feels completely justified about his actions, and therefore, doesn't feel remorse - like a normal person would feel. But he's not crazy. So, he says it wouldn't necessarily take that much for him to get angry enough to kill somebody."

"Huh . . . Well, I think Sarah Grayson was very credible. So, obviously, you think Mattox lied to her about the affair."

"Sure. Mattox probably got a thrill out of telling her that, too, shocking her."

"Yeah, makes sense . . . Brother, what a mess. Are you gonna write about it?" asked Shea.

"No," Reed shook his head, "my editor's a moron. He doesn't want to touch it, and he couldn't care less anyway. He's already wanting me to go to Birmingham to cover a civil rights story after the verdict."

"You're not going to do anything with it?"

Reed exhaled slowly. "Doesn't look like it."

Friday morning, with even the standing room occupied, Mr. Harvey Buck, the district attorney, began the closing arguments for the prosecution. He would be followed by the defense team, and finally, again for the prosecution, Mr. Burgin. The room was as quiet as a graveyard while he spoke. This was a critical time for both sides. The accused could sometimes be convicted, freed, or saved from the death penalty, based solely on a powerful closing argument.

"Someone always thinks they can commit a perfect murder and get away with it." Buck began. Then he went into detail and reminded the jury of the evidence and testimony presented, and took care to reinforce the credibility of their star witness, Sarah Grayson:

"Miss Grayson was telling you the facts. She had the courage to face up to her responsibility, and she did. Now, she was cross-examined on Saturday afternoon about everything - from the day she was born, up until the present time, and the defendant's attorneys had Saturday afternoon, all day Sunday, Sunday night, and up until Monday morning, and what did they come up with against Miss Grayson? One little girl that got on the stand and said she had known her two or three months, and that one day, in broad, open, daylight, on the Mississippi State University campus, she saw her run up and hug this boy . . . That's all, gentlemen."

"Gentlemen, she was just nineteen years old. When I was nineteen, I was studying to become a farmer. About one more case like this, and I'm going back to farming."

Mr. Buck reiterated some of the key points of the prosecution's case and then ended his statement to the jury:

"We are hearing every day, all over the country - murders and rapes, drunkenness, getting in a car and running innocent people down, and killing them. Gentlemen, I don't know but one way to stop it, and that is to convict the guilty, and that is the only way I know how to stop it."

Mr. Buck returned to the prosecution table, and the elder state legislator and defense lawyer, Mr. Luther Sims, rose to face the jury. He spoke in a folksy, down-to-earth voice, at times with the fervor of a country preacher. His manner would change from confident and kindly, to stern, when appropriate. His task was to demonstrate the weakness of the evidence. And in almost an hour of talking to the jury, he covered many areas of the trial, as well.

"We try to fulfill our responsibilities as lawyers the best we can, because if we make a mistake, it might mean that young fella's life, so we have to be careful . . . He is helpless. He is as helpless as a baby. Nothing he can do. It depends on us. So if we make a mistake, he is the man who suffers, not us."

"I have seen a good many murder trials in this court room the past thirty six years. I have seen scaffolds built out there where people were hanged, two Negroes, right there." He pointed out a window. "Some of you boys, that was before you were born. I don't believe I've ever seen, in my life, a trial that has drawn as much attention and has gone as long as this particular trial. People have been here in this courthouse - it has been jammed every day, which you know, because it is an interesting proposition."

"There are good people on both sides. The fair lady who lost her life was one of the finest little girls that lived in Columbus, and we have tried to protect her good name all the way through this trial, which you know, and we are the only ones that did that, too . . . If ever I had anything to strike me so forcibly was Mr. Tate's testimony. This beautiful woman, who he married eleven years ago - who went down through the valley of the shadow of death to bring forth those four little children for him . . . He was the first man that attacked her reputation and her character. He said she was immoral in substance and in fact. Who else said that? That talking machine that marched in here last Saturday afternoon! Those are the only two people in the world, in the whole world, that said she wasn't above reproach and a good wife, a sweet mother . . . All the neighbors say that - and entered their testimony on this stand."

"He said that that morning he didn't understand why Gene didn't want little Genie to go to Sunday school . . . He insisted on that child going to Sunday school that morning, and the grandmother came by and picked her up and carried her to Sunday school . . . Where did he go?"

"He went to Sunday school, too . . . Where did he go then? He said he finally decided to go by the place and pick up his paper, and there he ran into this Montgomery - the man who had taken all those notes - written down everything in detail, carried them back to his home that night and gone out in his backyard and burned them, gentlemen of the jury! Why?"

"My God, there is a dead nigger in the wood pile around here somewhere! You can't get around it. You can't get around it! . . . Why, in the name of common sense and decency, would he want to take those notes and go back and get in his backyard, and not just tear them apart - but burn them up!"

"I am telling you, gentlemen . . . I am telling you from the very depths of my heart, that I have never in all my born days seen a case try to be framed on a young man like that - in all my experience in this courthouse, or any other courthouse. Not a single, solitary matter of direct testimony. Yet they tell you that you send this boy to the gas chamber? For what? For what! Gentlemen, I tell you, as I said a while ago, there is a dead nigger in the wood pile around here somewhere . . . Some of these days, it will come out, too."

Mr. Sims pointed out that the police had released Mattox from jail after the final fiber analysis was performed by the F.B.I. He argued that the defendant's release from jail was proof that the fiber evidence was too weak for them to consider. Then he stated that Sarah Grayson only came forward after she read about the reward in the newspaper.

"If she was over here tomorrow, if you convict this boy, she would buy a Cadillac and ride up and down the street - and knock down this boy's life!"

"I wish it were possible this morning that that lady who lies down there in her grave, six feet under ground, six feet due east and west, and six feet perpendicular, if it were possible for her to turn back the clock and walk down the aisle there, come right on up here, where I am standing, I feel like she would tell this jury, 'You have got the wrong man. That boy has always been a perfect gentleman. You have got the wrong man.' But her lips are forever closed. She can say nothing now."

"And then let a little old flippy girl like that - come in here and attack her character! I tell you, gentlemen, you ought to resent it! And personally, I do resent it."

"She said he was mentally ill," Sims scoffed, "Now, if there is anybody ill in this case, it seems to me, it is her . . . She may not be. She is smart all right . . . but, she may be mentally ill."

"Where is there one single iota of direct testimony? How did he get in that house? Whoever killed her, did they kill her in the house and then take her out there and lay her down, just as straight, and her clothes wasn't even wrinkled or nothing? The man that did do it - did he do it in the house, or did he do it out in the garage? I don't know. You don't know. And you have no right to say she was killed in the house. You have no right to say she was killed in the garage - because you don't know. That was where she was found . . . And how in the world have you got any right to say that, 'I know beyond every reasonable doubt, and to a moral certainty, that he,' Sims pointed at the defendant, 'is the man that killed her?' How can you say that, men?"

"I am going to leave it with you. I have gone as far with him as I can go. It is up to you gentlemen now. May your conscience be clear, and we submit this man to you . . . believing, trusting, that your verdict will be 'We, the jury, find the defendant, not guilty.' Thank you."

After Mr. Sims took his seat at the defense table, Judge Greene called for a brief recess.

Some of the people in the courtroom thought Sims was persuasive, and a few of the reporters commented that they would be surprised if Jon Mattox was convicted - just not enough to go on for a conviction. Those who had talked to Mattox had found him friendly, charming, and funny. A nice college boy. Couldn't imagine that he could have done it.

Many others expressed the opposite viewpoint. And such were the chatty conversations heard about the courtroom when the jury returned. It was then Mr. Stennis's turn for the defense. He also would talk to them for almost an hour and emphasize the defense case regarding the time-line, with the aid of a chalkboard, the lack of opportunity, and the lack of credibility of Sarah Grayson. Stennis moved back and forth in front of the jury box while he spoke - and frequently stressed certain points with dramatic hand gestures or striking facial expressions, enhanced by his dark, thick eyebrows.

"I am told that you jurors are fair, reasonable, intelligent men . . . I want to thank you gentlemen on behalf of this fine lady, Mrs. Mattox," Stennis turned in her direction. Worry appeared permanently etched into her face. "She has gone through the torments of hell since the finger of suspicion was first pointed on her baby boy."

"Gentlemen, there are some things I wonder about in this lawsuit. There are some things that have not been explained . . . I have nothing unkind to say about Miss Sarah Grayson. I have nothing unkind to say about Mr. Martin Tate. I feel sorry for both of them. I will say that I am a father of three children, and before I would blacken the name of my wife - the name of my children's mother, and before I would cast an eternal cloud over the lives of my three children, in their youth, that I would have just kept my mouth shut!"

"The testimony is from Mr. Tate that this affair started about a year ago, and that it lasted until sometime in November . . . During all that time, he didn't do a thing about it. It is passingly strange that he sat there, a young man, and that thing went on for that long, and he did nothing about it."

"Miss Grayson's testimony was like a melodrama, like one of those dime novels, if you please, a fantastical story! Come up here with a fantastic, illogical story like that and expect you people to send this young man to the gas chamber!"

"It is passingly strange that this young man had premeditated a murder, and on the only date that she ever had with this man, that he would unfold all the gory details . . . And it is also passingly strange that she sat over there, from November the 4th, 1959, until March the 31st, 1960, knowing all of those gory details, without uttering a word to anyone! . . . Only after she had read the notice of the reward did she say anything. Passingly strange."

"This is the first time I have ever seen in the courtroom, and I have practiced 29 years, except for four years when I was in the Marine Corps in World War II - this is the first time I have ever seen a privately hired prosecutor of an interested witness. Why he is interested, I don't know. I wouldn't insinuate anything."

"And I will say this - there is another thing that has made me wonder: why it is that this man, Montgomery, who so meticulously wrote out the details, and the movements, and what was done and said on the day of this great tragedy - why it was that after he wrote it out on a Sunday, the Sunday of the tragedy - that he took it out into his backyard, in the darkness of the night, on the following night - and burned it up! . . . That causes me to wonder . . . That causes me to wonder, as Mr. Sims so aptly put it about 'the Negro in the wood pile.'"

"Another thing is about blood hounds. If they had roped the whole area off and got on the telephone and called Parchman Penitentiary, they would have brought some of the finest blood hounds that has ever tracked a person up here. If those dogs had been taken to the body of Mrs. Tate, and smelled the odor of Jon Mattox - they would have immediately gone to the Mattox house, and if they had smelled the odor of one of those three Negroes up there . . . they would have immediately followed the route that that party took! But nothing like that was done."

"Perhaps I have talked too long. If I have, it is a mistake of the mind, not of the heart . . . With all of the sincerity, with all of the heartfelt concern that ever went through my body, we are asking that you discard this dime novel stuff and bring in, on behalf of this defendant, a verdict of not guilty."

The men of the jury filed out of the courtroom for a lunch break. The mood of the courtroom was heavy, as was the burden felt by these men. Judge Greene ordered the arguments to resume at 1:15 p.m. Bill Burgin would give the final prosecution argument.

Outside of the court house, the spectators on their way to lunch were more subdued, engrossed in serious conversations, about the arguments so far - about a possible conviction and the death penalty. The weather, although very humid, was contrastingly bright and sunny. Here and there, shopkeepers and professionals came out of their businesses to catch whatever news they could from those who departed the courthouse. Was a verdict coming in soon?

Special Prosecutor Bill Burgin was prepared and ready to go when the jury returned after lunch. The argument he prepared was designed to rebut each point made by the defense and persuade the jury to accept the theory of the prosecution's case, based on the evidence. His suit was crisp, unwrinkled, his hair neatly trimmed in a clean-cut, short fashion. His voice, as usual, deep and steady. He first explained to the jury that in the past, as a lawyer, he had represented Gene Tate and her mother, Mrs. Baker, and that, at Martin Tate's request, he was happy to prosecute the person responsible for his wife's murder, whoever that may be.

"I have no apologies to make, in spite of the aspersions cast by Mr. Stennis." Then, he immediately began a recitation of the evidence: the statements by Jon Mattox made to Sarah Grayson, the shirt he wore, the fiber evidence, the opportunity afforded the defendant that was shown by the time-line.

He reminded them that Mattox had gone to the gas station, the day after the murder, to ask if the police had been there about him. He covered the chronology of the events, much like the defense attorneys had, but he argued that the evidence proved the guilt of the defendant.

"Who got killed? Whose blue fibers were on her blouse? Who was standing on the brick right after it happened? He wasn't seen by his mother walking out of the house. He was standing on the brick when she returned from church. And remember the gate that opened into the Tate's backyard was only a few feet away? He was standing there," Burgin pointed directly at the defendant, " right after it happened! At the same time, she was taking the agonal - trying to get the agonal gasp in the garage."

"'You know, I have figured out a way to commit a perfect crime - to use a coat hanger because they don't leave fingerprints, and it is strong,' Burgin quoted the defendant's alleged statement. There weren't any fingerprints on the coat hanger, and it was strong enough to crush Gene Tate's neck down over two inches - just like he said he was going to do."

"They turned Mississippi State University upside down over the weekend. They called California and Illinois, and they didn't produce any testimony to the effect that Sarah Grayson's reputation for truth and veracity was bad, that her moral character was bad, that she was a loose or promiscuous girl . . . And don't you know if they could have found it, they would have brought witnesses here to the stand, to testify to you? . . . Insinuations, slurs, innuendo, aspersions by inference. Why this desperate attempt?" His voice boomed. "Because they knew - that you knew she was telling the truth!"

"Oh, they make much of the fact that Chief Vickery turned him loose after the second F.B.I. analysis of the fibers. What good are fibers if, as at that time, you don't have the testimony to establish the motive? And what was the motive, gentlemen? Gene Tate made a mistake. She realized her error and repented. She corrected her mistake because of her love for those children and her husband, and she paid the supreme penalty. Vengeance! Vengeance! The vengeance of Jon Mattox."

"Oh, they say Martin Tate said that Gene was an immoral woman. He didn't say that. He said they had difficulties because of the attention Jon Mattox paid her - standing there, eyeing her, and that that got worked out. Why didn't he leave her, they say. Even if he had known, which he didn't, do you go off and leave four minor children, on suspicion?"

"Oh, he would say Montgomery is a scoundrel because he burned some notes . . . What has that got to do with it? What was the testimony relative to that? Montgomery said they asked him to make some notes. He made some notes. He said they asked him to give a statement, and he gave a statement that contained everything he had in his notes. They had the statement. He didn't think it mattered . . . Did you ever burn trash? . . . Yet, now that becomes some kind of sinister act or path that they hope you will be led down!"

"I ask you gentlemen, when you consider the verdict - to keep in mind the health and safety of others. Because if you are misled by these paths, which go down without reasonable basis . . . who knows where the coat hanger will strike next? . . . I wouldn't give you a plugged nickel for the life of Sarah Grayson . . . It might be your wife or my wife, or your child or my child - next time."

"How much mercy did this defendant show Gene Tate when he wreaked his vengeance on her? . . . Gentlemen, as men of reason, the state humbly asks a verdict of guilty, as charged in the indictment." He looked each juror in the eye and then returned to his place at the prosecution table.

There was a sudden rustle of activity and talk in the court room.

"Let's have order now," said Judge Greene, "Now, Mr. Clerk, let's get the exhibits and the necessary papers to the jury so they may retire." He turned to the jury box. "Now gentlemen, let me make this statement to you. While you are in the room deliberating on the case, if you want any water, come to the door, and we will have water sent to you. Don't come out anymore. All stay together in your room there . . . And all right, gentlemen, you may retire and consider your verdict."

After the jury left the room, Mr. Stennis objected to the condition of some of the clothing evidence and asked that it be retrieved from the jury room for examination. Upon inspection, it was determined that the evidence was properly submitted to the jury, and it was returned to them.

"I apologize to the court for delaying the matter and find that I have been mistaken about it," admitted Stennis.

"It is not the first time," grumbled Judge Greene.

The jury retired at 2:28 p.m., and at five o'clock, they were brought out into the courtroom, and the judge made the following statement to them:

"Now, gentlemen of the jury, it is time to take a recess until in the morning, and I am going to send you to your rooms. It is more comfortable up there. You can rest better, so the court will take a recess until in the morning at nine o'clock."

Now it was a matter of waiting . . . For the reporters and the public at large, it was an exciting time. For some, an entertaining and absorbing distraction. But for the victim's family, Sarah Grayson, and the Mattox family, it was a time of dread and anxiety that would be punctuated briefly with an inexplicable optimism. A tortuous roller-coaster of emotion.

For better or worse, the next morning the parties returned to the courthouse. There were few people there on Saturday morning. It was expected that the jury would continue their deliberations throughout the weekend.

When Judge Greene took his place at nine o'clock, the jury knocked on the door to indicate they were ready to report . . . The men exited the room and were seated in the jury box. Tension filled the room. Even the judge appeared somewhat nervous.

"Gentlemen, have you reached a verdict?"

"We have, sir." The room was weighted with silence, and everyone exchanged looks of disbelief.

"Pass it to the clerk . . . Mr. Clerk, you read the verdict."

Circuit Clerk Jack Wiggins read the verdict to the court:

"Judge Green, May 13th, 10:15 p.m., . . . We, the jury, find the defendant guilty, as charged in the indictment . . . and fix his punishment at imprisonment in the penitentiary for life."

Mrs. Mattox began to weep and was comforted by her ashen-faced husband. Their son, Jon Mattox slumped forward. At the prosecution's table, hand shakes were exchanged quietly.

"Now gentlemen," the judge addressed the jury, "you are finally discharged. I know you have had a hard two weeks . . . and we appreciate it, and you are finally discharged." Then he addressed himself solemnly to the defendant:

"Jon, you will have to stand up . . . Jon, you heard the verdict. They have convicted you, as charged in the indictment, and fixed the punishment at life in the penitentiary. So it will be my duty, as Circuit Judge, to sentence you to the state penitentiary for your natural life, at hard labor. That will be your sentence."

After a few moments, Mattox, his family, and some friends who were present, were all escorted to the witness room, where they could have some privacy until the defendant was taken to the jail. His attorneys immediately filed a motion for a new trial.

"I repeat the words of John Paul Jones, 'I have just begun to fight!'" declared Jesse Stennis to a local reporter. He added that an appeal would be filed. "We are confident of a reversal!"

THIRTEEN

For the first time since his arrest, Jon Mattox was handcuffed. And for the first time, he noticed, uncomfortably, that the deputy who escorted him back and forth, from the court to the jail, was wearing a gun. That night, he was transported to the county jail in Meridian, 90 miles southwest of Columbus. Sheriff Spruill explained that the facilities there were more suitable for the prisoner while he awaited the result of his appeal.

Sarah Grayson left Columbus when her parents came for her on Friday, before the jury began deliberations. While she tried to sleep, stretched out on the backseat of her father's car, she listened to the final arguments on the radio. "I wouldn't give you a plugged nickel for the life of Sarah Grayson!" Bill Burgin's frightening warning to the jury would haunt her in the days ahead.

She went to bed early after the Grayson's arrived at their home in Bay Springs, and the next morning, her mother woke her with the news of the jury's verdict. Mrs. Grayson had heard it on the radio. As Sarah and her mother sobbed in each others arms, the phone rang. And for the next week, reporters would hound her with phone calls, and requests for interviews. A few showed up on her front porch. Sarah declined them all but was overwhelmed by the attention and her sudden fame - not only in Mississippi, but throughout the South. Letters began to pour in. One of the first, and the most moving to her, was from Martin Tate:

"I have thought a great deal about what I might say in writing you about the way you came forward under, I am sure, trying conditions. This is all still like a nightmare to me; it shows that truth is many times stranger than fiction. I do hate to see other peoples lives affected by something like this; it seems as it has no end."

"If it is true that some good must come from everything somewhere in the future, I sincerely hope it will come to you. It was Divine Providence that placed this information in the hands of someone who had the moral character and the mental ability to testify under such grueling circumstances."

"Our children and I are deeply grateful for what you have done, for if you had not, it would have completely changed their life and mine. Words are inadequate; we sincerely thank you." Another letter that touched her was from one of the jurors:

". . . I can't express in words what a courageous thing you did. I know that it was a hard thing to do, and I'm sure it has caused you a lot of embarrassment and humiliation, the way the defense tried to make some things dirty and ugly, but I think you stood up to him fine and told him so. I believe you to be a very nice girl, and I know your parents are very proud of you. I hope if my children are ever faced with a decision like yours, they will be able to make the right one, like you did."

Many people wrote to praise Sarah, and several neighbors of the Tate family also wrote. For example:

"My husband and I want to thank you for your courage in exposing Jon Mattox . . . We appreciate what you did for our neighborhood and community . . . We are very thankful that the potential danger has been removed from us. We hope that you can resume a normal life and believe that you will succeed in whatever you strive for."

Some others, unsigned, were very critical, and Sarah categorized them as "crackpot" letters, even though they were hurtful to her, such as this one from Memphis:

". . . IF he committed a murder, you are worse than him, for you have given Jon and his parents a living death which is far WORSE than the one who passed on. I could get plenty of people to sign, who feel the same way as I do. I would hate to place my confidence in a LOW DOWN PERSON like YOU. You will suffer the TORTURES of HELL, before the end of this. I hope I'll be around to hear all about your suffering. Your parents must be very proud of you. (Ha Ha) You dirty low down double crossing skunk. From Somebody who don't think very much of you. P.S. The jury must have consisted of your boyfriends. Not very intelligent men I would say."

And there was:

"Lets hope that you some day do not accidently bite your self and die of the poison in your tongue. Despite the bounty, when you look at people hereafter see if they don't want to shun you like an adder."

There were also newspaper editorials about her pivotal role in the famous trial, and the one that Sarah found most heartwarming was written by the respected Mississippi journalist, Oliver Emmerich, the editor of the *State Times*:

"The Mattox trial was a deeply moving drama. Thousands of miles away from Columbus, it aroused human compassion. Written into its script of life were fear, devotion, apprehension, resentment, revulsion, doubt. It matched in real life what William Shakespeare assembled in *Hamlet*, *Julius Caesar, Merchant of Venice*, and *King Lear*."

"The courtroom of Lowndes County stole the news headlines from Nikita Kruschchev and the approaching summit meeting. It even caused people to forget the downed American pilot held in the solitude of a Soviet prison cell . . ."

"This trial was no Western drama to be turned off, or on. It was no phantasy. The characters were flesh-and-blood real, and in their opinions, millions of people turned thumbs up or thumbs down, as spectators did in the arenas of ancient Rome."

"The decision as to the guilt or innocence of a defendant is within the province of the court. This is the prerogative of jurors who search their souls and the evidence and gulp a verdict. But there is one witness of this case who falls within the province of the editorial writer."

"The witness, Sarah Grayson, is a Mississippi heroine."

"The severest test of courage is when the test is within ourselves."

"This 19-year-old, Mississippi State University co-ed, won a struggle with herself and for law and order, good government, and high idealism . . . For years to come there will be opinions and counter-opinions concerning the complexities of the Mattox trial and the parts played by the various people involved in it. But despite the kaleidoscope of public opinion, we believe that Sarah Grayson will be able to live with herself for having upheld a high concept of individual duty as a citizen of civilized America."

Sarah met a similarly mixed response from the folks in her hometown that summer. While most were proud of her, she did encounter the sullen stares of a few, and a couple of them even accused her of lying. For the most part, however, her greatest discomfort was her celebrity status. Old friends suddenly seemed awkward in her presence. She soon found it impossible to return to the normal life she had anticipated in Bay Springs, and her longing to transfer to the University of California in Berkeley dominated her thoughts.

When Jon Mattox arrived for his stay in the Lauderdale County jail, a misleading news article described him as "just another jailbird." It failed to report that on Sunday, the day after he got there, a local cafeteria and a local paint contractor had meals sent to him at the jail. Mattox was quoted as saying, "Well there's one thing about it, they're not going to let me starve down here." Jailer Willie Gunn described him as a model prisoner and a "cool, calm kid." He predicted that the young man would soon be allowed more freedom if his current actions continued, and he stated he was impressed that Mattox made his own cot. Regarding his conviction for the murder of Gene Tate, Mattox told the jailer:

"It felt like somebody just took a bottle of ice water and turned it over my head. It just doesn't look like people can get justice. I just didn't do it."

One quiet summer afternoon, while Sarah and her mother sewed together in the living room, Mr. Grayson answered a phone call. It was from U.S. Senator John Stennis. He and Mr. Grayson had become friends when Grayson had run as a candidate for county superintendent of education. Over the years, Mr. Grayson had helped the senator with his campaign activities in the county. Grayson was happy to hear from him. John Stennis was a respected and well-loved political figure in the state, and many Mississippians regarded him as their friend not only because of his accessability but also because of his warmth and down-to-earth personality. He was also attorney Jesse Stennis's cousin.

Suddenly there was a noticeable change in Mr. Grayson's tone of voice, from one of light-hearted friendliness to great anger. Sarah had seldom heard her father raise his voice.

"No!" he declared indignantly, "I will do no such thing! My daughter did the right thing. You don't know what this family's been through!"

Soon her father stormed past them and went out of the front door to cool off on the porch.

"My good friend, John Stennis!" Mr. Grayson sarcastically remarked on his way out. The incident was not discussed after that, and Sarah could only guess as to what the senator wanted her father to do, but it seemed fairly obvious that it had to do with the Mattox case.

By August, Sarah had written to Bill Burgin and asked him about the possibility of a reversal, due to the Mattox case appeal. Burgin wrote to her and explained that the odds were largely against a successful appeal, that only 2% of those filed were granted. He also informed her that an investigation had begun regarding what role, if any, Jon Mattox had played in the burning of the Old Main dormitory in 1959, which had destroyed the building and resulted in the death of Henry Williamson, a Columbus native.

"I doubt if anything will come of this, in view of the considerable time lapse, but in any event, the investigation is being made," Burgin wrote.

A Columbus newspaper article explained that State Deputy Fire Marshall Bill Harpole, at the request of District Attorney Harvey Buck, would question convicted murderer, Jon Mattox, at the Lauderdale County jail about the burning of the dormitory.

"It is in the best interest of everybody to clear up these rumors once and for all," he said.

Six weeks later, in late September, Harpole reported that no evidence had been uncovered which linked Mattox to the Old Main dormitory fire.

"He wasn't even living at Mississippi State at that time. He was living at Columbus with his parents," Harpole concluded.

By this time, Sarah Grayson had moved to Berkeley, California to study at the university. She had not been questioned by the fire investigator before she left, as no one knew of Mattox's statement to her, less than a year after the fire, that he had been in a fight with Henry Williamson, and that later that night he had been at the Old Main dormitory when the fire broke out. "Whew! Almost didn't get out myself!" She had clearly remembered his statement to her.

Reluctantly, and out of desperation, Sarah had accepted a partial advance of $1000 of the reward money, which would help pay for her California schooling. Chief Vickery had told her that only after all appeals were final could the money be distributed in full. Arrangements to get the money were made, and Sarah was to meet Lowndes County Attorney Lowery Lucas in Jackson, where she planned to catch a flight to California.

Sarah's friend, Henry McCrory, drove her to Jackson the day before her meeting with Lucas and took her to her former Mississippi State roommate's house where she would stay the night. When they got to the house, her roommate's mother told Sarah that it was very strange that a car had been parked across the street from the house all day - a man reading a newspaper sat in the car. Sarah and Henry decided to see if the man was there because of Sarah, so they got back in Henry's car, and sure enough, the man pulled out behind them. He followed them all around Jackson until they reached a lake where Henry was able to drive in a circle to get behind the man's car to copy his license plate number. However, before they could get his number, the man sped away and lost them.

The next day, when Sarah met with Mr. Lucas, he said he knew nothing about it, that the man was not connected with law enforcement. Naturally, this caused both of them some concern, and even more so when Sarah realized that, as far as she knew, only the Columbus Police Department was aware of where she would be staying in Jackson . . .

When Sarah got to Berkeley, troublesome thoughts were put to rest as she quickly became involved with the campus social life and was elected president of her sorority pledge class. Weeks later, she had decided that sororities were not for her after all. She had changed and wanted a more independent life. Soon, she moved out of the sorority house and into an apartment off-campus, which she shared with another female student.

As Christmas approached, Sarah made arrangements to ride home for the holidays with some other Mississippians who lived in Berkeley. Once home, she enjoyed the winter weather, the fireplace, and seeing her family and old friends. She was full of enthusiasm and news regarding her adventures in California. She had found Berkeley very stimulating intellectually and culturally, and was quite happy there.

In Columbus, the holidays were difficult for the Tate family. Almost a year had past since Gene had been murdered, but it was their first Christmas without her. Martin Tate made a special effort to spend more time with his children during this time, and Mrs. Baker decorated the house, baked holiday cookies and treats. Then a week before Christmas, Martin Tate received an ugly surprise in the mail, a Christmas card from Jon Mattox. It was a photograph of a puppy and a holiday candle. The printed message was "Have your nicest Christmas ever!" Mattox wrote, "Dear Martin, You won't be so happy this time next year, when you're sitting here. Jon." The card was turned over to Bill Burgin.

A similar surprise interrupted Sarah's holiday in Bay Springs. One night, as she and an old boyfriend returned to her house after a date, they found a sheriff's deputy's car parked in her driveway. When Sarah went inside, her parents and the deputy somberly awaited her. He had come to warn them of a murder plot by Jon Mattox against Sarah's life! Apparently, Mattox had arranged to have two cellmates in Meridian kill her when they were released on bond that month. The plot had been interrupted by the authorities, but the conspiracy was still under investigation. There was also serious concern that Mattox may have hatched more than one plot against her.

"Miss Grayson, it is absolutely vital that you not tell anyone about this until we give you the go-ahead," the officer told her. He further warned her to be extremely vigilant, as there may be other plots against her life that were not yet discovered - that perhaps Mattox had more than one plan.

She and her parents would be kept informed as the investigation progressed, and they were encouraged to contact the officers if they needed anything, or had any questions. So once again, within the blink of an eye, Sarah's life seemed to collapse around her. And, as before, she had to remain silent about the very real danger that threatened her.

A few days later, on her automobile trip back to California, she became very ill, and so concerned were the couple with whom she rode, that they took her to a hospital. She was diagnosed with a virus, given some medication, and then continued on her miserable trip back to Berkeley.

For the next month, Sarah was careful never to be out alone at night. Her father had given her a gun to take back with her, so she slept with it in the nightstand next to her bed. It was a minor comfort, but did nothing to prevent the return of her horrible nightmares - dreams of her own murder. The student who shared her apartment noticed Sarah's peculiar behavior, and her professors at the university chided her for the drop in her grades. In fact, she was placed on academic probation, which added to her anxiety.

Back home, her parents were beside themselves with worry over their youngest child, so far from home and the target of a murder plot. They both wrote to her frequently. Her mother wrote on January 15, 1961:

". . . Nothing has come out about this other investigation . . . Hope to hear from you soon. We miss you. The house seems too quiet. You are on our minds - hope nothing has upset you out there. Anything suspicious? Much love, Mother."

January 21st:

"Dearest Sarah, I was glad to find your letter here when I returned yesterday. I'd checked my box every day, for I was getting anxious to hear from you . . . I'm sorry you were sick again. Daddy talked to the district attorney in Meridian, and he was assured that everything was being done, and it must be kept a secret until they were ready. Three counties are in on it, so surely they will do the best thing. It is hard on you, but I feel the danger there is slight now . . . They'll have to make a move soon. We'll let you know as soon as we know anything. I hope it will soon be over for us all. Try not to worry and trust God. I feel He has a purpose for your life and will use you in service. Much love, Mother."

January 29th:

"Judy Grayson told me at church that someone called her house yesterday wanting you. Rosamond had a call, too, with the same question. We've wondered what this could mean. It was a man's voice from Jackson . . . I think some protection there might be in order. Daddy is going to talk to Bill Burgin. A policewoman could move in with you for these next weeks. You must be careful in every way for something may be tried before the appeal. I wouldn't be out after dark at all. We love you very much, and we're worried. I pray for you almost 'without ceasing.'"

Her father wrote:

"I hope this finds you doing fine and making adjustments to anything that might come up. It is always easier said than done. I have had my share of trials in life, but I have also had lots of pleasures. That is life, I suppose. Don't let anything lick you . . . If he is given a new trial, I haven't made up my mind for you to testify again, so please don't make any commitments to anyone, or promise to come back or anything, until we've talked it over and know that they are going to give adequate protection . . . Please be cautious, cautious, and say nothing. Write often. Your Dad."

Tuesday afternoon, February 7th, Sarah walked across the Berkeley campus toward her apartment. Other students walked past her, up and down Bancroft Avenue. Down the street, on the corner of Telegraph, shoppers milled around on the sidewalks. Usually, there were one or two people who were unusually dressed, in bohemian or beatnik attire. There were poets, artists, musicians, and Sarah was intrigued by them. She expected that her friends back home would consider her bohemian in her taste now, compared to her conservative style of only a year before.

A huge, bold, black headline on a newsrack caught her eye: "TERROR GRIPS U. C. CO-ED; CON PLOTS HER DEATH." It was the *Oakland Tribune*. California surely had more than its share of craziness, she thought.

As she walked down her street, she noticed an unusual number of cars parked in front of her apartment building and saw some men dressed in suits standing around. She looked them over with curiosity and went into her apartment. Her roommate greeted her emotionally.

"Sarah! Where have you been? The dean of women wants you to call her!" Then there was a pounding on the door. She peeked out of the blinds, as had become her habit. The men were reporters, and now she saw that police cars had also arrived. My God! Had the Berkeley police caught someone this close to her apartment house? What's going on!

"Miss Grayson, I just want a statement from you about the murder plot. Won't you please let me in, just for a minute?" . . . The murder plot? . . .

Oh, so that's it! The story about her was out - The headline she had seen was about her! The reporters wanted an interview, but she was not interested at all and politely, through the cracked door, declined their insistent pleas. Sarah had already had enough publicity to last her a life time. She only let the police enter her apartment.

The Berkeley police officer told her that the story about the Mattox case and the death plot against her was all over the news, and that she should be safe now that the investigation was over. The Mississippi authorities had been unable to reach her before the story got to the press.

Later, Sarah called the dean who expressed regret that Sarah hadn't told her of her situation, maybe she could have helped. In the least, she offered, Sarah would not have been placed on academic probation. Sarah was grateful for her call. Finally, on the advice of the police, "the reporters won't go away until you give them an interview," Sarah changed her clothes and invited the press in to hear her story and take pictures.

The next day, the Mississippi murder case was again splashed all over the San Francisco area newspapers, and eastward across the country. Sarah was headline news again.

It was reported that Mattox had offered $1500 to two brothers, Fred and Dan Wilkerson, who were being held on armed robbery charges. The brothers had expected to make bail, and Mattox, allegedly, had instructed them to shoot Grayson three times with a shotgun at her home in Bay Springs when she came home for Christmas. When the brothers were transferred to another jail, two weeks later, Mattox mailed them a photograph of Sarah Grayson. Pursuant to Jon's request, Mrs. Mattox had brought him his college annual, and he had cut Sarah's photograph out of it. Along with her photo, Jon had given the Wilkerson brothers Sarah's address in Berkeley in case she didn't come home for Christmas. But instead of cooperating with Mattox, the Wilkerson's had informed law enforcement of the plot once they were transferred to the other facility. Even so, all three were indicted for conspiracy to commit murder.

"I remember Jon telling me once that if you didn't kill something three times, you couldn't be sure it's dead," Sarah had sobbed to the reporters. "Jon wanted to get me out of the way so I couldn't testify against him again."

In Meridian, Deputy Sheriff Alton Allen said Mattox showed no sign of emotion when the indictment was served in his jail cell, and at arraignment later, he pleaded "Not Guilty." Lauderdale County District Attorney Paul Busby said talking to Mattox was "like talking to a damn door."

Since he had been in the jail in Meridian, Mattox had a radio and television set in his jail cell and had meals carried in from local restaurants, unusual privileges for a prisoner - particularly one convicted of first degree murder. However, the privileges were discontinued after the revelation of the murder plot.

"He's a prisoner of Lauderdale County now," Busby said, "and therefore not entitled to any special favors. He's my prisoner now and no damned celebrity anymore!"

Six days later, the Mississippi State Supreme Court was scheduled to hear arguments on Mattox's appeal of his conviction, and there was a new member of the appellate defense team, Judge Malcolm Montgomery, a former state supreme court justice. Judge Montgomery was a law partner of Mississippi Governor Ross Barnett.

A few weeks after the hearing, on March 20th, 1961, the Court issued its ruling which overturned Mattox's conviction and ordered a new trial. The justices determined that the evidence regarding the lie detector test taken by Sarah Grayson was reversible error, even though the results of the test were not presented to the jury. On the whole, however, the Court noted that the prosecution presented a strong circumstantial case against Mattox:

"The evidence justified the jury in finding that appellant was present in, or around his home, which was located about six feet from the garage where the deceased was found . . . and that he had the opportunity to commit the crime . . . The evidence was sufficient to go to the jury on the theory that the defendant was the guilty party, having as a prompting force behind the act the victim's termination of an affair that had existed for some time."

When informed of the state supreme court's decision, Mattox was said to have grinned slightly. The sheriff asked him if the news made him happy, to which Mattox replied:

"Yes and no. It could've been better, they could have turned me loose. But I'm happy that I'll get another trial. Other than that, I have no further statement."

Sarah Grayson was devastated by the news, and when questioned by reporters in Berkeley, she told them she didn't want to comment:

"I have nothing to say," she sobbed, "You reporters have done enough to me. Just leave me alone."

Because of the strong likelihood that Mattox would go free without her testimony, Sarah, in consultation with her parents, decided she must return to Mississippi and testify at the second trial. They felt it would be far more dangerous for her if Mattox was acquitted, than the risk she would take by testifying. Her school work would be almost impossible under the circumstances, so Sarah dropped out of the university and returned home a month before the trial, scheduled to begin April 24th with jury selection.

The second trial was basically a repeat of the first, with significant exceptions. Dan and Fred Wilkerson were brought in from Parchman Penitentiary where they had been sentenced to serve fifteen years for armed robbery, a capital offense in Mississippi. The two had admitted their guilt upon arrest, shortly after Thanksgiving, and thus had avoided the possibility of a death sentence.

On Tuesday, May 9th, they were seated at a table in the witness room at the pre-Civil War courthouse in Columbus, where they waited to be called as witnesses for the prosecution. Law enforcement officers and lawyers stood around the room, and the lawyers appeared to be engaged in a heated exchange with the brothers when Sarah Grayson, also scheduled to testify that day, was escorted in. She took a seat in the corner and realized that the brothers did not want to testify after all! They were afraid of retaliation for being identified as stool pigeons by the other inmates at Parchman. Harley McNair was also present in the witness room. He and Sarah had greeted each other warmly. Now they both watched the crisis unfold before them.

The two brothers, Fred, 24 and Dan, 19, sat motionless and stared at the top of the table. They were nice-looking young men, both with short brown hair, blue eyes, and friendly faces under different circumstances. But their family background of poverty and hard work revealed itself in the pallor of their skin - it had acquired a yellowish tanned stain from years of exposure to the sun and outdoors, and their bodies were lean and wiry from manual labor. Fred and Dan came from a family of fifteen children, none of whom had any education. Reading and writing were not necessary skills for hauling gravel, hunting, or growing food for too many mouths.

"You boys were brought here to tell the truth, and you damned well better do it! I'm tellin' you, now's not the time to start having doubts," said one of the lawyers, a vein bulged in his neck.

"Yes, sir, I know, but I'm just afraid we'll get kilt if we do," Dan answered while Fred frowned and silently picked at the cuticle of his left index finger. It had been rumored that one of the brothers had already been threatened with a knife by a prisoner at Parchman, and death threats had been made against them. It was a rough, bleak prison located in the Mississippi delta. In the summer, the hot temperatures and heavy humidity alone had caused violent episodes in the prison population. Stool Pigeons, much despised by the other inmates, would be at a particularly high risk in such an explosive environment.

Yet, if the brothers did not testify about Mattox's failed murder plot against Sarah Grayson, the star witness, the jury would be deprived of important evidence of his guilt. It could prove catastrophic to the prosecution. What if Grayson did not hold up as well this time - given her trying ordeal of the past year? What if Mattox testified and charmed the jury? All the defense needed was for one juror to have a reasonable doubt, and Jonny Mattox would be acquitted of the murder of Gene Tate. Without the Wilkerson brothers, it could happen.

From her corner in the back of the room, Sarah Grayson could not listen to any more of the debate. For over a year, she had lived a nightmare, her education had been disrupted, and she had, for much of that time, feared for her very life.

"How do you think I've felt this past year!" she blurted out.

Everyone was silenced momentarily, and Fred Wilkerson, who had not noticed her presence until then, walked around the table and humbly extended his hand to her.

"Are you Miss Grayson?" he asked her.

"Yes, I am." She hesitated and then briefly shook his hand.

"I'm Fred Wilkerson, and I just want you to know that I would never have killed a pretty little girl like you," he said. Sarah looked in his eyes uncomfortably, but decided that she believed him. Then a deputy nudged his arm and asked him to return to his seat.

"You know, Mother would want us to do the right thing, Danny," he said quietly after he sat back down next to his brother. Dan half-nodded in agreement. They were like two draftees in a foxhole: reluctant heroes. "Okay, we'll do it!" Fred announced with conviction, and a collective sigh flooded the room.

The proceedings were well underway, and there were few reporters and no radio coverage in Judge Greene's courtroom during the second trial of Jon Mattox. However, the crowds of attendees were still a problem most of the time. Sheriff Spruill had announced that there would be no standing in the doorways, but soon told a reporter that he could not control the situation. There were virtual mobs of female college students, who tried to fight their way into the courtroom.

"I just can't keep the crowds from standing, there's too many of 'em. But," he declared, "there'll be no dinner-bringin' this time." At the first trial, some of the spectators had brought in meals. "They can come at their own risk, too, because the courthouse is too old," he warned.

And Jesse Stennis was no longer a member of the defense team. He had been replaced by Hugh Cunningham, another partner in the law firm of Governor Ross Barnett. The prosecution team remained the same and had already presented a number of witnesses to the jury when the Wilkerson brothers arrived. Sarah Grayson had just finished her testimony, which the prosecutors felt had gone very well, and her cross-examination was much shorter than at the first trial. Dan Wilkerson followed her to the stand, and then Fred.

Each brother testified that they had spent 22 days in the Meridian jail with Jon Mattox, where the three of them had shared a common large cell, called a bullpen, which was adjacent to their individual cells. No other prisoners had been housed in that area. The men had spent hours where they had talked together, seated at a table in the bullpen. Jonny had shared his hunting magazines and gun catalogs with Fred and Dan, had written letters and Christmas cards for them, and had shown them the pictures of deer he had painted there at the jail. Because the brothers could not read or write, Jonny had tried to teach them the alphabet and arithmetic. The Wilkerson's testified that they had never heard of Jon Mattox, or the murder of Mrs. Gene Tate prior to meeting him at the jail.

District Attorney Harvey Buck questioned Dan, the first of the two to testify. He asked him, what, if anything, the defendant had said about Mrs. Tate.

"Well, he said, sir, he loved her, and said if he couldn't have her, no one else could."

"Now, what, if anything, did the defendant tell you about Miss Sarah Grayson?"

"He said, sir, he wanted us to kill Mrs. Sarah Grayson."

"And why," asked Mr. Buck, "did he tell you why?"

"Yes, sir, said she was a eye witness against him."

On cross-exam, by Mr. Cunningham, he was asked how long he had been in jail before Mattox spoke to him.

"Well, he come to the cell the first day we was there and asked us what we was in there for, and we told him armed robbery, and we asked him, and he said it wasn't none of our damn business."

"All right, none of your business?"

"None of my 'damn' business. That is what he said, that is the way he put it."

"And now you tell this court and jury that he told you he loved Mrs. Tate, and if he couldn't have her no one else could. When did he tell you that?"

"Soon as we went out in the bullpen with him, he begin to tell us about it. We told him our history, and he begin to tell us his."

"All right. How long had you been there before he told you?"

"Well, we was there, we was turned out in the bullpen after about three days. We never said nothing to him, hardly, while we was in that cell, and then we was turned out in the bullpen, and then he begin to tell us about Mrs. Tate."

Mr. Cunningham asked Danny if he remembered meeting with the defense lawyers at the Newton County jail in Decatur. The Wilkerson's had been arrested there and, due to overcrowding, had been temporarily jailed in Meridian. Then after a few weeks, they were sent back to Decatur. It was at that time that they had told the authorities about Mattox's murder plot and were later visited by the lawyers.

Dan acknowledged the meeting in Decatur with Cunningham. Defense Attorney Cunningham then challenged Dan with the allegation that the brothers had stated to him, during their meeting in Decatur, that Jon Mattox had not told them anything about killing anybody. Dan denied the allegation. Later, on redirect by the prosecution, it was brought out that the prosecution lawyers and law officers had also been present at the meeting. The clear implication was that Cunningham's allegation could be easily disproved.

Fred Wilkerson was called in as the next witness and questioned by Special Prosecutor Bill Burgin. He generally repeated his brother's story about Mattox, but provided more detail about the conspiracy to kill Grayson. Burgin asked him to tell the jury about the defendant's statements in that regard.

"Jonny Mattox tried to hire me and my brother to do, that is, kill Sarah Grayson - a eye witness against him. And if she was out of the way, that he would be set free. And he was going to pay us fifteen hundred dollars to kill her - when she come home at Christmas time."

"Did he tell you where to find her?" asked Burgin.

"He told us, when she came home on Christmas, to go to Bay Springs where she lived at, and he told us if she didn't come home at Christmas time, he would pay our way there and back to Berkeley, California, to kill her there at school. She was going to school there."

"Did he say how he was going to get the money to you?"

"Yes, sir. Said he had a young lawyer that would bring it up there to him, and he would give it to us."

"How were you going to know Sarah Grayson?"

"He sent me a picture. I left there on Tuesday, if I ain't mistaken, on Tuesday, from the jail, and I got the picture on Friday."

"How did you get it?"

"Through the mail. Sent it to my home, and my mother brought it to me."

"What was in that? Was it in an envelope?"

"Yes, sir, he put a Christmas card in there and sealed it on the back of the Christmas card, between the Christmas card."

"Have you seen Sarah Grayson since that time?"

"Yes, sir, I seen her just a little bit ago, this morning. First time I ever seen her."

"Was the picture that he sent you in that Christmas card, a picture of Sarah Grayson you saw this morning?"

"Yes, sir. Only except, she has got her hair fixed different, that's all."

"Fred, did you know he was going to send you a picture?"

"He said he would, sir, that morning we left from there."

"Did he say anything about where he would get it?"

"He said his mother would bring it up to him from his home. Said he had to cut it out of a book of school pictures."

"Has anybody promised you any reward, or anything, to testify in this case?"

"No, sir."

"Fred, when you were first placed in the Meridian jail, was anybody going to try and get you a bond?"

"Yes, sir, my brother."

"When you were talking to Jonny Mattox, did you think you were going to get a bond?"

"Yes, sir. My brother come up there that following Sunday and told me he thought Mr. John Jones was going to sign a bond to get me out."

"Did Jon Mattox, did the defendant know that?"

"No, sir, I didn't tell him. I told him I was hoping to get out under bond."

Fred said that when he left the Meridian jail, Jon gave him Sarah Grayson's address in Berkeley. He explained that he had told Mattox that he couldn't read, so Mattox copied it in block print, and then he could read it "a little." When he and Dan were taken to Decatur, he gave the address to the county attorney there, and later, gave him the Christmas card from Mattox that contained Grayson's photograph. On cross-exam by the defense, Mr. Cunningham asked an important question on behalf of the defendant:

"Now, let's clear up a point for the jury. Jon Mattox never confessed to you that he killed anybody, did he?"

"He didn't say he killed nobody, no, sir."

"And Jon Mattox didn't tell you that he killed anybody with a coat hanger, did he?"

"No, sir, he didn't. He just said that Mrs.Tate was killed with a coat hanger, and that she was found on the garage floor on Sunday morning."

Finally, on redirect, Mr. Burgin had Fred identify the note paper containing Grayson's address, and the Christmas card with her photo. Both were entered into evidence for the jury. Before the state rested its case, he asked a few more questions.

"When you were in the Lauderdale County jail in Meridian, with the defendant, did he send any Christmas cards?"

"Yes, sir, several of them, just like this right here, every one of them."

"Where did he get them?"

"Just like the one he sent to Mr. Tate."

"Sent to who?"

"Mr.Tate."

"How do you know he sent one to Mr. Tate?"

"He stood there and read it, and said, 'This is the one I am going to send him.' His mama and daddy also read it."

"Who mailed the one to Mr.Tate for him?"

"His mother."

"How do you know?"

"I saw her when she carried it out and . . . put it in her purse and carried it out - taken all of them, even the ones he sent for me to my mother and another friend."

"What kind of cards were those?"

"Just like this. He mailed two to Dan's girlfriend and mailed two for me."

The state rested after Fred's testimony, and the defense put on its case much like they had before. On Wednesday afternoon, May 10th, however, the defense team surprised everyone and called the defendant, Jon Mattox, to the witness stand.

FOURTEEN

Jon Mattox, now almost 22 years old, took the witness stand, dressed in slacks, sports shirt, and loafers. He nodded amicably at the men in the jury box and appeared relaxed and confident, although his color was pale from his jailhouse confinement the past year. Luther Sims, the older member of the defense team, was tasked with the direct examination of his client, and his demeanor with Mattox was like that of a kindly, but protective, grandfather.

He was led through a long series of questions by Sims regarding his activities the morning of the murder. Basically, but in extraordinary detail, and despite some contradictions revealed on cross-exam, Mattox told the jury that he had left his house around 9:45 a.m., had run several errands, and had returned home again at approximately 10:35 a.m. This admission by the defendant placed him at his home at the approximate time that the murder occurred. However, Mattox insisted that he had not been home for more than five minutes before he had left again to go to Otho McDaniel's. The clear implication was that he could not have had time to commit the murder. But, in the final analysis, there was no evidence to support his account of when he left his house, and his parents, whose credibility was brought into doubt in the first trial, did not testify.

In addition, Judge Greene allowed into evidence a four page statement, hand-written by the defendant a few days after the murder. The police had found the statement in the defendant's clothing at the time of his second arrest the previous year. The statement was a blow by blow account of how he had spent his time on the day of the murder, and it contradicted some of his testimony.

Next, the defendant denied having ever told Sarah Grayson anything about his personal life. He stated that he had never told her anything about any affair, and certainly had never said anything to her about a perfect murder plan. In fact, Mattox characterized Grayson as having been a pest, a college girl who chased him relentlessly. He had difficulty avoiding her, and several times he was finally forced to just walk away from her.

"Did that happen on many occasions, Jon?"

"Well, any time she would catch me somewhere that she would just latch on, just like a leech or something, and you just couldn't hardly get away from her. I mean she would just . . . well actually, she would actually hold you by your arm, just stand there and talk to you."

"Did she ever invite you to go spend the weekend in Memphis with her?"

"She begged me to go and spend a weekend in Memphis."

"Did she ever invite you to go out to a dance, or picnic, or anywhere else with her?"

"Yes, sir."

"Did you ever go with her, other than this first picnic you went on?"

"No, sir, I did not. I didn't want anything to do with that young lady. She just acted like a tramp," Mattox responded emphatically.

Jon testified that he went on a picnic with Sarah on November 4th, and that while he was stretched out under a tree, Sarah had twice gotten on top of him and tried to kiss him, but he had rejected her advances. He contended that he had only accompanied her there, because she had offered to help him study for an exam he had to take that night. At that time, Jon explained, he had a high opinion of her, but that favorable opinion had evaporated after her forward behavior on the picnic.

"After you were arrested here, Jon, and went back to "State," I believe she called you up after that time, did she, or was it before that time?"

"Both before and after."

"Did she ask you to go out on a picnic with her?"

"She asked me to go with her, and I can't hardly remember where she asked me to go the second time, the time at "State." She called me up over there a couple of times, and I cannot remember now where she asked me to go, but she asked me to go somewhere, and I told her at that time I was sorry, but I did not want to go with a young lady. And she said, 'Well, you will be sorry,' and hung the phone up!"

"Hung the phone up in your face?"

"Yes, sir. She sure did."

Later, during the prosecution's rebuttal case, two police officers testified that, pursuant to a search warrant, they had found a two page, unsigned, handwritten letter in Mattox's bedroom dresser drawer. It was later identified by Sarah Grayson as a "poetic essay" she had mailed to Jon in the fall of 1959. She stated that she had written it with the hope of inspiring him to end his alleged affair with the married lady. The letter was entered into evidence. Mattox's response was to insinuate that the letter had been planted.

"I have never seen that letter before in my life!" he declared.

When asked about the testimony of the Wilkerson brothers, Mattox said that he had told them nothing about his case, and he denied that he had offered them money to kill Sarah Grayson. He did admit that he had mailed a Christmas card to Martin Tate, and that his parents had read the card. But when asked by Mr. Burgin, whether or not he and his parents had laughed about the card, Mattox testified that he could not remember.

"Now," said Defense Attorney Sims, "the Wilkerson's claim you gave them the address of this fair damsel, Sarah Grayson. Did you give them that?"

"I did not."

Sims showed the defendant Sarah Grayson's address printed on a piece of paper, that had been put into evidence by the prosecution. Mattox admitted that he had written the address, but stated that a friend, whose name he could not remember, had sent him the address, and he had subsequently copied it on to the piece of paper. He said he then had put the address in a box containing his Christmas cards. He asserted that the address was later stolen by one of the brothers, along with a few of his cards. Mattox stated that he had not given them the address, or mailed them the photograph of Sarah Grayson. He acknowledged that the envelope addressed to Fred Wilkerson had been written by him, but he stated that he had mailed a magazine picture of a deer to Fred, and nothing more. However, on rebuttal, the sheriff of Newton County testified that the envelope, with the Christmas card containing the photograph of Grayson, was opened in his presence by Fred Wilkerson at the jail in Decatur.

Finally, the old defense lawyer addressed the heart of the matter:

"Jon, I want to ask you now, if you ever, at the time of Mrs. Tate's death, or any time previous to that, was having affairs with Mrs. Tate?"

"I was not."

"Did you ever in your life have any affairs, or anything to do with Mrs. Tate, except just as a neighbor there, like the other ladies?"

"No, sir, I never touched that lady."

"I will ask you this, Jon, and I want you to tell these gentlemen . . . Did you kill Mrs. Gene Tate?"

"So help me God, I did not kill that lady," he said and looked squarely at the jury.

"Was there ever any complaint, or anything said in reference to you, about you, by Mrs. Tate or anybody familiar with Mrs. Tate?"

"No reference was ever made to me in any way whatsoever."

"Now, Jon, I will ask you this: When was the last time, if you recall, about the last time you was ever in that garage - Mrs.Tate's garage?"

"It was the first of the week, prior to her death. My mother sent me over to get the clothes from the dryer."

On rebuttal by the prosecution, Lieutenant Louis Harper of the Columbus Police Department and Investigator Gwin Cole, Assistant Director of the Mississippi Highway Patrol, would testify that they had tape recorded Mattox's statement to them, during an interview the day after the murder - that he "was sure" that he had not been in the Tate garage since before Christmas of 1959.

"I want to say to you now," said Luther Sims at the end of his direct exam, "if there is anything else you want to tell this court and jury, you have the liberty to do so."

"There certainly is," Jon replied, "I did not kill Gene Tate."

"Anything else you want to tell them?"

"So help me God, I did not kill her."

Special Prosecutor Bill Burgin relished the cross-examination of the defendant. It was an opportunity any prosecutor hoped for, but rarely was afforded. In addition to the elements of the crime, Burgin was allowed to explore areas of Mattox's credibility, and one of the areas he questioned him about was his alleged acts of cruelty and violence:

"You know the Higgins child?"

"Yes, sir, I do. You mean Dexter Higgins?"

"That's right."

"Do you recall the occasion when you beat the child in a scout meeting?"

"I gave Dexter Higgins, on one occasion, a paddling."

"A what?"

"A paddling."

"With what?"

"With a stalk from a cattail reed, I believe."

Mattox said that the scout leaders were not present at the time, but several other boys, whose names he could not remember, were also present. He said it had happened "six or seven years ago," when he was about fourteen or fifteen, and Dexter was about two years younger.

"What kind of pets have you had?"

"Oh, just about all kinds. Let's see, I have had, of course, dogs. When I was a boy, I collected snakes, turtles, had a flying squirrel once upon a time, and . . . "

"Did you ever choke a dog to death with a rope?"

"No, sir, I have not."

"You ever choked a dog to death with a coat hanger?"

"No, sir, I have not, sir."

"You ever cut a dog's feet off, after choking him to death?" There was a gasp in the courtroom.

"No, sir, I did not."

"How did you kill Mrs. Dave Lavender's dog?"

"The dog had been laying around the yard for some three or four days, or she informed me to that fact. The dog had been hanging around the neighborhood, and she had called the police and asked them to come and move him, and they had come up there and shot the dog three, or four, or five times, and left him there. The dog had run off after the police had shot him."

"I came through the yard, some three or four days after the dog had been shot by the police, and Mrs. Lavender raised the window and informed me that it would not be safe to stay in that yard, that the police had shot a dog, and he was still around, and he had not died. And so I said, 'Well, why don't you just shoot him?' And I said, 'Why don't you call them and tell them to come get him?' And she said she had called them, but they had not come back at that time, and I said, 'Well, do you want me to kill the dog for you?'"

"She said, 'Well, I would be scared for you to fool with him,' and I said, 'Well, if he is hurt bad, you ought to go on and kill him.' And she said if I would, she would certainly appreciate it. I said, 'Do you have a gun?' and all this time, she was in the house talking, and she informed me that she was afraid to let her dog out in the yard for fear this dog would jump on him. She informed me that she had a gun, but that we could not shoot inside the city limits."

"The dog was lying, I believe, next to a concrete block wall going down beside the driveway, just lying there watching everybody go by. He wasn't bothering anybody in particular, but his head was swollen up, until it was almost this big," Mattox formed a big circle with his hands to demonstrate the size to the jury, "I mean he was a pretty big dog, but his head was swollen up nearly double the size. His eyes were swollen closed - and pus and all coming from out of his head."

"He looked pretty bad, and it was a length of lead pipe laying there. And I took that piece of pipe and hit the dog across the head," Jon continued, much to the revulsion and horror of many, "and I took my pocket knife and cut his jugular vein, and the dog bled to death there on the ground."

"What did you do with it then?" asked the prosecutor, his own stomach a little queasy.

"I left the dog there."

"Left him there?"

"Yes, sir, and she told me that she would have her husband move the dog."

"How is your temper, Jon?"

"Just about like everybody else."

Burgin changed to a different line of questions.

"Date any girls prior to the death of Mrs. Tate?"

"A few."

"How many dates did you have from the beginning of your school semester in the fall of 1959, until the death of Mrs. Tate?"

"I would say just two or three."

"With whom did you have those dates?"

"I do not remember at this time."

"You don't remember the names of any girl that you dated during that period?"

"No, sir."

"What boys did you run around with during that period?"

"Well, I don't, what you call, 'run around' with anybody."

"Did you hunt alone most of the time, or did you hunt with someone?"

"It depends on what kind of hunting I am doing. If there is a big drive, or a party - just like you and I, and Otho, and several other people use to go on, Douglas and Gentry - now, if that is what you call - we hunt together like that a lot of times. But a lot of times, I would hunt alone."

Regarding his contact with the murder victim, Gene Tate, Burgin continued.

"When was the last time you talked to Mrs. Tate?"

"Well, I couldn't give you a definite date on that."

"You can't tell the court and jury when the last time was you talked to Mrs. Tate?"

"No, sir, not for definite."

"Well, was it a month prior to her death, or two months . . . three months?"

"No, sir, just a few days."

"Can you tell the court what was said?"

"I remember one time. We were taking exams that week, and she was at my house when I came home. I believe my mother and Mrs. Tate were having coffee in the kitchen of my house, and I came through, going to my room, and some conversation struck up. I informed her that I was taking exams, and she asked me were they hard, and I said they were pretty rough, something to that effect."

"Was that the last time that you talked to Mrs. Tate prior to her death?"

"To have a conversation with her, it was."

"When was the last time you talked to her prior to that occasion?"

"I could not give you a definite date. One thing is for sure, and you can put this in your book - I did not kill Mrs. Tate!"

"I tell you what you did do, Jon," Burgin replied heatedly and pointed his finger at the defendant, "you got mad when she wouldn't return your advances, didn't you?"

"I did not."

"You got mad about it . . . "

"I never made any advances, whatsoever, to Mrs. Tate."

"And you brooded about it, didn't you, Jon?"

"I did not."

"'She can't do this to me!' And, 'If I can't have her, nobody else will'?"

"I have never made that statement to anyone."

"And you were there that Sunday morning, and you saw Martin Tate and those boys going to Sunday school?"

"I did not see Martin Tate that morning at all."

"And then you came back, and you saw Mrs. Baker. You knew Mrs. Baker's car, didn't you?"

"I did not see Mrs. Baker, or her car, that morning, to the best of my knowledge."

"You were familiar with her car, weren't you?"

"I am familiar with her car, yes, sir."

"And you saw them, as you went up Military Road going home, and you knew Mrs. Gene Tate was in that house alone?"

"I did not see Mrs. Baker."

"And you met her there?"

"I did not know Mrs.Tate was in that house alone. I did not know Mrs.Tate was in that house, period."

"And you knew that you had met her there on Sunday morning before, when they were all gone?"

"I have never met Mrs.Tate in that house on Sunday morning, or any other place."

"And you took the coat hanger, and you choked her to death?"

"I did not! So help me God, I did not."

"In vengeance."

"No, sir."

"And when your mother came home from Sunday school, you were standing on the brick, within twenty feet of the body of Mrs. Gene Tate?"

"I was standing . . . I came out of that door right there, and it is a brick, it is a platform that you have to stand on when you step out of the door. When you turn to close the door, you are standing on that platform. And just as I turned from closing the door, I turned back toward the street, my mother walked down the sidewalk, around the corner."

"And you were within twenty feet of Mrs.Tate's body?"

"At that time, I do not know where Mrs. Tate's body was. That is where I was at that time. Now where Mrs.Tate's body was, I have absolutely no knowledge, whatsoever, of."

"That's all."

Closing arguments were made to the jury on the afternoon of Friday, May 12th, after the defense had finished its case, and the prosecution had presented the rebuttal case.

"You owe a debt to society, you owe a debt to yourselves and your families to see that he is not turned loose on society . . . ," District Attorney Harvey Buck admonished the jurors. He reminded them of the evidence and pointed out that the defense had had a full year to bring in a witness against Sarah Grayson to call her "a liar," and had been unable to do so.

Then the defense argued to the jury. Luther Sims compared Grayson to Pharaoh's wife, who said, "Come lay with me." And he compared his client, Jon Mattox, to young Joseph, whose brothers had plotted his death.

"They're out to get Jon Mattox!" he charged, "And they don't care how."

With the closing statements concluded, Judge Greene read the instructions to the jury. They were sent out to deliberate the verdict around 4 p.m.

The local newspaper reported that, as had happened at the first trial, students from Mississippi State College for Women were banned from attendance that day. Over three dozen of them had stormed Mattox's jail cell after the proceedings on Thursday, and at least one had succeeded in kissing his hand.

The next morning at 9:00 a.m., the jury returned to the courtroom and announced that they had reached a verdict. Reporters and attorneys on both sides were predicting a hung jury.

But the clerk read the verdict, and for the second time, Jon Mattox was found guilty of the murder of Gene Tate, and again he was sentenced by Judge Greene to life imprisonment at hard labor. The defendant showed no emotion.

However, after the jury was released, and filed out of the courtroom, one disappointed spectator was overheard by a deputy when he cursed one of the jurors: "Go home, you damned dog!" the angry man hissed. The deputy reported the man, and Judge Greene charged him with contempt.

Before the court adjourned, Defense Attorney Hugh Cunningham filed a motion of appeal that included a charge of jury tampering, and in response, Bill Burgin wanted him to tell the court to whom he was referring.

"I imagine that Mr. Burgin knows more about that than anyone within the sound of my voice," Cunningham remarked. Later he produced no evidence of tampering and apologized to the court.

Sarah Grayson was on a train headed for California when the verdict came in. She had arranged for her brother to tell her the news - with a code they had created. She had told him that she didn't want to talk, but she had to know the outcome. If the verdict was "not guilty," he would tell the operator that "She will be coming back soon." If it was "guilty," he would say "She's gone on to California, Operator," and if it was the death penalty, he would talk to her.

The train was in Kansas City before it stopped for a short while. The wait had been difficult, and Sarah scrambled to find a phone when the train pulled in the station. Her fate depended on one phone call. When her brother answered the phone, she heard the words she had prayed for: "She's gone on to California, Operator." She returned to the train in a daze of tears, pain, and relief.

Sarah felt very much alone, but was determined to rebuild her life, away from the South.

Over a year later, Sarah received a letter from Bill Burgin which informed her that the rest of the reward money would soon be disbursed to her. In the end, after she repaid some loans, she would actually keep $750.00 out of over four thousand dollars.

Also in his letter, Burgin passed on some news about Jon Mattox: "James Mattox died suddenly on June 11th . . . Jon Mattox was in town for two days immediately prior to his father's death - on leave without any guard or supervision whatsoever, other than the fact that he was 'paroled to Luther Sims.' This, as you can well imagine, created quite a furor, and when he came back for the funeral unattended, Governor Barnett suddenly realized he should be under guard and rushed two guards from Parchman to return him."

Some twenty years later -

Several men were seated around the polished hardwood table, in a small conference room outside the minister's office. They were church elders, dressed in business suits, some expensive, some not. It was a happy, but serious occasion: the selection of a new church deacon - chosen from among the large congregation, as a man of proven faith and unblemished reputation. Their candidate sat across from them in humble anticipation of their decision. His name, along with others, had been submitted to the elders by other members of the church.

"We all want to welcome you here this morning," the senior elder addressed him. "And I think we are all agreed that we don't know of a man we have been more proud to consider as a deacon in Our Lord's service." The other elders smiled at him and nodded in agreement.

"You have been a faithful member of the church for many years and have always offered yourself as a volunteer to help with our youth projects, and as a teacher, and on church outings. And you have always cheerfully made yourself available to help, in general, as our brother in Christ."

"But, aside from all of that," he continued, "and as I am sure you know, we are guided and directed by the Holy Scripture as to those qualifications we are to consider, when, as elders, we think the Church has need of a new deacon to assist us."

He opened a Bible, "In the book of I Timothy, chapter 13, verses 1-13, it reads in part: 'Deacons must be reverent, not double-tongued, not given to much wine, not greedy for money, holding the mystery of faith with a pure conscience.' And verse ten says, 'But let them first be tested, then let them serve as deacons, found blameless.' "

"You know, I don't think we know of anyone who has been so sorely tested in his lifetime. Almost beyond endurance at times, I imagine?" the elder asked him sympathetically, and the man slightly nodded.

"You were a young man when you were confronted by great tragedy: your family life was destroyed and snatched away from you. Your bright future dulled and dimmed, or so it seemed, I'm sure. And yet, over those harsh and trying years, you rededicated yourself to Christ, and your faith sustained you. You overcame it all: an innocent man, falsely accused. A victim of injustice. And in spite of it all, here you are now without any bitterness. A professional man, a family man, and a much beloved Christian man, an example of faith to us all."

"So, Brother Jon Mattox, if you are willing to join us in greater service to Our Lord, and your brothers and sisters of the Church, we would be honored to have you."

AUTHOR'S NOTE

About a year after the murder, my friend, George Witt, and I were playing down in the woods across from the Tate's and Mattox's. There is a seasonal creek, we called a ditch, that we liked to jump across, whether as cowboys or army men. In the growth along the creek, tree roots jutted out of its banks, and one of them, I happened to notice then, had about a half-dozen coat hangers wrapped around it, twisted tightly. The root had formed a thick knot, as big around as someone's neck. It was clear to me, at the time, how the coat hangers came to be there.

"Looks like the place Jonny must have practiced," I said to George, and he agreed.

At the time, the only thing that caused me some doubt was that I had never seen Jonny down in those woods. But when I read the trial transcripts, Mattox himself had mentioned, in passing, that he sometimes had gone down there, in the woods across from his house.

EPILOGUE

In 1971, Jon Mattox was released on parole from Parchman Penitentiary to Alabama, where he remains today on unsupervised parole. He is a deacon in a large fundamentalist church. In 1990, based upon his claim of innocence, Mattox applied for a full pardon from the governor of Mississippi, but was denied.

He has never admitted his guilt for the murder of Mrs. Gene Tate, or for the conspiracy to murder Sarah Grayson. After his second conviction for murder, the charges of the conspiracy were dropped. At that time, the maximum sentence that could have been imposed would have been six months in jail and a $25.00 fine.

In 1996, Mrs. Elizabeth Mattox died.

In the mid-sixties, Fred and Dan Wilkerson were released from Parchman Penitentiary.

Two years after his wife's murder, Martin Tate married a young widow.

The Tate boys have since become successful business and professional men.

In 1988, Genie Tate committed suicide by hanging, and was survived by a six year old daughter. She was the same age as Genie when her mother was murdered.

Since she left Mississippi in 1961, Sarah Grayson has remained in seclusion until the writing of this book, in which she agreed to participate. Today her whereabouts continue to be kept confidential, out of her concern for safety.